The Anatomy of
Relationships

The Anatomy of Relationships

And the rules and skills needed
to manage them successfully

Michael Argyle and
Monika Henderson

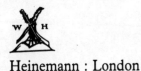

Heinemann : London

William Heinemann Ltd
10 Upper Grosvenor Street, London W1X 9PA

LONDON   MELBOURNE   TORONTO
JOHANNESBURG   AUCKLAND

First published 1985
© Michael Argyle and Monika Henderson 1985
SBN 434 02500 3

Filmset by Deltatype, Ellesmere Port
Printed in Great Britain by
Redwood Burn Ltd, Trowbridge

To
Sonia Argyle and Peter Henderson

Contents

Preface

The systematic study of relationships has made rapid advances during recent years. Social psychologists have concentrated on friendship and love, sociologists on families and kinship, workers in social medicine on the effects on health, amongst others. We have made use of these and other lines of research to provide an account of the anatomy of all the main relationships. Our own research has been mainly into the rules and skills needed to manage relationships successfully.

We are indebted to the ESRC for financing this research, and to a number of our collaborators and colleagues at Oxford, especially Adrian Furnham, Peter Collett, David Clarke, Jos Jaspars, Peter Bryant, Mansur Lalljee, Rosalie Burnett and Robert McIlveen.

We are also indebted to our overseas collaborators in the rules study – Ralph Exline (Delaware), Michael Bond (Hong Kong), Yuichi Iizuka (Hiroshima) and Alberta Contarello (Padua).

The volumes on *Personal Relationships* edited by Steve Duck and Robin Gilmour have been very helpful for certain chapters, as was the conference on the same subject organised by them in Madison in 1982.

We are also grateful to John Hutton of MORI for making recent survey findings available, especially the one on Neighbours.

Finally we are grateful to the staff of the Bodleian and the Radcliffe Science Library, and to Ann McKendry for her work on the 'word protester'.

Michael Argyle
Monika Henderson

Department of Experimental Psychology
Oxford
June 1983

1

1

Introduction

This book is about social relationships – friendship, marriage, kinship, workmates and the rest. We are by our very nature social animals, but some relationships are quite puzzling. Why do people fall in love, for example, what exactly happens and what purpose does it serve? Relationships at work are odd too – there is a lot of joking and teasing, a lot of help and social support too, yet this is often regarded as a superficial kind of relationship. And how about the weakest of all – relationships with neighbours? We shall find that these have some very interesting features. And as for the most intense relationship – marriage – why does it go wrong so often, and could this be avoided? We believe that some marriages and other relationships break up because people do not understand the true nature of these relationships. People may not realise, for example, that conflict is inevitable in marriage, or that parents and children are usually bonded together for life. Another reason for breaking up is a lack of the social skills needed to handle each relationship.

The research by ourselves and others which we shall describe provides much information about the basic properties of each relationship, and the skills needed to sustain them. We shall describe how each one actually operates, what people do together, how they interact, how one helps or annoys the other. We shall look in particular at the informal rules we have found to operate for each relationship. We shall ask how far friendship, marriage and the rest take different forms in different social classes, cultures and historical periods, and whether men and women, older and younger people, have different relations.

The practical applications of all this involve sketching out the basic features of each relationship, listing the rules to be followed, showing how to acquire the skills needed to sustain them, and how to avoid common sources of difficulty.

In addition to our own research findings, we have used a consider-

able amount of other published material, taking for our main
examples in figures and tables the best and most recent British studies,
though we have also made use of the extensive American work on this
topic.

What are relationships, and how do they work?

'Relationships', 'personal relationships', or 'long-term relationships'
refer to regular social encounters with certain people over a period of
time. They would generally be taken to exclude the more superficial
contacts, such as with postmen, bus conductors, etc., though these
may be the most important contacts for isolated individuals, and we
shall describe research later on the social support provided by contact
with, for example, hairdressers and barmen. In many cases there will
be 'attachment' or 'bonding'; this means that the other is missed when
absent, and that distress is caused if the relationship is ended. There
does not seem to be much attachment in this sense to many people at
work, or to most neighbours, so this is not an essential feature. In the
same way, there need not be a feeling of positive emotion, though in
close relations with spouse, kin and friends there usually is. The
easiest way to define relationships then is in terms of regular social
interaction over a period of time, together with the expectation that
this will continue for at least some time in the future.

Surveys have been carried out in which people have been asked to
list 'the persons outside the home that you feel closest to'. It is
assumed that the spouse or equivalent is the closest attachment. In a
study in Toronto[1] the results were as follows:

	First five named	First person named
all kin	50%	65%
child	6%	13%
parent	9%	19%
sibling	15%	21%
other	20%	12%
friends	38%	28%
neighbours	6%	4%
co-workers	6%	3%

It can be seen that the closest ties are with friends, followed by
siblings, parents and children. Co-workers and neighbours come out
very low, though some workmates are also friends; neighbours may be

friends, kin or workmates, and so on. Professional relationships, with doctors, clergy, tradesmen, postmen, barmen, hairdressers and so on, are important for some people.

These relationships can be placed along dimensions such as

intense—superficial
friendly—hostile
equal—unequal
task—social

Myron Wish and colleagues[2] have found that work relationships, for example, are relatively *superficial*, definitely *task-oriented* and often *unequal*. Marriage of course is *intense*, *equal*, and *friendly* (see Figure 2, p. 240).

However, we think that such dimensions do not reveal the full intricacies of different kinds of relationship. It is rather like trying to describe a game in terms of dimensions. Squash could be described as *competitive* and *intense*, but this would not tell someone how to play it. In order to play one would need to know the *rules* for a start, the *goals* (how to win), the *environmental setting*, and the *repertoire* of moves. One would then require instruction in the *skills* needed to play successfully. We want to argue that the same applies to relationships, and in later chapters we shall discuss the different kinds of relationships in terms of their rules and other components. To give one example, no account of marriage would be complete if it did not mention shared property, sex, and the production of children, none of which comes into the dimensions listed above.

Relationships are also unlike games, in that in most cases they are cooperative rather than competitive, and no one is trying to win. But they are like games in that certain goals are being pursued, within limits set by the rules, only certain activities are permitted, they take place in particular arenas, and they need certain skills.

The benefits from relationships

The main reason for psychologists' interest in relationships is the strong link with health and happiness. As we shall see in the next chapter, gaining a relationship is one of the pleasantest, most positive life events, while losing one is the worst and most distressing. Furthermore, those who are married, who have lots of friends, or who in other ways have a supportive social network, are happier, in better physical and mental health, and live longer. In the case of marriage, men for some reason seem to benefit much more than women. But how exactly does all this happen? It turns out to be a rather complex issue, and it will be gently taken apart in Chapter 2.

In addition there are characteristic sources of satisfaction – for example, family members providing help – and there are common sources of conflict and annoyance – for example, husbands not helping in the house, wives being reluctant on Saturday nights. These will be examined in later chapters.

The rules of relationships

This is the central theme of the book, and the main object of our own research. All relationships are governed to some extent by the rules of law. In addition there are a lot of informal rules, which members of a culture believe should be followed. Some of these rules, when broken, lead to the collapse or disruption of the relationship. Some of these rules are familiar, others are less obvious.

Most of human behaviour is governed by rules, and this is particularly true of relationships. The book will deal with these rules in some detail, and present the rules we have found. Rules are 'functional', that is they enable us to deal with life better in some way. The rule of the road enables us to use the road without head-on collisions, for example. Rules often appear to be restrictive – don't do this, don't do that. But they also make whole spheres of activity possible – from the more obvious rule-governed activities, such as games and sports, to our relationships with other people. These rules emerge gradually, by slow trial and error, as an achievement of the group. The evolution of the rules of rugby football, for example, can be traced in this way. The rules are then taught to members of the group, children are taught them by their parents, and group members are made to conform to them.

Donald Campbell[3] has argued that moral rules are needed in society, in order to control our basically selfish biological nature. Modern urban life in particular is made possible by the existence of rules, restraining dishonest and antisocial behaviour. Without them life would be a chaotic, antisocial jungle. On the other hand the rules tend to be related to the past, and constantly need to be altered to keep up with changing conditions. We discover new rules by trying out variations to see if they will work. Campbell believes that the social evolution of rules is more important than biological evolution for human social behaviour. There may also be political pressure to change the rules – women want to change the rules governing the relations between the sexes, young people have managed to change the rules about sex.

On the other hand sociobiologists have argued that there is an innate tendency to look after the welfare of our genes, including the welfare of children and other kin who share a percentage of our genes. So there may be a biological basis for some of these pro-social rules. And we shall see that in close relationships people develop a concern for one another, and may not need rules to compel them to be nice to one another.

Rules often lead to longer-term advantages for the individual, at the expense of short-term losses. Not eating or drinking too much are examples. Following the rules also results in advantages for others; not stealing is an example. In this second case there is an advantage for the first person too if the second engages in similar, or reciprocal, action. Sometimes the rules that primarily benefit others need further backing, and this is provided externally by the power of the law and from moral and religious leaders, and internally from the conscience. The conscience consists of prohibitions and ideals derived from the parents and punishes with guilt feelings, or rewards with the satisfaction of having acted rightly.

Variations with sex, age and class

Obviously not all marriages are the same, nor are all friendships. One of the most interesting sources of variation is that between men and women. There are some surprisingly strong sex differences in the nature of the relationships formed. We shall show that men gain more from marriage than women do, though women gain more from having children. The explanation for the first difference is probably that women provide more social support than men do. Women also form closer same-sex friendships than men, and keep up closer contacts with kin. It has been suggested that the reason women live longer is that they are able to form closer and more supportive relationships. When we look at parent–child relationships we shall discover at least part of the explanation for these later sex differences, in the different ways that boys and girls are brought up.

Age differences are equally important, and we shall trace for each relationship the different forms it takes at different points in the life-span, from childhood to old age.

No account of social behaviour in Britain would be complete without some account of differences due to social class, and we shall also examine these. For example, it has been found that many working-class people in Britain do not have friends on the middle-class pattern; they do not invite them home, but see them in particular settings such as church, football, or the pub. On the other hand working-class people live closer to their kin, and mothers and grown-up daughters, or sisters, may see each other every day.[4] British studies, especially those using social-survey methods, have provided evidence on relationship differences from classes I to V.

We shall see that there are some interesting variations in the pattern of relationships inside our own culture. However, rather greater differences can be found if we look at relationships in different cultures. It is well known that the family may take a variety of forms in other parts of the world – up to four wives for Muslims, a concubine among the Chinese, for example. One of the greatest differences is that in many non-Western countries kinship bonds are more important – a larger range of kin is recognised, and obligations to help them are stronger. There have also been changes with history: our current conception of romantic love is fairly recent, and quite different from ideas in earlier epochs. Traditionally marriage did not involve such intense affection or intimacy, traditionally the wife was very sub-servient to the husband. And husband and wife were part of a much larger household.

Clearly there are variations with class, culture and history, in the forms relationships take. However there are also universal features, which are found in all times and places. This is partly biological – it takes a man and a woman to produce a child; the woman needs economic support and protection during the years of child-rearing; and so the nuclear family predominates, even though extra wives may be added to it. We shall see that the marital roles of husband and wife have taken a similar form in most cultures so far, though they are changing in our own time. Friendship is found in all cultures, between people who are not kin, and this too seems to be universal. People have to work in groups, and this creates supervisor–sub-ordinate and workmate relationships, though these people may be friends and kin as well.

Sometimes relationships take a form that is sufficiently different for a new name to be coined for it. For example, 'blood-brothers' are a kind of spurious kin, created by a ceremony of cutting fingers and mingling blood, between friends or business partners who want to establish a more binding relationship. This could be regarded as a kind of extra kin relationship. In Japan there is a kind of godfather relationship called *oyabum kobun*, formed between pupils and sub-ordinates. This is a special kind of supervisor or teacher relationship, with special obligations added.

We shall look briefly at historical differences in the forms relation-ships have taken, from primitive men to the present age. However we shall look particularly at changes in Britain in the present century and especially at the changes that are taking place now.

Current changes in the form of relationships

The traditional pattern of relationships shows signs of changing in a number of ways. The main changes are to do with the most intense relationship – marriage. We do not hear much about radical changes in friendship or between kin, although there has perhaps been a change in one of the main work relationships, towards greater equality between supervisors and subordinates, and towards more consult-ation.

Changes in marriage 1. More couples live together now before marriage, or without marrying at all. In fact the majority of people in Britain still do get married in the end – 92%. We shall discuss living together in Chapter 5, and see how it compares with marriage in terms of the benefits it provides. It can be revealed here however that the level of stability is rather low, i.e. there is a very high 'divorce rate', with its attendant distress.

2. The divorce rate is now very high – about one-third of marriages in Britain end in divorce. It has been suggested that the Western world is moving into a new era of shorter-term relationships. To some extent this observation is correct, but we resist the further view that this is a desirable state of affairs. As we shall show, the disruption of relationships of several kinds is a source of great distress, indeed it has a physical impact. And in the field of marriage, females still have a strong interest in relationships that last long enough to support and sustain them during the long period of child-bearing and rearing.

3. Dual-career marriages. There has been a strong trend in advanced

countries for women to work more than they used to, and to earn more money. When this happens the traditional marital roles undergo some modification, in that the wife has as much, or nearly as much, power as the husband, and the husband does more domestic work. We discuss the benefits and problems of this kind of marriage in Chapter 6.

Smaller families   Another general change has been towards a smaller domestic unit. The number of people in Britain who live alone has increased to 8%, and is still increasing. The number of single-parent families is also increasing, to nearly a million such families, usually consisting of a young mother and one or two children. Grandparents are less likely to be living in the family and more likely to be in institutions. This can entail a greater degree of social isolation than before, which we have seen is bad for health and happiness.

The psychology of relationships

How can psychologists explain the existence of long-term relationships, the benefits they convey, and the ways they work? Can psychological theories help us to understand relationships? One theory that is popular here is 'exchange theory', which states that people will stay in a relationship if the balance of rewards minus costs is as good as they think they can get from the various alternatives open to them, making allowances for the costs of making the change. We shall see that this theory has some application to friendship, and that it has been influential in the design of marital therapy. Some versions of exchange theory now take account of the fact that in close relationships an empathetic concern for the other develops, so that it is a source of satisfaction to see them happy, and a source of sorrow to see them suffer.

There is also evidence that kinship does not depend on a balance of rewards in this way, and that kinship links can be kept up over many years with very little contact and presumably little reward. We shall discuss the basis of kinship attachment in Chapter 9, and the various explanations for this form of attachment. One is in terms of 'selfish gene' tendencies, as described above. Another is in terms of bonding based on early childhood experience, and another is the social learning of proper behaviour towards kin. Work relations are different again, and are partly due to the supports and restraints of the working environment whereby we have incentives to sustain working relationships. What about marriage, the most intense relationship of them all? This will be discussed in Chapter 6.

To some extent there are biological dispositions towards particular kinds of relationships. The mother–child relation is the most instinctive; the need of men and women for a permanent mate may be another innate pattern. More important for the other kinds is socialisation, whereby we learn the concepts of 'friend', 'love', and the rest, and the rules of proper behaviour in each case. This explains why different ranges of kin are recognised in different cultures.

Practical applications

There is another psychological approach which can help us – the analysis of social behaviour in terms of the social skills needed. People often have difficulty with social situations of various kinds; they can be helped by the discovery of the styles of behaviour that are most effective, and then by training in these skills. Special techniques have been developed for such training. Research into social skills has shown how they are similar to manual skills like driving a car, in that certain goals and sub-goals are pursued, corrective action is taken in response to feedback, and it is necessary to learn detailed skills of performance and the best strategies.

A certain amount of training for relationships is already being given, such as marital therapy, and supervisory training. Marital therapy is mainly based on exchange theory, and emphasises exchange of rewards and negotiation of better exchanges. The research that we shall present in this book suggests a number of new ways in which people could be trained for relationships – not only to maintain or improve problematic ones, but to enhance and enrich well functioning relationships.

The main new contribution we have to make is to list the most important rules for each relationship, some of which have been found to lead to the loss of the relationship if they are broken. In addition we aim to provide a map, a set of descriptions of the key features of the main forms of relationship. As we said before, this may be useful to help readers to understand a little better the central and underlying features of these relationships from various points of view.

FURTHER READING

Duck, S. & Gilmour, R. (1981–1984) *Personal Relationships* (Vols 1–5)
    London: Academic Press
Hinde, R. (1979) *Towards Understanding Relationships* London: Academic
    Press

2

The Benefits Derived from Relationships

This book is about relationships: how they work, why they go wrong, and how to maintain them. But first we want to show why relationships are important. The answer is simple: they are good for us. If we have the right kind of social attachments we are likely to live longer, to have better physical and mental health, and to feel happier. Of course relationships are not the *only* source of health and happiness, but they are a very important factor. Most people know this already; what we shall do in this chapter is to sample some of the research findings, which show how strong these effects are, and who benefits most. In later chapters we shall go into marriage, friendship and so on in more detail.

Meanwhile it is worth noting that health and happiness are affected more by social relationships than they are by income, social status or education.[1]

The most positive life event – gaining a relationship

A new field of psychological research is the study of 'positive life events', i.e. events that make people happy. We tried to find out which are the most positive life events by asking samples of subjects to rate a number of pleasant events on a scale from 0 to 100, according to how much happiness, satisfaction or well-being they believed each event would bring most people. Some of our findings are shown in Table 1.

Gaining a new mate, friend or child, staying with friends or kin, are estimated to be very positive social events. The only others that come into this range are going on holiday, obtaining a degree and recovering from a serious illness. All other positive events, even winning a lot of money, come lower on the scale. And there is quite a large sex

TABLE 1. Ratings of Positive Life Events (out of 100)

	Males		Females	
	under 21	21+	under 21	21+
Getting married or engaged	47.0	72.5	71.3	71.4
Falling in love	75.7	72.9	87.0	73.1
Birth of a child	41.4	57.8	60.5	70.1
Making a new friend	63.0	58.3	75.6	73.4
Friends visiting or staying with friends	52.1	54.7	68.9	65.2
Staying with a brother, sister, or close relative	52.9	48.2	65.7	68.3
Going on holiday	64.0	72.0	74.2	71.0
Obtaining a degree	61.6	58.5	80.2	72.9
Recovering from serious illness	82.1	60.4	66.6	77.3

difference: women value gaining relationships more than men do.

Freedman[2] asked over 100,000 people which aspects of their lives gave them greatest happiness. For single people 'friends and social life' and 'being in love' were ranked most important for women, and first- and third-most important for men. However, 'being in love', 'marriage' and 'partner's happiness' were rated as the three most important items for married women, and were ranked second, third, and fifth for married men. 'Friends and social life' rated at eighth for both sexes.

An experiment was carried out which showed the impact of gaining a relationship. Forty-eight subjects were asked to increase the level of positive events over the period of a month, for example by starting a love affair, beginning to date someone, improving relationships with kin, finding new friends, increased participation in a club or voluntary organisation. The result was that at the end of the month those concerned reported a more favourable quality of life, a more pleasant outlook. Individuals who had a previous history of negative life events benefited most, feeling less depressed and having fewer other psychiatric symptoms.[3]

The most stressful life-event – losing a relationship

As everyone knows, the death of a spouse or of a child, or of other close kin, getting divorced, or losing a job, are extremely distressing and disturbing experiences, and can make us ill in mind and body. In this section we shall look carefully at the effects of losing a spouse. One way of tackling the question is to compare the widowed and divorced with the still married for their levels of happiness, health, and so on. Figure 1 gives examples of the *ratios* of, for example, death from various causes for widowed and divorced or separated to married people. So the first bar shows that widowed men aged 47 have an overall death rate over a given period which is 77% greater than that of married men of the same age.

Fig. 1   MORTALITY RATE OF WIDOWED AND DIVORCED/ SEPARATED TO MARRIED MALES AND FEMALES[4]

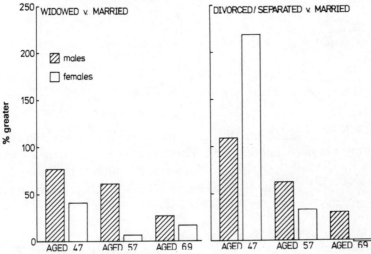

It can be seen that younger widows and divorcees suffer more, probably because most of them are nearer to the event than the older ones. At the younger ages, divorce is more traumatic than bereavement, especially for women. The death rate is 3.19 greater than for married women of the same age (219% more).

The effects of bereavement or of divorce are greatest shortly after the event takes place. For men the death rate rises by 40% in the six months following the wife's death, though this falls off rapidly, as Figure 2 shows.

For women the pattern is rather different, and the greatest death rate is during the second or third year after the husband's death. The most common cause of death is heart attack. There is also an increased rate of suicide, especially for men, during the first six months after bereavement.[6]

Fig. 2

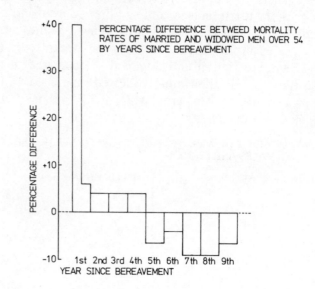

PERCENTAGE DIFFERENCE BETWEED MORTALITY
RATES OF MARRIED AND WIDOWED MEN OVER 54
BY YEARS SINCE BEREAVEMENT

Physical illnesses   Susceptibility to a wide range of illnesses is greater among the widowed and divorced. They are ill more often, have more days off or in bed, and see the doctor more often than either the married or those who have stayed single.[7] They are more likely to die from a number of diseases, as Table 2 shows.

TABLE 2. *Ratios Widowed/Married and Divorced or Separated/Married for Death Rates from Different Causes, U.S. Population 15+, Age Adjusted*[8]

	Widowed Married		Divorced or Separated Married	
	Males	Females	Males	Females
TB*	6.00	2.00	10.00	2.50
Cirrhosis of the liver	4.36	3.25	7.18	4.42
Pneumonia	4.17	1.75	7.33	2.50
Breast Cancer	2.50	1.02	2.50	1.13
Cancer of mouth and throat	2.12	1.47	4.10	1.67
Diabetes	2.00	1.57	2.83	1.14
Stroke	1.92	1.63	2.42	1.47
Coronary	1.56	1.52	2.06	1.41

* These ratio figures show that, e.g., 6 widowed males die of TB for every one married male of the same age.

It can be seen that for a wide range of fatal illnesses, the widowed and divorced have rates of death which are on average 1½–2½ times as high as for the married. The ratios are somewhat higher for the divorced and separated than for the widowed, rising to 7 to 10 times as high for some illnesses.

Mental illness   The figures are similar for mental disorders, as Figure 3 shows. It can be seen that the divorced and separated in particular are more likely to be mentally ill, become in-patients, or commit suicide (which is linked with depression) than the married. They also suffer more from alcoholism. The effect is again greater for men and is less for the widowed. Part of the explanation of the high rate for the divorced and separated is that many of them get divorced *because* of these mental disturbances.

Fig. 3   RATES OF MENTAL ILLNESS AND SUICIDE OF WIDOWED AND DIVORCED/SEPARATED TO MARRIED MALES AND FEMALES

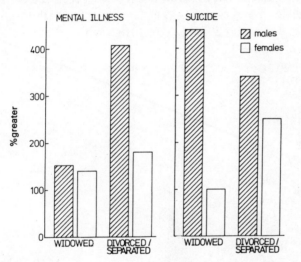

What these people are suffering from in the majority of cases is *depression*. Indeed loss of a close relationship is one of the main causes of depression.

Happiness   It is not surprising to find that of all stages of life, being widowed or divorced is typically the least happy. Among the divorced and separated only 33% say that they are satisfied with life as a whole, compared with 89% of young married women without children. For men the figures are 42% and 72%. Widows are a little happier than divorced women, and happier than widowed men.[11]

The benefits of a supportive social network

We have seen that gaining a relationship is a source of joy, and that the loss of a relationship is a cause of distress, depression and heart attacks. But do marriage or other relationships actually make people happier, give them better health, or make them live longer?

Length of life   The more strongly attached we are to others, the longer we are likely to live. In a famous study in California, 6,900 adults were followed up over a nine-year period. Altogether 8% of them died during this period. Within each age group those with the fewest social attachments were more likely to have died. An index based on marriage, friends and other links was devised. In each age group, individuals who were 'most connected' in their social relationship had lower mortality rates than those who were 'least connected'. This was most obvious for males aged 50–59 at the beginning of the study: 9.6% of the closely connected died, compared with 30.8% of the least connected, as Figure 4 shows.

Fig. 4   AGE AND SEX SPECIFIC MORTALITY RATES FROM ALL
CAUSES PER 100

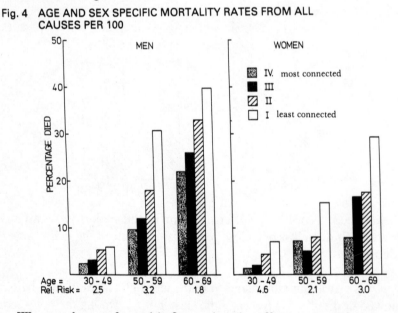

We can also see from this figure that the effect seems to be stronger for men than for women, a point to which we shall return later.

The relationship that has the strongest effect here is marriage, and some of the findings will be given in the next section. For married couples children convey similar benefits, as Table 3 shows. For example, childless wives between 35 and 44 are 2.4 times more likely to die during a given year than those with children. It can also be seen that the benefits of children are greater for younger people and for women.

TABLE 3. The Effects of Children on Mortality Rate[13]

	Age	35–44	45–54	55–60
ratio childless/those with children	Males	2.1	1.3	0.9
	Females	2.4	1.6	1.1

Other studies have shown that physical health is better for the employed than the unemployed, the married than the single, and for those with children compared with those without.[14] So here is something to add to those predictions of length of life that can be found in magazine quizzes and insurance company offices, based on smoking, exercise, weight, blood pressure and the rest. It appears that social attachments may be just as important a factor as any of those.

However there are still unanswered questions here. Why do some people have weak social networks? For the widowed it is beyond their control, and some forms of illness may lead to isolation. In the case of the divorced and those without friends, the cause may be partly in their own personality, such as lack of social skills, or emotional disturbance.

Physical illness. The married are less likely to die from a range of illnesses than those of the same age who have stayed single.

TABLE 4. Ratios Single/Married for Death from Various Illnesses[15]

	Males	Females
TB	5.67	2.50
Pneumonia	5.17	3.75
Cirrhosis of the liver	2.82	0.86
Breast cancer	2.50	1.41
Diabetes	2.17	1.00
Cancer of mouth and throat	2.16	0.87
Stroke	1.75	1.21
Coronary	1.34	1.16

These effects are again quite strong, especially for men. Other research shows that they are stronger for the young than for the elderly, and that living together is nearly as beneficial as being married. However the explanation could be that single people have remained single because they were ill or predisposed to ill health. But in a prospective study of 10,000 married men of 40 and over in Israel it was found that for those who felt that they had a loving and supportive wife the risk of angina was reduced from 9.3 to 5.2%, over a five-year period.[16]

Another case of relationships benefitting physical health is during recovery from operations, injuries or other serious illness. A considerable number of studies have found that spouses, parents or other kin, friends, and health professionals can all accelerate the patient's rate of recovery, as measured by his or her loss of physical symptoms such as high blood pressure, resumption of work and other social roles and emotional recovery.[17]

Work relationships can be good for health too. Simply being employed rather than unemployed is associated with better health. In the case of women the benefits of employment are particularly marked for those who are single, widowed or divorced, who are of low social class, have a poor non-work environment, and who are involved in and satisfied by their work.[18] Friendship does not have much effect on health, but among the young friendship is the most important bond, and the quality of social contacts with friends is associated with physical health.[19]

Mental illness　Single people, who have never married, have higher rates of mental disorder than the married. The ratios of single/married are 3.13 for men and 1.74 for women – the averages for fourteen large-scale studies.[20] This difference arises partly because the single actually live alone, partly because they live with other people, such as parents, who provide less social support and more conflict than most spouses.[21] The lower rate of mental illness for the married is probably not due to selectivity – that they were less disturbed than the single in the first place. This is shown by the fact that the widowed and divorced also have higher rates of mental illness than the single. The effect of stress on mental disorder is less for the married, suggesting that marriage in some way provides protection against stress.[22]

It has been found that weak social support predicts depression and other forms of mental disorder at a later date. However it is also the case that mental disorder predicts later lack of social support.[23]

Experiments have been carried out in which some patients have been given social support as a form of treatment, with rather mixed success,[24] though the amount of such support provided sounds rather weak.

Research on women shows that having a husband, especially one who acts as a confidant, reduces the rate of depression; so does having a job, another form of social support. However, having small children at home *increases* the rate of depression.[25] Evidently, children are more a source of stress than of social support, at least until they become older, and part of the adult supportive network (see Fig. 1 p. 130). Children are affected in a similar way: it has been found that disturbance in adolescence is associated with stressful life events and with lack of support from the family.[26]

Happiness So far we have been able to refer to 'hard' data, such as death rates and hospital admissions. Happiness is more difficult to measure, and a great deal of research has gone into how to assess it. Sometimes a single question is used, such as 'Taking all things together, how would you say things are these days?', to which the answers in an American study were:

Very happy   24.5%
Pretty happy   65.5%
Not too happy   10.0%

'Here are some faces expressing various feelings. Below each is a letter. Which faces come closest to expressing how you feel about your life as a whole?'[27] Another way, which uses a non-verbal index of happiness, is:

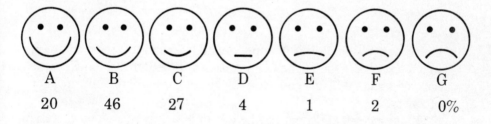

A	B	C	D	E	F	G
20	46	27	4	1	2	0%

We can now see how relationships affect happiness. We need to compare for example married and unmarried people of the same age, both with or without children, since that is another factor. This was done in a famous study of *The Quality of American Life*[28], with the results shown in Figure 5. This diagram shows that the married are happier than the unmarried, for both men and women, especially those couples without children.

Research into loneliness shows that people who feel lonely also feel unhappy, depressed, worthless, lacking in self-esteem, and so on. Feeling lonely is mainly due to lack of friends or other social

Fig. 5 SATISFACTION IN SINGLE AND MARRIED MEN AND WOMEN WITH AND
WITHOUT CHILDREN[28]

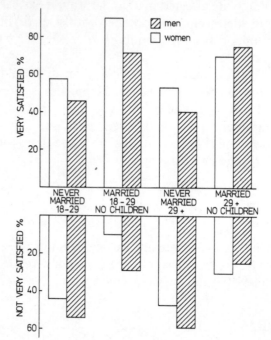

attachments, though it is not only due to this, and it is most common in adolescence. One of the main causes of isolation and loneliness is lack of social skills,[29] and we will discuss this more fully in later chapters.

Of course relationships can be a source of stress, indeed there is often conflict as well as satisfaction, especially in marriage. However the overall effect is positive in most cases.

Stress versus social support

In order to understand further the benefits due to social relationships, we need to go into the battle between stress and social support. In a nutshell, stressful life-events make us ill, but if we have a good spouse or other forms of social attachment and support, the effects of stress are greatly reduced.

The usual way of finding out how much stress someone has been exposed to is to ask how many of a list of stressful experiences they have had in the last six months. The importance of each kind of event can be assessed by asking a number of people to judge them for the perceived degree of stressfulness, and then averaging their ratings, or by interviewing individuals carefully who have undergone these events and finding how stressful each had actually been for him or her. Table 5 shows average ratings by a sample of British judges, using the first method.

TABLE 5. How Upsetting Different Life Events are Estimated to be (0–20)[30]

Death of child	19.5
Death of spouse	19.1
Sent to gaol	17.8
Serious financial difficulties	17.6
Spouse unfaithful	17.3
Court appearance for serious offences	16.9
Divorced	16.3
Fired	15.9
Fail important exam or course	14.4
Demotion	14.3
Begin extramarital affair	13.7
Child marries without approval	12.7
Move to another country	11.1
Retirement	10.1
Move to another city	8.6
Promotion	5.9
Marriage	5.4

The main types of stressful life-event are: bereavement or other loss of attachments, loss of job, moving house or to another country, trouble with the law, illness or accidents to members of family.

However in addition to such major upheavals, the number of everyday annoyances is also linked to mental disorder. These are such things as troublesome neighbours, being short of money, not liking current work, problems with children, and bad weather. It has been found that the number of such annoyances predicts psychological symptoms like anxiety and depression, and that this was a better prediction than the major life-events. The most frequent annoyances are shown in Table 6.

Many studies have shown that those people having a high life-events score for the previous six months are likely to be ill, mentally or physically, in the following year. This includes physical illness, such as arthritis, heart disease, and the rest which can be detected by physical measures, e.g. of cholesterol level.[32] On the mental disorder

TABLE 6. Ten Most Frequent Annoyances [31]

Item	% of times checked
1. Concerns about weight	52.4
2. Health of a family member	48.1
3. Rising prices of common goods	43.7
4. Home maintenance	42.8
5. Too many things to do	38.6
6. Misplacing or losing things	38.1
7. Yard work or outside home maintenance	38.1
8. Property, investment or taxes	37.6
9. Crime	37.1
10. Physical appearance	35.9

side one theory is that people are particularly upset by events being unpredictable or beyond their control. This leads either to frantic efforts to gain control or to giving up the attempt to do so and relapsing into depression. This particularly applies to 'Type A personalities' – see below.[33]

On the mental disorder side there is a 'reverse causation' problem. Perhaps being mentally ill is a cause of divorce rather than the other way round. Both possibilities have been investigated, mainly by seeing which comes first, and it has been found that *both* processes operate.[34] So some life-events may be caused, or partly caused, by the individual himself, and this has been found to be part of the story.[35] However many life-events, including some of the most stressful, are beyond the individual's control – such as death of child or spouse, losing one's job owing to factory closure, retirement, illness of family member, having to move to another town to work. These are sources of stress which on the whole are *not* self-generated.

But not everyone who experiences these stressful events becomes ill, and there are forms of susceptibility on the one hand, or 'hardiness' on the other, determining whether or not an individual will become physically or mentally ill.

Hardiness is the name that has been given to a number of personality qualities which distinguish between those who are and those who are not made ill by stress. It has three components, which can be assessed by questionnaire.

1. Commitment – 'the ability to believe in the truth, importance, and interest value of who one is and what one is doing, and thereby to involve oneself fully in the many situations of life, including work, family, interpersonal relations, and social institutions.'

2. Control – 'the tendency to believe and act as if one can influence the course of events.'

3. Challenge – 'the belief that change, rather than stability, is the

"Oh, Gerald—you haven't failed the entrance test for Mensa again?"

(Punch)

normative mode of life . . . much of the disruption associated with the occurrence of a stressful life event can be anticipated as an opportunity and incentive for personal growth, rather than a simple threat to security.'[36]

Others who are relatively resistant to stress are those who are high in 'internal control', that is people who believe that they are in control of what happens; 'external controllers' think that what happens is more due to chance or to other people.[37] The reason internal controllers do better is that they use more active methods of coping with problems, and are more flexible in their ways of coping; these include seeking help and advice from others.[38]

Type A personality   This is a type of person who is particularly prone to coronary heart disease. They are people who are competitive, aggressive, impatient, and with a strong drive to achieve. They react to stress by increasingly vigorous efforts to succeed and to gain control of events. They become physiologically over-aroused, with raised blood pressure; if they fail to regain control they become depressed. Their pattern of social relations is also disturbed, they withdraw from social networks and are tense and hostile at home.[39]

Social support   However the kind of stress-resistance in which we are interested is that due to social support. Part of the 'hardiness' syndrome, 'commitment', includes involvement in social relation-ships, as part of self-confidence and a sense of purpose. Internal control includes seeking help from others. Type A personalities are found to withdraw from their main social support systems. In this book we shall show how it is possible to maintain supportive social relations, for example by keeping to the right rules and learning the necessary skills.

How social support reduces the effects of stress

Studies of coping behaviour have been conducted by asking questions like 'What do you do when you are feeling depressed?' The most popular answers include seeking tangible help from others, and seeking sympathy or advice.[40] Many studies have found that social support can alleviate the effects of stress on health and mental health. There is quite a lot of support for the 'buffering hypothesis', that is that social support comes into action when it is needed, when there is stress.[41] This can be likened to the benefits due to sun-tan lotion which are only felt when the sun is shining.

A well-known study of complications during pregnancy found this interaction of stressful life-events and social support.[42] They found high levels of complications (91%) for the combination of stressful events and lack of social support, compared to 33% for high support and high stress, 49% for low support and low stress, and 39% for high support and low stress combinations. Other studies found that becoming unemployed produced higher levels of arthritis and cholesterol, but the effects were very small for those with good social support.[43] The effects are illustrated in Figure 7. Another way of putting it is that stress affects health only when there is *low* social support, or that social support affects health when there is *high* stress, or that ill-health is due to the combination of *high* stress and *low* social support.

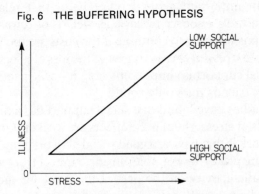

Fig. 6   THE BUFFERING HYPOTHESIS

Similar findings are obtained for mental health. In their study of working-class women in South London, Brown and Harris found that women who reported stressful experiences were likely to become clinically depressed. However the effect was much reduced if they had a spouse to whom they could talk about themselves and their problems, as Table 7 shows. This shows that having a spouse who acts

TABLE 7. Effects of Life-Events and Social Support on Depression (percentages)[44]

	Spouse who is confidant	No such confidant
Stressful life-events in last 6 months	10	41
Few stressful events	1	4

as a confidant can ward off the effects of stress. The presence of the spouse has little effect when there is no stress.

However this is not the end of the story, and recent research has brought up some more complications. Here are some of them. One study has shown that neurotic mental illness is due to the *perception* of social supports as inadequate, which in turn is due to having a neurotic disposition.[45] Another study shows that people with weak social networks have a distinct kind of personality – rigid and authorit-arian.[46] Another possibility is that depression, or other negative states, leads to a weakening of the social network. However it should still be possible to break into the causal network by showing people how to improve the quality of their social support system.

It has also been found that social support can have negative consequences: too much help from others can reduce self-reliance, create more worry, or distract attention from tackling the problems.[47] There is an important general point here, that relationships with others are always a source of costs as well as of rewards, though the relationship is unlikely to continue if the costs are too high. Of course some of these stressful events consist of the loss of a social relationship, so that social support is simply replacing it – when someone loses his/her spouse, friends may rally round.

Other studies have found that social support has a direct effect even at low levels of stress, though the effects are weaker. One way in which this may work is that having a good social network may prevent certain events taking place; for example, strong support from workmates may reduce hostile activity on the part of the boss. Or the availability of help from the network may simply render events less stressful, since they can be coped with more easily.[48]

Which social relationships produce the greatest benefits?

It is found that those people who are happier, and in better physical and mental health, tend to have good relationships of all kinds. But which of all these relationships are the most important? A number of investigations have succeeded in separating statistically the effects of different parts of the network.

Marriage, Cohabitation and similar relationships are found to be the most important, especially for mental health. This is why we selected marriage for closer inspection in the earlier part of this chapter, and were able to show large differences between the married and the divorced, widowed or single. Those who are cohabiting, or in a similar close relationship, are nearly as well off. And among the married it is those who enjoy a close relationship, where each acts as confidant for the other, that are in best shape. It is the *quality* of marriage which counts, and this is not simply living in the same house, or engaging in sexual activity.[49]

Family and kinship Those who have children tend to live longer (see Table 3). But while the children are at home the parents are less happy than before or after, and the wife is more likely to suffer from depression.[50] When the children have left home, however, the parents' health is better if they see the children more often. Contacts with brothers and sisters and other close kin are important, since they are one of the main sources of serious help in time of need. Studies of mental patients have found that they are particularly short of family relationships, rather than being short of friends.[51]

Friends Contact with friends has been shown to be important for the young and the old; it may be less important in between. What is important is not the quantity of social interaction with friends, but its *quality* – the level of intimacy, the amount of self-disclosure, the pleasantness of contact and the satisfaction derived from it.[52] And the wider social network, outside the family, can be a source of different kinds of help in times of crisis.

Studies of mental patients have found that they tend to receive some support from others, but give nothing in return.[53] Research on helping behaviour has found that if the person helped is not able to reciprocate in some way, his self-esteem is damaged, and he feels hostile to the helper.[54]

Work relationships People at work are in better mental and physical health, and experience a greater sense of well-being, than the unemployed, or women who are housewives.[55] Most women who have jobs are happier than those who have not, and they are more resistant to stress.[56] Work can be stressful in a number of ways – because of long hours, repetitive machine-paced work, time pressure, responsibility for other people (in the case of, for example, managers, doctors, air traffic controllers), competition with colleagues, career and promotion problems, difficult superiors or colleagues. All these forms of stress have been found to be associated with physical and mental ill-health. However when people have good relationships with their work superiors or colleagues, the link between stress and ill-health is either much smaller, or is broken.

Relationships with both workmates and supervisors can be sources of stress or of social support and satisfaction. Work superiors are in a position to solve problems directly, workmates can back the individual up and add to pressure to solve problems, as well as listening to troubles and offering advice. When a person at work sees that he has social support this dampens the perceived level of stress.[57]

Neighbours and local organisations These are the weakest kinds of relationship, and provide the least in the way of benefits. Nevertheless, among old people in particular, good contacts with neighbours, and belonging to churches or other local organisations, does have some effect on health and well-being.[58] In addition, integration with, and attachment to, the neighbourhood can be important, especially for members of ethnic minority groups.[59] The local network, of neighbours, friends, and acquaintances, is an important source of help. There is someone in the network who can either provide help or knows where it can be found. Groups of individuals who face a similar problem may get together to provide mutual help and support.

How do relationships help?

There are a number of different ways in which social support from relationships can work. The rather different kinds of benefit obtained from different relationships provide us with a useful guide. A general finding is that it is *close* relationships which are important. A small, helpful network is more useful than a larger, more diffuse one.[60]

1. Intimate close attachments – caring, trust and empathy. These play an important role for young children. When mother is near they feel secure enough to explore strange environments. In later life a close attachment may provide similar benefits.

2. Confidants. The relationship with a confidant may be different from that already mentioned, though it often occurs with the same people. There is a lot of evidence that having a confiding relationship with a spouse or friend is good for mental and physical health. The process involved – disclosure and discussion of personal problems – may be akin to psychotherapy. This has been found to be the main reason that

marriage is able to protect against stress.[61]

3. Affirmation, giving confidence, increasing self-esteem, and the belief in ability to cope. Favourable evaluation from others may lead to the expectation of similar evaluation and confidence in getting our own way; belief in one's ability to cope results in confidence to tackle problems.[62]

4. Tangible help. We shall see that help in minor, everyday matters is often provided by neighbours; major help by kin, help at work by workmates. This is the most direct kind of support.

5. Informational help. Social networks, as we have seen, are one of the main sources of information. Large and heterogeneous networks contain experts, or provide access to experts on a great variety of topics.

6. Social integration. Being accepted by a group of friends, being able to participate in regular social activities, may be a distinctive form of social support.

Some of these processes are more important than others. A recent study managed to separate the effects of different ones on mental and physical health. The most important were found to be the availability of a confidant, and the opportunity for positive evaluation of self by others.[63]

How do social relationships affect physical health? There are some simple explanations: spouses look after each other, for example people living alone have bad health habits, such as drinking and smoking more.[64] There is probably a more important process however. There is now evidence that stress makes people ill by weakening the immune system, the natural defence against germs.[65] It seems very likely that by reducing stress social support can help to keep the immune system operating. Another possibility is that the relaxation response is activated by social support: this in turn reverses the biochemical effects of stress.[66]

Sex differences

In general women benefit more than men from social support.[67] However in the most important relationship, marriage, it is men who do better. The tables on the benefits of marriage given earlier indicated that marriage does a lot more for husbands than for wives. This has been found in a large number of carefully conducted studies, and is not affected by the complexities of reverse causation which we discussed. So what is the explanation?

The most likely reason is that wives, indeed women in general, provide on average more support than husbands do. It has been found for example that wives are more affectionate, appreciative, encouraging, more inclined to share intimacy, and behave equitably in the marriage relationship.[68] Many more husbands use their wives as confidants than vice versa (p. 129). And, as we shall see later, marriage is somewhat inequitable. Men usually have more power and interesting jobs, their wives do more boring housework.

Bereavement has a smaller effect on women, perhaps because they lose less. They also have a better network of friends to fall back on. Less is done for widowers, partly because there are fewer of them, and they can be very isolated. In addition widowers may not be able to cope domestically – though widows often have financial problems.

Benefits for women from friends and kin may be greater, since they maintain closer attachments to both than do men, as we shall see later. On the other hand men have more attachment to workmates, and this is more predictive for the mental health of men than for women.[69] Men form less close attachments to friends, with less self-disclosure. Their attachment is often formed with a group of people, and they spend their time on shared activity rather than intimate conversation. It has been found that women are more likely to seek help, men more likely to withdraw, and that women receive more social and instrumental help (though no more professional help) than men.[70]

In any case men seem to be biologically more susceptible to many diseases, some of them fatal. Women are more prone to depression and anxiety, and have more minor illnesses, but they live longer. Perhaps their greater facility for creating supportive networks helps.[71] Some common female attributes, such as social skills and the desire for intimacy, may be good for their health. It has been found that intimacy motivation in men aged thirty predicted various measures of happiness and adjustment seventeen years later.[72]

Class differences in the benefits from relationships

Social class is one of the main sources of variation in way of life. If we look at different indices of health and well-being, it is found that on average working-class people are more mentally disturbed, more ill, less happy, and so on; though the effects of class are *less* marked than the effects of social relationships. Part of the explanation is that

TABLE 8. Percentage of Males with Small Networks (Defined Two Ways) by Income and Education Levels [74]

	N	Non-kin isolation		Kin isolation		Total isolation	
		Severe	Moderate	Severe	Moderate	Severe	Moderate
Household income							
0–$9,999	(97)	15	50	13	40	23	54
$10,000–$20,000	(162)	5	22	21	52	6	34
$20,000 and over	(189)	2	20	14	39	4	29
Education							
Less than high school	(54)	15	59	6	28	19	38
High school graduate	(122)	9	31	18	42	10	62
College	(199)	4	24	15	42	9	67
Post graduate	(96)	1	14	25	60	3	73

working-class life is more stressful – people are less well off, and more prone to unemployment, one of the most stressful life events.

It is also found that the effects of stress on mental and physical ill-health are stronger for working-class people.[73] In other words they are more vulnerable to stress than the middle classes.

Do working-class people receive weaker social support than middle-class people? Surveys of loneliness show that those with lower incomes, and especially those with little education, are less likely to have confidants (Table 8).

Which relationships do working-class people lack? There are class differences in nearly all social relationships, and these will be discussed in detail in later chapters. Briefly, working-class marriages are less happy, with less time spent together, and are more likely to end in divorce. Working-class friendships are on the whole weaker, though links with kin are stronger. Links with neighbours are not weaker, except at the lowest levels of society. And work relationships vary with the type of work: they can be stronger for working-class people, since managerial jobs involve a lot of stressful relations with others. Blue-collar workers see a more restricted range of people; professional workers have a more varied network, and it has been argued that this provides more varied help and social feedback.[75]

Further light is cast on these issues by the finding that social support reduces the likelihood of depression for working-class people only when stress is high, while it has no effects at lower levels of stress. For upper- and middle-class folk social support has positive effects at all levels of stress.[76] It looks as if social support is not a regular part of (American) working-class life, but that it comes into action when it is clearly needed. We will examine the role of social class in more detail in the following chapters dealing with specific relationships.

How to obtain social support

If social support is so good for us, how do we get it? The answer is: get married and stay married, make friends and keep them, and so on. So it is a matter of the social skills of managing relationships, which is what this book is all about. In Chapter 12 we describe how to train people in the necessary skills.

How to get help, advice, and the rest is a further skill, though it is much easier when one has an established network. It is necessary to seek and ask for whatever help is needed. Infants do this, and support-seeking skills develop during childhood for most people.[77]

FURTHER READING

Brown, G. & Harris, T. (1978) *Social Origins of Depression* London: Tavistock
Lynch, J. (1977) *The Broken Heart* New York: Basic Books
Peplau, A. & Perlman, D. (eds) (1982) *Loneliness* New York: Wiley

3

Social and Relationship Rules

The components of relationships

Social relationships are in some respects like games. Both are miniature social systems, producing cooperative behaviour which leads to the attainment of goals, by play within the rules. The analogy between games and social situations has been worked out already, and the basic components of each described.[1] Social relationships have similar features; we shall use these features in this book to analyse different relationships. They are:

1. Goals, sources of satisfaction. People will not play a game, or stay in a relationship, unless they receive sufficient satisfaction from doing so, and satisfactions that are greater than the costs involved. These differ in character between different relationships.

2. Repertoire. These are the moves permitted and accepted as relevant in a game, or the forms of activity typical of some kind of encounter or relationship. These moves are steps towards the goals.

3. Roles. In cricket there are batsmen, bowlers, and so on. In a similar way there are roles at work, e.g. those of doctor, nurses and patients, and roles in families.

4. Environmental setting. Most games have their special courts or pitches. In the same way relationships are pursued in characteristic settings, e.g. those with friends and those with family.

5. Rules. Above all, games are defined by their rules, and in order to play a game of football, croquet, etc., it is necessary for a number of people to follow the same rules, otherwise no game is possible. Children's games provide a good example of creating rules as you go along – 'you're not allowed to hide in the next-door garden', etc. These rules develop over time. The rules of football are complex, and cannot be explained simply as functioning to help people get some exercise on Saturday afternoons. The game existed in many countries in the

ancient world, and usually consisted of large mobs, often from different villages, kicking a ball about with virtually no rules, and often with great violence, so that the game was sometimes suppressed by law. Over a long period the different versions of the game developed, with gradual additions, changes and refinements to the rules, which have now developed into an elaborate system in each form of the game. The designers of board games such as Monopoly invent the whole set of rules at once, but these have to be tried out and modified so that they produce a satisfactory game.

Similarly the rules of social relationships form a complex whole. Changing the rules can be tricky, since they are all related. For example, the rules of rugby football were changed to reduce the extent to which games were won by penalty kicks. The change was to give a free kick (i.e. a drop kick rather than a place kick) for certain minor infringements. This did not reduce the number of points won from penalties, so the nature of a free kick was altered, so that the ball had to be played with the foot before being kicked at goal. This in turn has led to the strategy of passing the ball to the best kicker – but a third change of rule has not yet been made.[2]

A great deal of human behaviour is governed by rules, indeed is made possible by rules. Some of these rules are formally outlined and legally sanctioned, as in incest laws or rules about human rights. Others are more informal. They carry normative rather than legal penalties. In this book we shall discuss the rules that apply to the main social relationships. We want to argue that they provide a key to the skills needed to cope with them successfully, and that these rules enable us to understand relationships better.

But what exactly is meant by a rule? By a rule we mean behaviour that most people, i.e. most members of a group, neighbourhood, or sub-culture, think or believe should be performed, or should not be performed. Rules can apply to particular situations, e.g. what should or should not be done at meals, or at the doctor's. Rules can also apply to particular relationships, e.g. they can specify what should or should not be done with friends or workmates.

We are concerned in this book with a particular kind of rule – informal rules applying to relationships. They are somewhat different from, though they sometimes overlap with, other kinds of rules, such as:
Laws, e.g. it is not allowed (in Britain) to marry your sister, or to be married to two people at the same time. We shall mention some of the

laws governing relationships later, but on the whole these do not deal with styles of behaviour, or ways of handling relationships.

Etiquette. We give some examples of some of these rules on p. 45f. They are similar to relationship rules in that they have the function of avoiding offence or other problems, but usually in minor matters and in particular situations.

Morals. Some of our rules do have a 'moral' content, in that some behaviour is approved or disapproved, e.g. one should keep confidences. However the degree of approval or disapproval is less than for traditional moral rules, and is based on the belief that breaking the rule is bad for the relationship.

How rules work

What we propose is simple: rules are developed so that people's goals in different relationships or situations can be attained. It is a familiar psychological principle that an individual person or animal will discover routes to desired goals, either by trial and error or by other forms of problem-solving. We are now proposing an extension of this principle: groups of people will find routes to their goals, and these routes will be collective solutions, including the necessary co-ordination of some behaviours and the exclusion of other behaviours by means of rules. Unless such co-ordination is achieved, group goals will not be attained.

An example is the rule of the road, which enables people to travel in both directions without colliding. Leon Mann[3] studied the emergence of rules governing behaviour in Australian football queues, which last for twenty-four hours or more. He found that rules developed, and were enforced, to control such behaviour and to make the queues tolerable, e.g. by allowing some time out. Indeed these were the main rules governing behaviour in the queues. He does not report that there were any rules to stop people making a noise, making love or getting drunk (as there are in many other situations); these are not necessary, since such behaviour would not interfere with the goals of queueing. In these cases the rule works primarily through co-ordinating the behaviour of a number of different people – the rule only works if they all follow it. In other cases the rule applies to individuals, and represents the most effective way of handling a situation. Recommended styles of leadership would be rules of this kind.

Rules are not always followed. We do not, for example, live in a world 'in which men tip their hats to ladies; youth defer to old people in public conveyances; unwed mothers are a rarity; citizens go to the aid of law enforcement officers; chewing gum is never stuck under tables and never dropped on the sidewalk; television repairman fix television sets; children respect their aged parents'.[4] However, a rule that many people break may still be deemed important, as we shall see later on.

Rules are not quite the same as conventions, which refer to arbitrary customs such as fashion in clothes. It is a rule in cricket that the batsman should use a bat (rather than, say, a tennis racquet), but a convention that he shall wear white trousers. The rules we are interested in are more like the rules of cricket, in the sense that the game is impossible or seriously disrupted if the rules are broken. If they are not kept, people will not find it interesting or sufficiently rewarding to continue playing or to come again.

Behaviour shared by members of a family can be regarded as rules in our sense. However, we shall find that many rules are much more widely shared than this. The reason is that all families share similar problems, and need similar rules to deal with them, and these rules are in any case learnt as part of the culture.

Rules often sound restrictive, but as we have seen, these restrictions often bring obvious benefits – for example, driving on a certain side of the road, or not talking during concerts. But rules do far more than this – they make whole realms of behaviour possible. 'Using language, playing games, courting, getting married, reasoning in mathematics, making decisions in committees, buying and selling a house, passing sentences on a person convicted of crime and even fighting a war are all to a large extent rule-governed activities'.[5] These are all examples of what has been called the 'social construction of reality'.

Functional anthropologists have offered explanations of common social rules. For example, the strict rules of etiquette surrounding doctors, lawyers and other professional people have the function of maintaining a certain distance, so that doctors and others can obtain intimate information without becoming too familiar or involved.[6] We shall come across a number of rules for relationships which can be interpreted in this way. For example, the widely established rule about having to take a spouse from another clan or family has the function of binding different groups in a society together (p. 236).

It is sometimes possible to satisfy functions in more than one way, by more than one set of rules. For example, buying and selling can be done by 1. fixed-price sale, 2. bargaining, 3. auction sales, or 4. barter. Similarly there is more than one set of marriage rules and more than one set of work relationships. And the relationships that exist in the present have developed slowly over time, and are still changing now, as is the case with the relationship between men and women in marriage.

Attempts to improve the rules have not always been successful. Missionaries in Australia tried to help an Aboriginal tribe by giving them free steel axes, since they seemed to be very short of axes. However this seriously disrupted the life of the tribe since only older males had possessed stone axes, which were part of the status system; and they were obtained by a form of trading which integrated different groups.[7]

The trouble is that a rule may be shown to have an important function, but members of the society who keep the rule may not know how the rule works. People may not understand why they cannot marry their sister, or (in some societies) have to marry a daughter of one of their mother's brothers – they simply find that they are attracted to one and not to the other, as a result of the working of the social system.

So rules may have functions which are not very clear, and they also combine together forming integrated systems, like the rules of a game. However, we do not need to take a conservative view about rules –after all most of them have been different in the past, and there are other ways of doing things in other cultures. But it is the case that changing them can be very difficult, and may involve changing more rules than one.

How far can there be local variations in rules, for example between different marriages or pairs of friends? Obviously marriages differ, yet they also share certain basic features, as we shall see. Our studies show that there is a very widespread consensus over the rules of marriage and of other relationships, so that the scope for local variation is probably much smaller than is sometimes supposed.

Cultural variations in rules

Ignorance of the workings of social rules creates difficulty, however, when we are faced with a whole new set of rules. Etiquette and the appropriateness or inappropriateness of certain behaviours in particular situations vary greatly between different cultures. A simple exchange of greetings ranges from the handshake common in Europe, to bowing in many Eastern cultures right through to the traditional Maori 'nose-rub', as well as more esoteric varieties of greetings in different tribal cultures. Even the sorts of non-verbal behaviours that we tend to take for granted, such as eye contact when speaking, or how far apart we stand from others, have been shown to vary greatly in different countries.[8]

"You get used to the English Quarter."

(Punch)

While the goals may be similar, different sets of rules may emerge to achieve them. For example, in some countries, such as Africa, it is expected that people will help their relatives by giving them jobs, while in others such 'nepotism' is frowned upon. In many parts of the world it is normal to pay a commission to professionals and civil servants in exchange for some service, while in other cultures such 'bribery' is deemed unethical or even illegal. Rules about time are often highly culture specific. In Britain, for example, one should be strictly on time for an appointment, while in other parts of the world being an hour or two late is acceptable.[9]

Different kinds of rules

There are many different kinds of rules for relationships. Here are some of the most important types:

Rewardingness The basic tenet of 'exchange theory' is that people will not stay in some kinds of relationship unless the rewards minus the costs give them more than they could receive in any alternatives available – taking into consideration the costs of making the transfer.

Some kinds of relationship are difficult or impossible to leave – kinship, for example. However, it is possible to reduce intimacy, frequency of contact, or level of help in these cases. So we expect that there will be a number of positive rules aimed at keeping the rewards provided to others at an acceptable level, and we expect that some of these rules will be universal to all relationships.

In addition we expect that there will be rules about avoiding undue costs for others, and that some of these will also be universal to all relationships.

Intimacy rules   One of the most important ways in which relationships differ is in the desired and appropriate level of intimacy. We report a study below in which family and friends were found to be quite different from neighbours, workmates, etc., in the rules governing intimacy. With the second group many of these rules are reversed, in order to keep intimacy low.

Co-ordination and avoiding difficulties   We now come to rules which apply to specific relationships and which have the function of co-ordinating behaviour so that relationship goals can be attained. These rules will reflect the basic properties of relationships in a quite detailed way. Some will enforce the approved roles. Some will avoid common temptations or other common sources of difficulty. Some will co-ordinate behaviour towards specific relationship goals.

Rules of behaviour with third parties   Pairs of individuals do not generally exist in isolation, and rules are needed to control behaviour in relation to other people – to deal with problems of jealousy, keeping confidences, standing up for people, and so on.

Are there always rules?

Is behaviour in all relationships and situations governed by rules? We expect that all relationships will need to be regulated by rules, and we shall find that there are in fact rules for all of the relationships which we discuss later in this book.

In the same way it is expected that all situations will be rule-governed, even the most informal ones. Price and Bouffard[10] asked subjects to rate the appropriateness of fifteen forms of behaviour in each of fifteen situations. They found that situations varied in the range of behaviours which were acceptable, but that every situation prohibited some things.

In a number of studies of apparently disorderly behaviour Marsh and colleagues[11] found that these too were governed by rules. For example, he interviewed football hooligans about how to 'put the boot in' and allied matters. In these interviews a number of rules were stated more or less directly by informants, e.g. it was not acceptable to injure members of the opposing gang, though it was desirable to frighten them. Anne Campbell[12] asked Borstal girls for their views about various kinds of behaviour in connection with fighting. Examples of the rules obtained were:

Should not ask friends to call the police (85%)

Should not ask friends to join in (81%)

In another study we investigated the rules for behaviour in twenty-five situations commonly entered by Oxford psychology students.[13] People rated how appropriate or inappropriate 124 kinds of behaviour were in each of the twenty-five situations. We found that groups of rules occurred together for particular situations. The first group – 'should be friendly', 'should be polite', 'should not embarrass others', etc. – were judged to apply to all or nearly all situations. These were the universal rules we had been expecting – rules to keep up the level of rewards for others and so keep them in the situation.

Other groups of rules applied to particular groups of situations: for example, 'should keep to cheerful topics of conversation', 'should dress smartly', etc., applied to sherry parties and similar social events. Just as there are groups of rules, so there are groups of situations, where each situation in a group shares much the same rules.

Finally there were some rules that applied to one situation only. For example, when going to see the doctor there were two special rules – 'make sure you are clean', and 'tell him the truth'. In a tutorial – 'don't pretend to understand when you don't'.

This study illustrates some of the features we are expecting to find for relationship rules, and was a model for some of the studies reported in later chapters.

Rules and skills

Is keeping rules part of social skill? We defined rules as behaviour that people believe should or should not be performed. We expected that breaking rules would result in the failure of a relationship, and have used this as a way of checking the importance of rules. Social skills have often been discovered by a comparison of the styles of behaviour of successful and unsuccessful practitioners. The concepts of rule and skill thus have a good deal of overlap. Rules can therefore be a guide to skills, as we shall see in our concluding chapter.

The main difference is that when we speak of skills we include both the choice of a particular kind of behaviour and also the ability to perform it. A non-swimmer might be given a clear explanation of swimming strokes, of the rules that have been found to work; but in order to keep afloat some *skill* is also needed. More complex skills, e.g. gymnastics or musical performance, may take years of training before they are mastered. In some cases the problem is controlling anxiety or other emotions, as in public performances.

The rules for behaviour of parents towards children, or of supervisors towards work groups, will be discussed in later chapters. In both cases those familiar with these relationships have quite definite ideas on the rules, i.e. the right way of handling these relationships. This may be partly because they have found out through their own experience or observation of others what works and what does not. Their ideas come partly from reading books or magazines (e.g. about how to be a parent), or from training courses for supervisors. Such books and training courses are nowadays quite closely based on research into the skills in question, though this was not true until quite recently. So popular beliefs about rules are increasingly likely to coincide with effective skills.

However, it is found in skills research that certain aspects of social skills are *not* generally known, even by experienced practitioners. For example some of the more subtle aspects of non-verbal communication or of the conduct of conversations are not widely known, though no doubt they eventually will be.[14] So these are areas where rules give an incomplete guide to social skills.

Rules as the key to relationships

Rules are not only the key to the most effective skills to use in a relationship. They are also the key to *understanding* relationships. They are only one feature, but they are in many ways the most important feature, of relationships. If rules are functional in making it possible to attain goals, they can tell us what the goals are. If rules are functional in averting common difficulties, they show us what these are. However it should be remembered that rules often represent only one possible solution to a problem.

Can rules reveal the goals of relationships? We shall find that friendship rules include a lot about the exchange of rewards, such as affection and help, which other research has shown to be very important here. The rules of marriage contain little about the exchange of rewards, but many rules about maintaining intimacy, which is itself rewarding. In work relationships the main rules are concerned with the efficient conduct of business.

Some rules are clearly aimed at avoiding common difficulties of various kinds. This was a common theme in the rules we found for situations. For example, a queue makes it possible for people to obtain tickets in a manner which is orderly and fair, though any one person could do better for himself by pushing to the front, asking friends at the front to buy him a ticket, or asking people to keep his place for long periods of time. Some relationship rules have the same purpose: marital partners should be faithful, people should keep confidences. These are both rules about behaviour with third parties. Similar rules which are internal to a relationship are: 'should not nag' (for wives) and 'accept one's fair share of the work-load' (work mates).

Other rules enable people to avoid difficulties that commonly occur in a relationship. Rules of etiquette appear to be designed to prevent such difficulties. For example, sending invitations not more than three weeks before the event makes it possible for the recipient to refuse, and coughing before entering rooms containing young couples is recommended.[15] Some of the rules that apply to relationships are like this, and suggest that there are certain very general problems to do with relationships.

Debrett's Etiquette and Modern Manners, for example, lists appropriate rules for a variety of circumstances, ranging from courtship and divorce to 'royal, diplomatic and formal occasions' and 'business manners'. For example, upon divorce:

> It is considered correct to return presents exchanged during the marriage. A woman generally offers to return her engagement ring but this is seldom accepted; she keeps it, gives it to a daughter or sells it.[16]

Or under business manners, when dealing with Arabs:

> A business man is unlikely to meet his business contact's wife and should not enquire about her in person but rather to ask after 'your

house'. The surest way to avoid causing offence is to pretend that women don't exist at all.[17]

And in the case of Muslims:

It is also courteous to avoid party-giving during the first month of the Islamic year because Mohammet's grandson was murdered in that month.[18]

And, of course, as we all know, upon meeting royalty:

If the royal hand is extended, take it lightly and briefly, at the same time executing a brief bob with the weight on the front foot, or a bow from the neck (not from the waist).[19]

How to find the rules

We defined rules as shared opinions or beliefs about what should and should not be done. It follows that the way to find rules is to ask members of a group what they think should be done, and to find out where there is agreement. Simply asking people to state the rules is not necessarily the best approach. In the case of grammar only professional linguists could do this, though most of us know the rules well enough to follow them, and to recognise mistakes. Similarly, while we may all recognise when a style of behaviour is inappropriate, we may not always be able to outline what *is* appropriate for that situation.

People can be asked questions of the form 'Is it important for husbands to be faithful to their wives?' on a rating scale giving degrees of importance. Another way is to describe instances of rule-breaking and to ask people to rate their appropriateness or inappropriateness.

However, we shall see later on that asking about rules in this way yields a number of rules which are not necessarily very important. A further test of rules is to find out what happens if they are broken. If no one minds, perhaps the rule doesn't matter. It may be possible to break the rules in an acceptable way – by indicating that this is meant to be funny, or is an attempt at improving the rules, or by simply indicating positive affect, for example.[20] In addition some people are good at dealing with cases of rule-breaking and hence avoiding disruption – by laughing it off, or having a quiet word with the offender. On the other hand there is usually trouble if people try to jump queues, e.g. at Australian football matches. And industrial workers may be 'sent to Coventry' for breaking rules about the rate of work. In polite social circles on the other hand there may be little visible reaction, because of the operation of higher order rules governing politeness and tolerance.

A better way of checking the importance of relationship rules is to find out whether breaking them leads to the disruption of a relationship. We shall be describing studies in which we have compared the rule-following behaviour of divorced couples in the period before the divorce with the behaviour of those who are still married. However, it is possible that the relationship failure came first and led to failure to keep the rules. A method which counters this problem is to ask people who have experienced the loss of a relationship how far their own or the other's failure to keep rules was responsible. We shall report the results of such studies in later chapters.

Our Study of the Rules of Relationships[20a]

We began by compiling a list of thirty-three rules which could apply across most relationships. These included rules about what should or should not be discussed in conversation, about hiding or expressing emotions, about dress and personal appearance, and so on. We also drew up a list of twenty-two common relationships, ranging from the very intimate, such as husband–wife and parent–child, to those 'professional' relationships all of us have encountered in everyday life, such as doctor–patient and teacher–pupil.

One hundred and eighty English-born men and women from different occupational and social class backgrounds took part. Each person rated how important he/she believed the rules were in six to eight of these relationships. The rating scales ranged from very important, through fairly important, to not applicable. Because some of the rules might operate in reverse for different relationships (such as hiding one's anger being important for some relationships and expressing it being important in others), people could also rate whether the *opposite* of the stated rule was fairly or very important. The nine-point rating scale used is shown below:

1	2	3	4	5	6	7	8	9
Rule *very* important	Rule *fairly* important		Rule doesn't apply		*Opposite* of rule *fairly* important		*Opposite* of rule *very* important	

Since men and women might hold different beliefs about the appropriateness of certain rules, equal numbers of both sexes completed each questionnaire. We thought that there might be age or generation differences, so we divided our group equally between older (aged 30 to 60) and younger individuals (aged 18 to 25), assuming that each group would be relatively homogeneous in its ideas about relationship rules.

We were also interested in whether the rules of relationship we found would be specific to our own culture, or would also apply in other countries. So our questionnaires were translated and distributed to men and women by collaborators in Italy, Hong Kong, and Japan. In all, we obtained our results from 300 Japanese, 280 Hong Kong Chinese, 230 Italians, and 180 British informants.

We began by examining the number of rules that people in the four countries rated as important in each relationship. In Hong Kong nearly two-thirds (63%) of all the 726 combinations of rules and relationships were endorsed as important by our informants. The figure was slightly lower for British men and women (63%) and for our Italian sample (56%). In Japan just over half (51%) of the 726 rule-relationship pairs were deemed important.

When we divided our set of rules into prescribed and proscribed rules – what one *should* do and what one should *not* do – we found another difference between our four cultures. In Japan there was an almost equal division: of the 371 combinations of rules and relationships that the Japanese believed were important, 182 were about things an individual *should* do within the particular relationship, and 189 about things he or she should *avoid* doing in the relationship. In Hong Kong there was also an almost equal split, with 55% of the important rules being prescribed ones, and 45% being proscribed. But for our two European cultures the results are very different. In Italy nearly two-thirds of the important rules are about what a person *should* do, compared to 35% which are *should not* rules. This asymmetry is even stronger in Britain, with 70% of our important rules dealing with things we *should* do in that relationship, and only 30% about what we should *not* do.

In Italy and Britain the relationships with the highest numbers of important rules attached to them are the more intimate ones – husband and wife, parent and adolescent and siblings. In Hong Kong these intimate relationships also have a large number of important rules, but in addition work superiors and work subordinates have as many rules. And in Japan these work relationships have a greater number of important rules applied to them than any of the intimate relationships.

Universal rules

Are there any rules that apply to all relationships across all four different cultures? Only four rules were rated important in all, or nearly all, of our twenty-two relationships by British, Italian, Hong Kong and Japanese informants. These are:

TABLE 1. Universal Rules

Should respect the other's privacy.
Should look the other person in the eye during
  conversation.
Should not discuss that which is said in confidence
  with the other person.
Should not criticise the other person publicly.

Fig. 1 EXAMPLE OF A RELATIONSHIP RULE:

SHOULD RESPECT THE OTHER'S PRIVACY

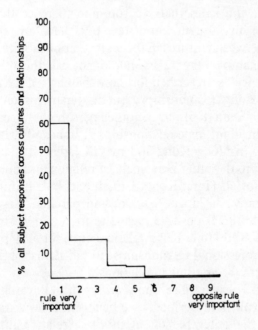

The most important rule across all relationships and cultures is the rule about privacy. This is shown in Figure 1. This rule is rated as very important in 60% of cases, and as fairly to very important in another 30%.

There are therefore rules that people from very different countries and cultures believe to be important in dealing with others in relationships ranging from the very temporary and task-oriented (such as Householder and Repairman) to the very intimate and long term (such as Husband and Wife).

In addition, there are rules endorsed by all four cultures in more than half of the twenty-two different relationships. These are:

TABLE 2. Rules Endorsed Across Cultures in More Than Half the Relationships

> Should not indulge in sexual activity with the other
>   person.
> Should address the other person by their first name.
> Should stand up for the other person in their absence.
> Should seek to repay debts, favours or compliments, no
>   matter how small.
> Should not disclose to the other person one's feelings and
>   personal problems.
> Should not ask the other person for material help.

These are the rules that are common to more than half of the relationships in all four countries, but there are also interesting *differences* between cultures in the general applicability of a particular rule. For example, the rule 'Should not ask the other person for personal advice' is prescribed for more than half of the British, Italian and Hong Kong relationships, but in Japan for only four out of twenty-two. 'Should talk to the other person about sex and death' is prescribed in all intimate relationships in Italy and Britain, compared to only four in Hong Kong and two in Japan. The same is true of 'Should talk to the other person about religion and politics', which is prescribed for all Hong Kong, British and Italian intimate relationships, but only for Japanese wives and parents. However, 'Should show unconditional positive regard to the other person' is strongly prescribed for all Hong Kong relationships, for all Japanese intimate and most professional relationships, for all British intimate relationships, but not for any Italian relationships.

Joking and teasing also show cross-cultural variation. While in Britain the rule is prescribed – we believe it is important to joke and tease with the other person in intimate relationships, with work colleagues, neighbours, and those we are sharing accommodation with – this is not the case in any other country, for any relationships. In fact there is a no-teasing rule for many relationships in these cultures.

There are also differences in rules about expressing emotion. In Britain and Italy the rules 'Should show anger' and 'Should show distress or anxiety' are prescribed in intimate relationships. However, in both Japan and Hong Kong a no-emotion rule is endorsed, especially for professional and service relationships, neighbours, and work superiors and subordinates. The rule 'Should not use swear words in front of the other person' is prescribed for all twenty-two relationships in Hong Kong, for all except close friend, siblings and husband in Japan, for fourteen relationships in Britain, but for only six in Italy. Rules about personal appearance also vary, and the rule 'Should appear neatly or smartly dressed when with the other person' is prescribed for only teachers, pupils and doctors in Italy, and for these plus work superior, subordinate and dating in Britain. But in Hong Kong and Japan the rule is prescribed in over half of the relationships, including work colleagues and son/daughter-in-law.

While we have some general rules across relationships in different countries we also have some interesting patterns of cross-cultural variation. Rules about respecting another's privacy and confidences are common to all. But rules about expressing emotion, self-disclosure, discussing intimate topics, and making requests for material help or personal advice are more strongly applied among our two European groups, particularly in Italy. Such intimate behaviour may actually be *pro*scribed in Hong Kong and Japan, particularly for professional and work relationships. Japanese rules tend to be more formal – e.g. those about not swearing, neat dress, and first-name usage, particularly in work relationships.

Cultural differences

How similiar are the relationships from each of our four countries? Are there similar patterns of rules for husbands and wives, for example, regardless of the country from which they emerge, which would distinguish the marital relationship from all other ones? To look at the overall patterns of rules and relationships we used a statistical technique called cluster analysis. This takes account of the pattern of similarity and differences among a set of items as a whole, and groups these together according to how similar they are on all the measures used simultaneously. We wanted to examine the grouping of relationships based on the scores of the thirty-three common rules for each relationship in each culture. If we find that most of our clusters or groupings comprise the same relationships regardless of the country from which they derive, then we shall be able to say that the same pattern of rules distinguishes these relationships, regardless of culture. But if we find that our clusters comprise many different relationships from the same country, then we shall be able to say that the cultural differences in the use of rules outweigh the similarity between relationships.

Fig 2.   CLUSTERS OF RELATIONSHIPS

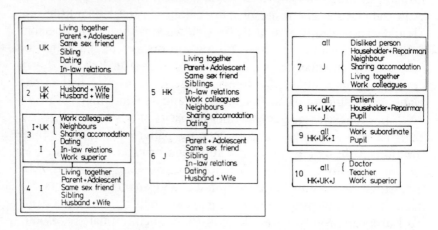

Figure 2 shows in diagram form the ten clusters that emerged. Some of the clusters are relationship-consistent regardless of country of origin, and some are culture-consistent, regardless of relationship. For example, cluster 1 contains only British relationships, cluster 4 only Italian ones, cluster 5 only Hong Kong, and cluster 6 only Japanese. However, cluster 10 contains doctor and teacher relationships from all four countries, and work superiors from three of the four, while cluster 8 comprises the patient relationship from all four countries, householder and repairman from three of the four, and pupil from Japan.

We can see from this diagram that there are fairly consistent patterns of rules across all four countries for certain relationships. Doctors, teachers and work superiors (cluster 10) tend to have the same rules applied to them, regardless of which country they are in. And this pattern of rules is different from the rules applied to pupils and work subordinates (cluster 9) or to patients, householders and repairmen (cluster 8). And while in all four countries we tend to apply the same pattern of rules to those people we 'don't get along with' (cluster 7), these are the same sort of rules that the Japanese also apply to neighbours, work colleagues, householders and repairmen, and those of either sex who they share accommodation with.

It is in the more intimate relationships that we find greater consistency within cultures than within relationships and across cultures. For example, Japanese intimate and marital relationships (cluster 6) are defined by rules different from those defining Italian intimate and marital relationships (cluster 4). Yet British and Hong Kong rules for husbands and wives are more similar to each other (cluster 2) than either is to its own country's other intimate relationships (clusters 1 and 5 respectively).

What are these different patterns of rules? The major differences are between the more intimate relationships on the left of our diagram and the service and professional relationships on the right. Not surprisingly, we prescribe more of the intimacy rules for the more intimate relationships, and proscribe their use in the less intimate ones: in particular, discussion of personal finances, disclosure of personal feelings and problems, and requests for personal advice or material help. In addition, we apply certain privacy rules more strongly for our service and professional relationships, in particular, not discussing confidences, not visiting socially unannounced, not touching and not joking with or teasing the other person. But for both intimate and non-intimate relationships, certain rules apply equally strongly. These are rules about eye contact, about repaying debts and favours, not feeling free to take up the other's time, showing positive regard, respecting privacy, not criticising the other person in public and not swearing.

Within the group of professional and service relationships there are also clearly defined patterns of rules in all four cultures. For work superiors and doctors and teachers certain intimacy rules should not be applied, while for work subordinates and pupils they are rated as simply not applicable. This is especially true of disclosing problems and feelings, not showing either anger or anxiety and distress in front of the other person, not requesting material help or discussing personal finances. In other words, work superiors, teachers and doctors should strive to hide their personal feelings and private problems from their subordinates and clients, while people believe that it is not really important for the latter to do the same.

When we look at the intimate relationships, we find that Japanese marital and intimate relations (cluster 6) are most similar to Hong Kong non-marital intimates and acquaintances (cluster 5). Both of these are distinguished from Italian and British groups by less emphasis on intimacy rules. For clusters 5 and 6 it is deemed far less important to discuss intimate topics, express personal feelings, show public affection, touch the other person, ask for material help or discuss personal finances, particularly in comparison with British and Italian intimate relationships, and even in comparison with British and Italian acquaintances such as work colleagues or neighbours.

It seems, at face value, that our European cultures place far greater emphasis on expressing emotions, giving opinions on intimate topics, affection and requests for help and advice than our Hong Kong and Japanese counterparts, at least as far as intimate relationships are concerned. Close relationships, whether spouses, family, friends, or kin by marriage, or even by virtue of heterosexual intimacy (as in dating or cohabitation), are viewed as sources of support, and rules exist about using them as such. We *should* ask for material help, disclose our personal problems and feelings, and ask for personal advice in our intimate relationships. And to a lesser extent, we apply similar rules to our less intimate acquaintances such as work colleagues and neighbours – and also use them as sources of social support. While the Hong Kong informants endorse very similar rules for husbands and wives, Japanese marriages are characterised by less emphasis on the overt expression of intimacy. And the same is true of other Japanese and Hong Kong intimate relationships.

When we cluster-analysed each individual culture we found that British subjects' ratings grouped into two clusters of relationships – intimate and non-intimate:

Intimate cluster: Husband–Wife, Parent and Son/
                                daughter-in-law, Parent–Adoles-
                                cent, Siblings, Close friends, and
                                Couples dating   and   living
                                together.
Non-intimate cluster: Work colleagues, Superiors and
                                subordinates, Neighbours, Re-
                                pairman–Householder,   Doctor
                                –Patient, Teacher–Pupil, People

sharing accommodation, and those who don't get on.

Rules about expression of personal feelings, attitudes and affection were highly endorsed for the Intimate cluster while rules about formal behaviour were common to both.

Three clusters emerged for the Hong Kong results, varying in level of intimacy:

High Intimacy cluster:	Husband–Wife, Sibling, Parent, Close friend, and Opposite sex living together.
Moderately Intimate cluster:	Parent and Son/daughter-in-law, Adolescent, Dating couples, Same sex sharing accommodation, Work colleagues and Neighbours.
Non-intimate cluster:	Householder–Repairman, Doctor –Patient, Teacher–Pupil, Work superior and subordinate and People who don't get on.

Rules about expressing feelings, opinions and affection are regarded as very important for the Intimate cluster, while there are rules about not displaying emotions in the Non-intimate cluster. Non-intimate relationships are also characterised by more formal rules about dress and appearance.

There were also three clusters for Japanese relationships:

Intimate cluster:	Parent–Adolescent, Close friend, Dating couples, Parent and Son/ daughter-in-law, and Siblings.
Non-intimate cluster:	Work colleague, Superior and sub-ordinate, Neighbours, Repair-man–Householder, Doctor–Patient, Teacher–Pupil, Same and opposite sex sharing accommoda-tion, and People who don't get on.
Marital cluster:	Husband–Wife.

Only the husband–wife relationship cluster endorses the expression of feelings, opinions and affection strongly. In the non-intimate cluster there is a prohibition on expressing feelings and affection.

Italians also show three clusters of relationships:

High Intimacy cluster:	Husband–Wife, Parent–Adolescent, Close friend, Sibling, and Couples living together.
Professional and commercial:	Householder–Repairman, Doctor–Patient, Teacher–Pupil.
Moderate Intimacy cluster:	Work colleagues, Superior and subordinate, Parent and Son/daughter-in-law, Neighbours, Dating couples, Same sex sharing accommodation, and People who don't get on.

Again, the high intimacy cluster is characterised by rules about expressing feelings, opinions, affection and requests for help and advice. Professional and commercial relationships have very few endorsed rules, while the third cluster endorses some of the rules about expressing opinions, but not those relating to feelings or requests for help.

To summarise, all four cultures distinguish between intimate and less intimate relations. But overall, the Eastern cultures, especially Japan, prescribe fewer of the rules about expressing emotions, opinions and affection across all types of relationship. And while all cultures place family and friends in a single cluster, Japanese endorse different rules for the marital relationship than for all other intimate relationships. And while in-laws are treated similarly to family and friends in Britain and Japan, they are viewed more like other less intimate relations like work colleagues and neighbours in Italy and Hong Kong.

Sex differences

We hypothesized that men and women might endorse rules differently, since, as we shall see in later chapters, there are sex differences in the way males and females behave in close relationships such as friendship and with kin. We found that there were major sex differences in the way rules were endorsed across the four cultures for almost all relationships. Only three relationships – with neighbour, parent and work superior – showed no consistent differences between men and women.

Many of the sex differences related to the use of intimacy rules.

Females, across all cultures, deem it more important to express emotions such as anger and anxiety, to disclose personal feelings and problems, and to share news of success. But females also prescribe certain rules that operate to diminish intimacy. For fifteen of the twenty-two relationships, they endorse rules about privacy more than men do, and believe that one should *not* 'feel free to take up as much of the other's time as one desires'. And they endorse rules about not touching and no sex more strongly than males in non-intimate, especially work relationships. Women also believe it is important to look the other person in the eye during conversation, and endorse this rule far more strongly than men do in twelve relationships, especially intimate ones. Men, on the other hand, endorse rules about obedience more strongly than women. These sex differences are particularly strong in sibling and dating relationships.

Age differences

We expected to find certain differences due to age or generation, in that male and female young adults (18 to 25-year-olds) would endorse different rules from those endorsed by older men and women (30 to 60-year-olds). We found major differences between our two age groups across the four cultures for all relationships except son/daughter-in-law, and even then there were age differences in at least one of the cultures. But the direction of age difference varied according to the particular culture.

In general, younger people were likely to endorse the intimacy rules more strongly, particularly in Japan and Hong Kong, while the older group were more likely to state that one should *not* disclose feelings and problems, discuss intimate topics, show public affection, or ask for personal advice. This is especially true of relationships with non-kin peers, such as close friends, dating couples and people of either sex living together.

Older subjects tended to endorse rules about neat dress and appearance more strongly, but mainly in Britain and Italy. Very few rules about personal appearance discriminated between young and older Japanese informants. Similarly, formal rules such as prohibitions on swearing generally failed to discriminate between the two age groups across all four cultures. Overall, British informants showed the greatest discrepancy between rules endorsed by young and older subjects, while the Japanese gave very similar answers across both age groups.

We do not know how far such age differences are due to the effects of the actual ageing process, and how far they may reflect historical changes in the rules endorsed by members of each culture. Age differences can be shown by longitudinal studies, historical differences by studies of groups of individuals of the *same* age at different dates. We shall be able to draw on studies of both kinds at several points later in the book.

The implications

What do these findings tell us about relationships in general? First, they show that people share a consensus about what behaviours are appropriate in which relationships. Secondly, while certain rules apply across relationships in all four cultures, others are more specific to individual relationships – sometimes across cultures, but more often within particular cultures. Things we should *not* do in one relationship are strongly prescribed in others, and may not apply at all to a third relationship or to the same relationship in a different country. This can obviously create difficulties and misunderstanding, as many Western businessmen have found, to their consternation, when dealing with non-Western cultures.

Brislin and Pederson[21] state:

> The cross-cultural factors that are most troubling are often not the most obvious differences of dress, gestures, or food, although the exotic aspects of these differences are cited to illustrate cultural differences. The adjustment process produces a re-ordering of daily behavior habits in subtle ways which might escape conscious awareness, such as different uses of the same word, different status symbols that must not be insulted, different traditional values that must be recognized or different views on the importance of personal relationships.

How do individuals within the culture itself, as well as foreigners who need to learn about a new set of interpersonal behaviours, function efficiently within a wide range of interpersonal relationships? We have already seen how rules operate to regulate relationships, but within each culture different values and traditions require the application of somewhat different rules. For example, in our own culture we endorse rules about keeping confidences *very* strongly across all relationships, more strongly than rules about public criticism. We would consider it an abuse of trust to disclose another's confidences and view the perpetrator as a less than honourable or moral character. Whether we actually apply the rule as strongly in practice is questionable, as the popularity of gossip shows. But we do endorse it strongly. In Japan, however, there is a far greater emphasis on 'face'. An honourable person would never cause another to 'lose face', so that there are very strict rules about not criticising another person in public. This rule is judged an important one across all relationships by our Japanese informants, and more important than rules about disclosing confidences – although these are also endorsed as important since breaking them would also involve a loss of face.

This emphasis on maintaining face is one that has led to many misunderstandings in business dealings. In Japanese culture, direct questions are avoided unless there is absolute certainty that the answer will not embarrass the individual, since, for example, admitting that one could not meet a production demand or performance schedule would result in a loss of face. So direct questions about the capacity or ability of a Japanese firm might be answered in the affirmative, even if the actual situation is the reverse, resulting in serious misunderstanding.[22]

Japanese culture also emphasises the control of an outward show of emotions in public. The ideal is to present an expressionless face to the world, especially in situations of great anxiety. Hence there are rules in Japan about *not* showing distress or anxiety or expressing anger. Both rules are endorsed in many relationships, and only in the marital relationship should one express anxiety or distress, and not even then in the case of anger. The same rule is also prescribed in our other Eastern culture of Hong Kong. However, for our two European cultures, expression of such emotions is endorsed in many relationships. There are no such rules about hiding possibly negative emotions in our own culture. And in Japan particularly, there is a similar restriction on the expression of other emotions in public. Public displays of affection, even between intimates, are less common, and even pleasant emotions may be controlled in public.[23] Japanese emotional expressions are, in fact, harder to identify accurately from non-verbal facial cues than from English or Italian faces, even for Japanese viewers, as we showed in an experiment.[24]

Another cross-cultural difference is in the nature of work relationships. As we saw earlier, Japanese informants rate as important a greater number of rules in work relationships than in any others. There are, apparently, more rules about appropriate behaviour between work superiors and subordinates than the Japanese would apply to any intimate relationship. For example, the rule about self presentation – 'Should strive to present oneself to the other person in the best light possible' – is rated important only for work superiors and subordinates, and not for any other relationship. In Western culture there tends to be a more egalitarian relationship between superior and subordinate – first-name usage is common for both parties. In Japan there is greater emphasis on hierarchical relations, but there is also a strong emphasis on group supportiveness, and there is an ethos of paternalistic care of subordinates – the oyabum–kobun relationship. This leads to rules such as 'Should show unconditional positive regard to the other person', which is important both for subordinate to superior, and also for superior to subordinate.

What of the more intimate relationships? We have already noted that the Japanese prescribe fewer intimacy rules than are found in our two European cultures, and we can see from Figure 2 that Hong Kong intimate relationships (except for husband and wife) are, overall, most similar to Japanese intimate and marital relationships. This is not surprising, since the two cultures share a common heritage (as do the Italian and English) – they certainly have more in common than either Eastern culture has with the West, despite the strong Western influence in Hong Kong. In both Eastern countries there is less emphasis on the importance of expressing emotions and opinions. In England, and more so in Italy, it is deemed important to discuss and express potentially negative emotions or topics which may lead to conflict. In the Eastern cultures, these behaviours tend not to be prescribed or proscribed for most intimate relationships. This may derive from a desire to avoid potential sources of conflict, since, it has been found that there is a strong emphasis on social conformity and harmonious group behaviour among Eastern (particularly Chinese) cultures. The Japanese have a motto of *Chowa* or *Wa* (Harmony) and a scroll bearing these Chinese characteristics is often hung on the wall of a room in the home, school or company. From childhood people are trained to value interpersonal harmony and to restrain themselves in order to avoid conflict.[25] The worst behaviour of older children is quarrelling with people outside the family. In Eastern and Latin American countries there is a general emphasis on maintaining good social relationships by reducing disagreement and being less assertive in non-family relationships, which may in fact extend to more intimate relationships, not by prohibiting the expression of potentially conflict-laden opinions or emotions, but by minimising their importance. In Japan there is also the concept of *amae* or the wish to lean on another's goodwill and to be dependently self-indulgent.[26] It has been described as the direct opposite of the Western ideal of self-reliance, and is expressed in families and with close friends, but especially between husbands and wives. Fewer things are prohibited within these *amae* relationships, so there are fewer rules.

The purpose of rules

What purpose do rules play in relationships? We have already proposed a functional theory of rules. Relationships determine, to a large extent, the sorts of situations that will be met. For the householder–repairman relationship, the range of possible situations is limited to the task at hand. It is unlikely that the two individuals would meet socially, or have the opportunity to disclose personal problems or their views on sex or death. Therefore there is little necessity for rules dealing with such matters to emerge for this relationship. For husbands and wives, on the other hand, the relationship involves large amounts of time spent in close contact, over a lengthy period of time, plus a high level of emotional involvement. Many more opportunities exist for a very wide variety of situations to occur, and also many more opportunities for a conflict of goals.

Rules, we believe, have two major functions in relationships. First, they regulate behaviour to minimise potential sources of conflict which may disrupt the relationship. These rules function to maintain the relationship itself rather than to meet any specific goals. Secondly, rules provide for an exchange of rewards that motivate the individuals to remain in the relationship. Regulating rules serve to channel behaviour in order to allow individual goals to be met by the maintenance of a relationship. Reward rules prescribe behaviours that meet individuals' goals, and thereby provide an inducement for relationship growth.

Relationships differ in terms of the number and range of goals, and therefore of the types of rules. In relationships which have very narrowly focused goals, such as householder–repairman or doctor – patient, there are few relevant rewarding rules. The main goal of the interaction would be task oriented, and there is little potential for relationship growth. Therefore the main rules operating are those that facilitate the efficient completion of the task at hand, and that allow the relationship to continue long enough and smoothly enough to complete the task. But for intimate relationships there is no single goal or task. The relationship must in itself be rewarding in order to continue. So regulating rules are also important to provide the framework in which reward rules can operate. And since the potential for conflict is greater, more regulating rules are thought to be important. We would therefore predict that for intimate relationships we should have many regulating and reward rules operating, while for less intimate relationships, only regulating and task-oriented rules would be endorsed as important.

What are these regulating rules that operate to maintain relationships by the avoidance of potentially disruptive conflict? One rule is respecting the other's privacy, and, as we have seen, this rule is regarded as important for all relationships, whether intimate or non-intimate, in all four cultures. Two related rules are not disclosing another's confidences, and not criticising the other person publicly, which are judged important in almost all relationships and cultures.

Other regulating rules are relevant to relationship-specific sources of conflict, such as rules about tolerance of third parties in intimate relationships, or about faithfulness in heterosexual relations. We shall examine these relationship-specific rules in more detail in later chapters, when we look more closely at the pattern of rules characterising individual relationships.

What about rewarding rules? Rules dealing with the specific exchange of rewards, such as sharing good news or repaying debts and compliments, or showing emotional support, are common to most of the ten intimate relationships in all four countries, and tend to be less strongly and less commonly endorsed for the non-intimate relationships. An exception is Japan, where such an exchange may be formalised, as in the ritualised exchange of gifts (*zoto*) or bonds of reciprocal obligations such as *on* and *giri*. In Japan this rule was most strongly endorsed among work relationships, neighbours, and persons of either sex sharing accommodation. Other rules dealing with the rewarding aspects of relationships, such as public support and self disclosure, are also common to many of the intimate relationships in all four cultures, while some, such as the expression of public affection or of positive regard, are more culture specific.

To summarise, we have given an overall view in this chapter of the similarities and differences in the patterns of rules across relationships and cultures. We shall examine the particular rules associated with specific relationships in more detail in the following chapters.

FURTHER READING

Argyle, M. (1983) *The Psychology of Interpersonal Behaviour* Harmonds-worth: Penguin, 4th edition
Bochner, S. (1982) *Cultures in Contact: Studies in Cross-Cultural Interaction* Oxford: Pergamon

4

Friendship

What are friends? The *Shorter Oxford Dictionary* defines 'friend' as 'one joined to another in mutual benevolence and intimacy'. Friendship in our culture is not established or dissolved by a ceremony, like marriage, and is not dependent on any role-relations, as workmates and kin are. Friends are simply people who like each other, and enjoy doing certain things together. Friendship is entirely voluntary, unlike kinship, and there are no clear rules about who may be friends or what they should do together.

Friendship takes a variety of forms, which vary somewhat with age, sex and social class. However, there is a common theme, and people seem to have a clear understanding of what friendship is like. In several studies samples of subjects have been asked what they mean by a 'friend'. Much the same answers have been found in different groups of subjects and in different countries. Friends are people who are liked, whose company is enjoyed, who share interests and activities, who are helpful and understanding, who can be trusted, with whom one feels comfortable, and who will be emotionally supportive.

Friendships have different degrees of closeness. There are 'best' or 'close' friends, and 'acquaintances'. Although research has often focused on close friends, these may be less typical than good friends. Certainly they are less numerous. The differences between these levels are that with close friends more intimate topics are discussed, more help is given, people feel more relaxed, and feel that they can be themselves.

If we may anticipate a later section (p. 75f), there is a consistent sex difference: for men, friends are people to do things with, for example, shared leisure, while for women, friends are people to confide in, who will be emotionally supportive. To anticipate again, for young people friends are expected to be entertaining, for old people friends are expected to be useful and helpful. So there are different degrees of friendship and different kinds of friends; in each type one aspect of friendship is emphasised while other aspects are less important. When we come to look at cultural variations in friendship, we shall find some quite interesting varieties of friendship, which have developed in particular settings. Nevertheless, for all stages of life, for both sexes, and in all classes and cultures, the friendship relationship is found, and is one of the most important relationships.

Friends are usually distinguished from kin. However, 7% or more of friends are also kin. In other words, a sufficiently friendly relation is formed, voluntarily, with a few kin, so that they are treated as friends.[1] There is also the reverse process whereby close friends are made honorary kin – 'she's like a sister to me'.

Similarly some people at work become friends. This is more common for teachers, social workers, and others, whose work overflows into leisure, whose contacts with customers or clients are important, and whose work is a central life interest.[2] Some neighbours become friends, especially for older people and in traditional working-class areas (Figure 1).

Fig 1. SOURCES OF FRIENDSHIP BY LIFE CYCLE

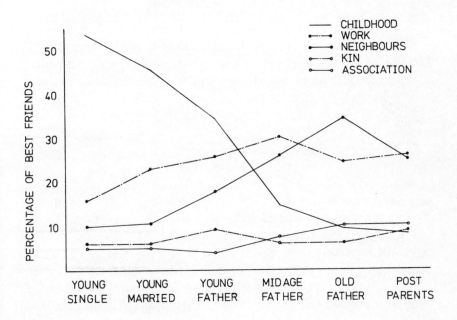

How many friends do people have, and how long do they last?

It depends what we mean by a friend. If we mean 'best friends', then people have one or two, though many people – many middle-aged men and working-class people for example – have none at all. The number of friends claimed, or named, increases rapidly if the degree of closeness is reduced:

'close friends' – about 5
'friends' – about 15
'members of social network' (includes kin) – about 20
named 'acquaintances' – variable, usually large, over 1,000 for some people.

Another way of answering the question of how many friends people have is to find out how many they saw in the last week (Table 1).

TABLE 1. Number of Friends Seen in Last Week[4]

	Men	Women
local friends (within 10 minutes' walk)	2.9	2.4
work friends	1.4	0.3
other friends	3.3	1.9
Total	7.6	4.6

Although women reported fewer friends than did men in this London study, this is not always found – and women do have more *close* friends. The people who have the most friends are those who are:

young (18–25)
middle-class
single
extrovert

While some individuals have a lot of friends, others have none or very few, or fewer than they would like. Adolescents often feel lonely – 10–15% are seriously isolated and lonely, over 50% report that 'I often feel lonely', girls rather more than boys.[5] Middle-aged people, especially men, often have few friends, but they do not feel so lonely, because they have other social contacts at home and at work.

The stability of childhood friendships is notoriously low – 'staying with the same old friends can be awfully boring'. As children grow older their friendships last longer, and those formed during adolescence and the early adult years before marriage are often the closest and the most long lasting. Number of friends varies quite a lot with living arrangements, as Table 2 shows.

TABLE 2. Number of Friends and Living Arrangements[6]

	married no children	married with children	married children grown up
close friends	3.8	4.1	11.1
total friends	17.4	14.6	29.4

	single living alone	single living with partner	single divorced, separated or widowed
close friends	4.4	5.6	7.8
total friends	22.4	20.0	18.4

	single living alone	with others	married living (together) on own	with others
close friends	4.4	4.3	4.6	8.8
total friends	21.7	25.5	14.3	29.4

Married people have fewer friends when there are children at home, and more after they have left. The divorced, widowed and separated have more close friends, and those who are living on their own have more friends. Other studies show that the unmarried spend much more time with friends than do the married.[7]

On the other hand young people make new friends, including new best friends, quite easily. Older people make new friends with more difficulty but hold on to their old friends longer. In a Canadian study of close relationships in a large city, it was found that overall 57% of these relationships had lasted for over eleven years (though these included kin), and 29% of choices (they were given six each) had not changed over five years.[8] Friendships last longer if people live near one another or meet regularly at work or in some other way. They are often broken if one person moves away.

Friendships last longest for those who are:

older
married and with children

living fairly near
part of a wider network
closer friends

Social networks

Friends do not usually come in pairs: A and B also know C. So the relationship between A and B is affected by their links with C and the wider network. Networks can be plotted by asking all the people in a neighbourhood or other grouping who their friends are or whom they see regularly. All the links are plotted, and the network can then be analysed in various ways. 'Density' for example is the percentage of the possible links between those concerned which are active. We tend to like friends of friends. This may be because it avoids a feeling of imbalance, but it could also be because members of a group share similar values and interests, or it may be a result of some people being more popular than others, so that we and our friends like the same people.[9] A friendship will last longer if both share the same friends, as in the friendship between A and B on the left-hand side of Figure 2, rather than that between A^1 and B^1 on the right-hand side.[10]

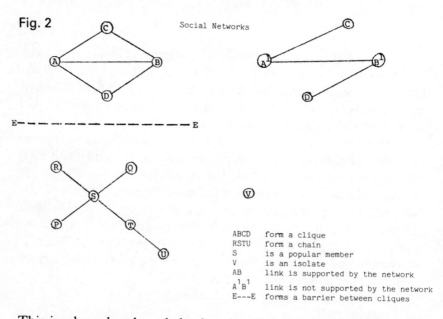

Fig. 2   Social Networks

ABCD	form a clique
RSTU	form a chain
S	is a popular member
V	is an isolate
AB	link is supported by the network
A^1B^1	link is not supported by the network
E---E	forms a barrier between cliques

This is why rules about behaviour in relation to third parties are so important in friendships – such as being tolerant and not jealous of other relationships (p. 92f), which is a major source of friction between friends. In Figure 2 we can see some other common features of networks – cliques, chains, barriers, as well as popular and unpopular people.

Networks are sometimes plotted in terms of friendship choices, the friends each person claims to have. These are often, but not always, reciprocated. Popular people receive a large number of such nominations; they in turn make a few more than others, but the choices they do make are reciprocated.[11] Networks are a more useful concept than *groups* for the study of friends, since friends usually form networks rather than clearly bounded groups, though networks do have dense clusters, corresponding to groups of friends.

Dense networks develop under certain social conditions – in the country rather than in the city, when people live close together, and in cultures where law and order are ineffective and people need protection. In India, for example,[12] it is very important to have a network of kin, friends, old colleagues, etc., to help get things done, since the official channels are often slow-moving, corrupt or inefficient. Networks are denser for young adults, married people, and those with children, and are denser if based on kin or on work rather than on friends or neighbours. Close friends form dense networks if they live in the same neighbourhood (cf. p. 278f).[13]

Networks also play an important part in the informal structure of firms, universities and other organisations, and are the basis for communication and help over and above the slow-moving official channels. They are important in the links between organisations, for example in the form of overlapping directorships and external examiners.

Networks have many effects on their members: 1. There are more frequent encounters in denser networks. 2. There is greater pressure to conform, and more conformity. 3. Pairs of friends, couples in love, husbands and wives, are held together if they both share the same network. 4. Individuals seek help through their network. Here a dispersed network, with varied kinds of members, is most likely to provide access to the right kind of help. This can include getting jobs, finding accommodation, getting the right medical attention, and pulling strings of all kinds. 5. The mental health of people with dense networks is better, partly perhaps because they have been able to enter such networks. Networks are, however, a major source of social support. 6. Ideas are diffused through networks, including ideas about politics, fashion, new films. Doctors learn about new medicines, farmers about new seeds, and research workers about new ideas, through their respective networks.[14]

There are a number of different roles individuals may play in networks. Some are leaders of thought in one area – politics, travel, or whatever. These 'opinion leaders' are better informed and in touch with other parts of the network connected with their field of expertise.

The growth of friendship

Making friends is a gradual process, which can be divided into three stages: 1. Forming impressions of the other at a distance, or during casual meetings at work, in the neighbourhood, etc. 2. Early meetings by arrangement or invitation. 3. Regular meetings and interdependence. This process can be seen as a kind of filtering or selection of possible friends, where some are rejected at each stage.

Forming impressions of the other, in the course of casual meetings. Friends are based mainly on contacts made at work, in the neighbourhood, and in clubs or at other leisure activities. They can also be introduced by other friends – part of the network – or encountered accidentally anywhere. Many are met through the normal pattern of activity – at work, for example – but with no voluntary choice of each other as companions, or special attention to each other.

The more frequently two people meet, the more they know each other, and in most cases the more they come to like one another. Frequency of contact in turn depends on proximity, so friendship develops more easily if people live near each other, work in the same office, or meet at the same church or club. This is the first 'filter' – sufficient frequency of contact.

Studies of students show that the closer together they live, the more they like one another. However in the case of adults rather a small proportion of neighbours become friends (p. 277f). The difference is that students have a great deal in common, they are sufficiently similar for almost any pair to become friends, while adult neighbours are much more varied. At work, or in other organised settings, we can get on perfectly well with a wide range of others. However for friendship we are more particular – we prefer people who are similar to ourselves. They usually need to be of a similar age, social class, and race, for a start, and these aspects of people can easily be seen at a distance.

We are attracted more to other people if we like the look of them, and at the early stages this may be all we have to go on. Physical attractiveness is important in friendship as well as in love, partly because of the stereotyped belief that attractive people are warm, sociable, interesting, kind, and so on. (It is not yet known whether they really are.) Physical attractiveness is discussed further on page 103f. Clothes are important too: they affect physical attractiveness, but they also send messages about social class, group membership (e.g. of a school, or a rebellious sub-culture), and attitude to life (e.g. conservative *v.* flamboyant, tidy *v.* untidy).

We can learn a lot about others by observing their behaviour. We can form impressions of whether they are warm or cold – mainly from their non-verbal behaviour, such as facial expression and tone of voice; their extroversion from their apparent sociability; their assertiveness or dominance, intelligence, tendency to conform or to deviate. Estimates of these and other personality dimensions can be made by simple observation of someone's behaviour. Each of us is particularly interested in some traits: we may want our friends to be warm, non-assertive and intelligent, for example. If a potential friend passes this filter, the embryo friendship may move on to the next stage.

Meetings by arrangement or invitation   This is a crucial stage in the growth of friendship. Meetings between two people are now sought voluntarily, and in a different setting from before, with the clear intention of getting to know one another better. Middle-class people ask each other home for a drink or a meal. Working-class people are more likely to arrange to meet at a pub or club. This is the first point at which social skills are needed, the skills of suggesting the first meeting, giving an invitation. These first meetings consist of talking, and often at the same time eating or drinking. And the talk consists of two people, or a group of people, exchanging information about themselves, the beginnings of self-disclosure. At first this is done very cautiously, revealing rather superficial aspects, but not basic values, problems, hopes or fears.

Many studies have shown that we like people who are similar to ourselves in background, in interests and in leisure activities, in beliefs and in values, in way of thinking, and in life-style. The main filter at stage 2 is discovering how similar the potential friend is in such respects. This is not very easily observable at a distance, though it can be assumed that people who are met at church have shared beliefs, and those met at Scottish country dancing have a shared interest. As we have seen, during early meetings people are rather hesitant to reveal too much of themselves, so the skill at this stage is to proceed cautiously, with increasing degrees of self-disclosure, which are reciprocated, and to discover common interests and values. The danger lies in revealing things that will not be approved of by the other, such as supporting a different political party or being too rich or too poor. There is a considerable amount of self-presentation at this stage of friendship: people tidy the house, dress carefully, conceal discreditable aspects of their past, and generally package themselves in an acceptable way. This can be seen as 'ingratiation' – trying to please the other by agreeing with them, flattering them, and avoiding conflicts; but it is really part of general 'self presentation' – trying to appear the sort of person who has good qualities and is therefore likeable.

It is most important that two potential friends should think about things in the same way; Duck[15] has found that close friends use the same dimensions for classifying people. It is also important that they should react to events in a similar way, so that they can share experiences and know that the other will have similar emotional responses and think the same things good and bad. We like people who share our beliefs and values, especially if they share relatively uncommon values with us.[16]

On the other hand it is generally found that friends are not necessarily similar in personality. Often they are not. In our own study of female friendships, we found that there was no similarity in personality measures for friends, but that they were similar in certain needs, particularly the need for nurture.[17] While some people choose friends for their general compatibility, others choose different people for different activities, and compartmentalise their social life more. These people also monitor their own behaviour carefully, and vary it more from one situation to another.[18]

Another filter at this stage is how rewarding the other is found to be. Similarity can be seen as part of this – we like to have our beliefs supported by others, and to meet people with similar interests and background and ways of thinking. Other people can be more directly rewarding, however, by their style of social behaviour – for example by non-verbal behaviour which is warm and friendly, by being cheerful, amusing, interesting, kind, helpful, and above all by apparently liking us, and being interested in us.

These are the strongest rewards. We like people who like us, and we like people who have a favourable opinion of us, and who see us as we see ourselves. For those who have stayed friends for a long time there is a close correlation between self-concept and perception by the other.[19] When our self-esteem is low, we are more susceptible to the effects of feedback from another, and experiments have shown that people whose self-confidence has been lowered prefer others who positively evaluate them more, and dislike rejecting or negatively evaluating people more.[20] Positive feedback directed at some area about which the receiver is unsure is most likely to be perceived as rewarding. In other words, if we pride ourselves on our sense of humour, but are not too sure of our taste in clothes, a compliment about our sharp wit is likely to be less rewarding than one on our appearance.

Friends are rewarding in more material ways too – inviting to meals, giving presents, providing material help, but on a much smaller scale than the presents and help provided by kin (p. 218f). While such rewards should be in some way reciprocated, if they are returned too soon or too exactly, this is taken as a sign of a rather superficial relationship in our culture.[21] We saw above that some individuals need their friends to be fun, to be entertaining, while others want them to be useful; some want to talk, others want to do things together. Being rewarding is a crucial social skill in making friends, and it has many components. However the non-verbal signalling of a warm and friendly attitude has been found to be particularly important.

We may find an individual attractive, not just from physical appearance, but from his/her ability to deal with other people – his/her social competence. The ability to initiate and maintain an interesting conversation, saying and doing the right thing, may affect how attractive we are to the other. We like being with people who put us at ease and make us feel relaxed rather than anxious and uncomfortable. We enjoy being with someone who holds our interest or makes us laugh, or makes us feel attractive. We shall discuss the role of social skills in relationships in more detail later in this book. But social competence is an important component of interpersonal attraction which the many studies on physical attractiveness have tended to overlook.

Regular meetings and interdependence constitute another important step forward in the growth of friendship; for example when two people decide to have lunch every Wednesday, or to play squash once a week. They may also be involved in more serious joint activities – over work or business, or buying property, for example, though this is less common. They now anticipate regular rewards from the other, because they can have a regular heart-to-heart talk or share regular activities. The reward is of two forms, based on the agreeable behaviour of the other, and the joint activity itself.

They have now each become dependent on the other for these regular rewards. The other is part of the normal pattern of life. Each gains from the relationship, though one may benefit more from it than the other. Meanwhile each has become fonder of the other, and has developed a concern for the other's outcomes as well as his own. In deciding how to spend their time together each will give some consideration to how much the other will enjoy things.

Self-disclosure has gone much further by this stage, and the friends have revealed a lot about themselves. They trust each other to treat this information as confidential, and begin to treat each other as confidants with whom they can discuss their problems, and from whom they can rely on receiving social support. The intimacy of self-disclosure can be scaled, from very non-intimate matters such as preferences for TV programmes to much more intimate ones such as money and sex. As people get to know one another they move up this scale to a point that defines the degree of intimacy reached. Examples of the levels of self-disclosure to friends and others on one of these scales are given in Table 3.

TABLE 3. Self-Disclosure to Friends and Others[22]

	by	Males	Females
to: same-sex friend		42	52
opposite-sex friend		40	43
mother		39	48
father		34	37
total		154	180

Activities shared with friends

We can ask how often each friend is seen. In an American study, the following results were found (Table 4). Most people see their close friends nearly once a week, especially if they live in the same neigh-

TABLE 4. Percentages Seeing Friends Weekly [23]

Friends known less than 8 years	56%
Friends known more than 13 years	34%
Best friends who live in the neighbourhood,	58%
Best friends who live in the same city	35%
Best friends who live outside the area	25%
Neighbourhood friends	60%
Friends at work	43%
Childhood friends	54%
No known roles	20%

bourhood. But they do not see so much of their old friends, probably because they do not live near enough.

What do friends do together when they meet? In our study of activities shared in different relationships in an Oxford sample, we found that the following activities were most characteristic of friendship, as compared with other kinds of relationship:

Dancing
Tennis
Sherry party
Joint leisure
Pub
Intimate conversation
Walk

This is quite different from the activities shared with spouses (p. 134), or with kin (p. 217f). The emphasis for friends is on leisure, eating and drinking and talking.

Sex differences in friendship

For women in particular conversation is important. Pairs of female friends spend most of their time together talking, discussing personal problems, giving and receiving social support, and with a high level of self-disclosure. Friends – especially female friends – often act as mutual 'therapists', and there is evidence that some of them are just as successful as professional therapists.

Men friends on the other hand are more likely to *do* things together – to play games or to engage in other joint leisure. A lot of friendship is between married couples, who may have meals together, or take part in joint activities. They often meet at each other's homes, especially if they are middle class. Some couples proceed to a further degree of closeness and have holidays together.

It has repeatedly been found that men and women see friendship differently. Women value intimate, confidential relationships, with a high level of self-disclosure, affection and social support. Men think that it is important to do things and have fun. Women have a greater number of intimate friendships, mainly with other women; men have friendships which are less intimate, often with married couples. Men often do not have any close friends at all, especially in middle age. On the other hand men often have a wider range of social contacts and acquaintances, partly because they meet people at work, and also because a wider range of leisure settings are accessible to them, such as pubs, clubs, and sport.[24] Men seem to form groups and clubs of all kinds more readily; jealousy of third parties is less of a problem than it is for women. A picture of the social life of married men is given in Figure 3. It can be seen that far less time is spent with friends than

Fig. 3   TIME SPENT PER DAY WITH FRIENDS
(MARRIED MEN)

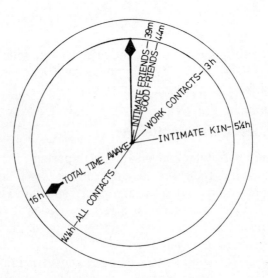

pg 325

with intimate kin or with people at work.

Why do women form closer friendships than men? <u>One possibility is that men are anxious about homosexuality. Another is that men spend a lot of time competing with one another at work and at games.</u>[26] And it is not socially acceptable for men to show feelings such as being anxious or depressed. There is approval for 'manly' control over such feelings. Research on masculinity and femininity has found that the qualities thought to be desirable for the two sexes are:

Men assertiveness, leadership, independence, self-reliance.
Women warmth, sympathy, kindness, gentleness, cheerfulness.

If people learn to value these qualities, it is not surprising that women make better friends.

A recent study of loneliness has found that the best predictor (for both male and female subjects) of not feeling lonely is frequency of interaction with *females*, and the reported 'meaningfulness' of this interaction. Time spent with males was not related to loneliness[26a]. Hence, it may be that females contribute meaningfulness and emotional closeness to an interaction regardless of whether they are interacting with another female or male. The only males who did contribute such emotional closeness were those with a high score on femininity scales.

We have seen that women form more intimate friendships, and that they are a better cure for loneliness in others. However we shall see below that people need another kind of contact as well, and feel lonely if they don't have it – they need to belong to structured groups which are engaged in worthwhile tasks, and this is something which comes more easily to males.[27]

Friendship at different ages

We can learn a lot about friendship by seeing the different forms it takes at different times of life.

Childhood   Children aged 3–5 have momentary playmates, based on who is available in particular situations. 'Friends' are evaluated by how near they live, and the activities shared with them. This is a simple and egoistic relationship, and it is very impermanent. From 4 to 9 a second stage develops, friends are valued for what they will do for the individual, and may be admired, but are expected to keep certain rules. This is based on short-term rewardingness, and is still quite unstable. As children grow older they are less likely to engage in negative behaviour such as crying, and more likely to produce positive behaviour such as laughing and talking. They are learning how to be rewarding. There is an increase in co-operation, but it is seen as a way of serving self-interests.

Between 8 and 10 there is an important development for many children, to where the child can see the point of view of the other and collaborate for mutual benefit. Children are aware of the needs of others, and will co-operate and reciprocate. They are aware of the possibility of friendship as a permanent bond. This shift in attitude towards friends is of great theoretical interest – it marks the point at which people go beyond concern with receiving immediate rewards.[28] The development of cognitive powers and social skills seems to go hand in hand. These older children understand what friendship is, can see others' points of view, and know the effects of different kinds of behaviour on a relationship. They are acquiring knowledge of social skills.

From 12 onwards, just before adolescence, children feel the need for a close friend, and are also prepared to allow the other some independence. They are moving towards a very important phase of friendship, where friends help them to become independent of parents, and to acquire further social skills. Friends now come in groups, or networks, and one of the main things they do is to have fun.[29]

Sex differences in styles of friendship can be seen in childhood. If pairs of boys are brought into the lab. to perform a task or play a game, they get straight on with the job; girls spend a lot of time on getting to know each other and exchanging self-disclosures.[30]

> From the games they play, boys learn both the independence and the organization skills necessary for coordinating the activities of large and diverse groups of people. By participating in controlled and socially approved competitive situations, they learn to deal with competition in a relatively forthright manner – to play with their enemies and compete with their friends – all in accordance with the rules of the game. In contrast, girls' play tends to occur in smaller, more intimate groups, often the best-friend dyad, and in private places.[31]

Adolescence This is the age at which same-sex friendship is most intense. During adolescence young people are becoming independent of their parents, undergoing physiological changes and having to cope with sexual impulses.

The main characteristic of adolescent friendships is their intensity. In fact they are so similar to love that some psychologists have thought that latent homosexuality is present. And when heterosexual relationships are taken up, the same-sex ones decline in intensity. At least we can say that they are a training or preparation for heterosexual intimacy.[32]

There is a close connection between the forming of intimate friendships and the establishing of identity. There is some evidence that for girls it is first necessary to have a close relationship, while for boys it is first necessary to establish identity, before a close relationship can be formed.[33] Adolescents choose as close friends people they admire, whom they see as similar to their ideal-self (the sort of person they would like to be), and they choose friends of the same age as themselves, who are facing similar problems. Great importance is attached to friends being trustworthy at 15–16, and friendships are very exclusive. There is a good deal of anxiety about jealousy and fear

Fig. 4 PERCENTAGE OF BOYS AND GIRLS IN EACH AGE GROUP EXPRESSING ANXIETY THEMES ON A SENTENCE COMPLETION TASK CONCERNING FRIENDSHIP

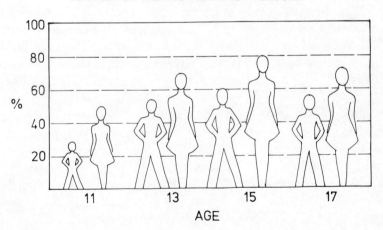

of losing friends at this age. Coleman,[34] in a study in London, found
that 15-year-old girls would say, for example, 'Often when three
people are together there is jealousy, I don't know why.' These fears
are strongest for girls, as shown in Figure 4.

Girls develop a need for a close friendship at an earlier age than
boys, and move on to dating sooner. They have a few close friends,
where boys have a group (or 'gang'); and pairs of girls are more
exclusive. Girls' friendships are like the romantic ideal of a tender
relationship, while boys are companions in shared activities.

Adult friendship Young adults, from 18 to 25, or until they get
married, have close friendships, like adolescents, and may see their
friends every day, as well as having telephone conversations. Young
married people similarly form close relations with others of the same
age and in a similar position to themselves, and see them a great deal.

From 30 to 60 the patterns of friendship change. Friends become
less important and are seen much less frequently. Instead of daily or
weekly they are seen monthly or yearly. Friendships fall off as people
marry, have children and become more involved with work. Friendships are based less on attachments formed in early life, and more on
neighbourhood and work contacts, which tend to be less intimate (see
figure, p 65).

Between 55 and 65 people make friends less easily; they hold on to
earlier friendships, which tend to be more intimate than the more
recent ones, but see these older friends less often. However if older
people go through a major upheaval – divorce, a new job, moving to a
new town – they make efforts to find new friends. Friends at this time
of life are not based so much on neighbourhood. They can be with
people of any age, and people have a greater variety of different
friends.

Friendship in old age After retirement there is a decline in contacts
with friends, though people have more spare time, and have lost the
social contacts at work. This disengagement is not voluntary, but a
result of the loss of work contacts, of illness and of transport
difficulties. However, the friends that do remain have often been
known for a long time. Friends among the aged mostly live near, and
are of similar age. Old people may have some younger friends too, but
the younger people may find that such friendships incur certain costs
(such as helping) and the older ones feel embarrassed about the

imbalance of rewards. For this reason they are more likely to turn to their kin, especially to their own children, for help (p. 219f). Elderly women have more friends than elderly men, and are more likely to have a confidant. Men lose a number of work-friends when they retire, but on the other hand it is possible that they have a less stringent definition of friend, and are quite happy with more superficial contacts.[36]

Old people see friends more often, and are helped by friends and neighbours more, if they are widowed, and if they have no daughter living near. Although many old people live alone (29% of those aged 65–74, and 47% aged 75 or over), few of them feel lonely, either because they are reconciled to being alone, or because they positively value privacy and some peace and quiet.

Friendship in different social classes and sub-cultures

There are clear quantitative differences between social classes in their patterns of friendship, in Britain and other countries. Middle-class people have more friends. These are more diverse and live at greater distances. However the differences are more subtle than this.

Middle-class people make friends cautiously, but efficiently – for example when they move into a new area. Their friends are drawn mainly from neighbours and work colleagues, or are met in clubs or leisure groups. Middle-class work contacts often have a strong social element, and this too helps in putting down roots quickly. Middle-class people invite others home, and see them in more than one environmental setting. Wives who do not have jobs entertain other wives during the day, which is an easy way to make friends. Otherwise husbands and wives have the same friends, usually other married couples, and see them together.

Working-class friendship is quite different. To begin with many working-class people in Britain do not use the concept of 'friend', and many say they have no friends. What actually happens is that women see a lot of their neighbours – they 'pop in', without invitation, or meet on the doorstep. Working-class women also see a lot of their kin. Working-class men have 'mates', men in the neighbourhood, who are met at pub or club, usually casually, without prior arrangement, and usually in a group. A minority have friends from work, especially in a company town, but this may be because they are also neighbours.

Husbands and wives often have different friends from each other, and they do not invite them home. Working-class friends are seen in different and specific environmental settings. Young and Willmott[37] quote someone who said 'I've got friends at work, and friends at sport and friends I have a drink with . . . I've always got on well with people but I don't invite anyone home.' Allan[38] maintains that the key difference between friendship in the two classes is that working-class friends are tied to specific settings, while middle-class friendships 'flower out' to more than one setting, and especially to the home. On the other hand working-class people do entertain their kin at home, more than the middle-classes do. Home is reserved for family and close kin.

We should mention here that people whom we choose as friends are quite similar to ourselves, and especially in social class. It is found that friends are particularly homogeneous in this respect at the top and bottom of society, for example among the highly educated or those in prestigious occupations.[39]

Friendship is found in all cultures, but there are some interesting variations on the theme. Australian 'mateship' developed in the early days between miners and stockmen, isolated in the bush, with very few women. They needed a friend who could be trusted to stand by them. The relationship of mateship was invented, and was said to be as intense and sometimes more intense than marriage, though probably little homosexuality was involved. Mateship is still important among men in Australia today. It is seen not only in the bush, but in the forces, and in men's bars, and in the segregation of the sexes at parties.

Another form of friendship is the forming of 'blood brothers', either by cutting the skin and rubbing in each other's blood, or by drinking some of each other's blood. This occurred in the ancient world, and is still practised in parts of Africa. The purpose is to create an alliance between individuals or groups, so that the other can be trusted absolutely, or perhaps to turn an enemy into a friend. It is believed that if a blood brother lets the other down, he will become ill and die, through the operation of the other's blood inside him. It is a way of creating a kind of kin out of friendship.

Blood brothership was suppressed by the Catholic Church in Europe, but was replaced in feudal times by 'Compadrazgo', or co-godparents. The ceremonies of baptism and confirmation were used to create this bond between the parents and godparents, and sometimes between parents and priest. This too was used as a means of creating alliances, with other families or with powerful individuals. Those involved were not allowed to marry, they were regarded as a kind of kin, and formed a strong co-operative group. Luther condemned the institution, and with the rise of capitalism society came to be based on impersonal contracts rather than on such alliances between families. It still survives in peasant society in Greece, Italy, Spain and South America. In Britain it has disappeared. Godparents are usually chosen from friends and kin, which has the effect of strengthening the existing bonds.[40]

Why do we need friends?

We tried to find out about the need for friends in a survey of sources of satisfaction in different relationships. We found three general needs which are met by relationships. These are: Help, Social Support, and Common Interests. The importance of these for different relationships, is shown in Figure 5.

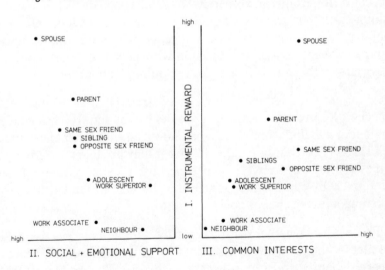

Fig. 5   RELATIONSHIPS PLOTTED ON SATISFACTION DIMENSIONS

Help   We shall see that kin are a ready source of serious help. Many studies have found that friends in our own society on the whole are not regarded as a source of such help. Friends are for fun and enjoying ourselves with, rather than to help us in trouble. There are, however, some kinds of friend who do rather more than this. For young people between adolescence and marriage, friendship is the most intense relationship, and they do reckon to provide help within their power to provide. This would not usually include much material help, such as money or accommodation, since they do not have very much. Workmates too, though not exactly friends in the usual sense, also provide and exchange help at work. In some other cultures friendship takes a form where serious help is certainly expected, as in Australian mateship and blood brotherhood.

Social support   This is one of the main things we need friends for – talking to them about our problems and receiving advice or amateur psychotherapy. On a more everyday level, simply comparing notes, sharing experiences, is important to us, to build a shared cognitive world, to put our private experiences into words and compare them with those of others. When we are alone, visiting a new place, or undergoing new experiences, we label these experiences with words, the words we may use when we tell our friends about it. This is especially important for women, who spend a good deal of time simply talking to their friends, especially if their husbands are poor confidants. It is important to adolescents, who are trying to understand new experiences and to cope with new problems. And it is important to the elderly, who like to reminisce about times past.

Common interests   Above all we need friends to do things with, especially leisure activities, going out and having fun. It is often nice to be alone, but being with friends somehow leads to greater cheerfulness and laughter. Children laugh a lot when they are together. Men play games with their friends. Sometimes we pursue common leisure interests with our friends, sometimes we just eat and drink while pursuing a further major goal – talking.

These needs together can be regarded as 'affiliative needs', which are met by the company of friends. One of the most widely accepted theories about friendship is 'exchange theory'. The main support for this theory is the extensive evidence that we like people who are rewarding, and that the most rewarding people are the most popular.

An important extension of this theory recognises that people are concerned with the outcomes or rewards for the other, as well as their own.[42] Such empathetic and altruistic concerns are strong and familiar in love and marriage, but are also important for friendship. We have seen that children advance beyond a concern with their own benefits, it is only disturbed adolescents without friends who act as 'exchange theorists'.

Some researchers have argued that the perceived balance of rewards and costs in a relationship will determine the continuation and quality of that relationship. This is known as equity theory. The basic principles of equity theory are:

1. People feel most comfortable when receiving exactly what they feel they deserve in a relationship.
2. Those who discover that they are in an inequitable relationship will attempt to restore equilibrium by:
    (a) restoring *actual* equity;
    (b) restoring *psychological* equity – that is, convincing themselves it is a fair relationship;
    (c) ending the relationship.[43]

In other words, people in a relationship will assess the costs and benefits of that relationship. If they believe that it is fair, and that they are receiving what they believe they deserve, the relationship will continue. Similarly, at the beginning of a relationship, individuals will evaluate the costs and rewards. This allows them to predict the potential rewards from a continuation of the relationship. If these are favourable, the relationship will continue to grow.

Equity theory has been used mainly to explain relationships that are in a particular state of inequity or equity at one point in time. It is less successful in predicting satisfaction or stability of relationships over time[44] or of situations that change from equity to inequity.[45] In fact, it has been found that half of the people who rate a situation as inequitable still see it as 'fair'. The most important factor was which partner had initiated the change: the person who is responsible for changing the situation to a state of inequity (whether he or she becomes over or underbenefitted) is generally expected to view it as fair, whereas the person who is not responsible is expected to think in equity terms, and to be less satisfied with such a situation.[46]

Other models have also attempted to explain relationship satisfaction. The investment model[47] states

$$\text{Satisfaction} = (\text{Rewards} - \text{Costs}) - \text{Comparison level}$$

$$\text{Commitment} = \text{Satisfaction} - \text{Alternative quality} + \text{Investment size}$$

In other words, we will be more satisfied with relationships that provide high rewards and low costs and exceed our general expectancies about relationships of that type. Commitment to maintaining a relationship is high if we are satisfied with it, have no acceptable alternatives, and have invested heavily in it. This model does not emphasise equal exchange of rewards as does equity theory, and gives us some understanding of why apparently inequitable relationships continue.

However there are considerable individual differences in the strength of affiliative needs. In the survey of *The Quality of American Life*[48] it was found that those who had lots of friends already wanted even more, and vice versa (Table 5).

TABLE 5. *Friendship Satisfaction, by Number of Friends and Interest in New Friendships*[49]

| | | Interest in making new friends | | |
		very interested	somewhat interested	not very interested
How many very good friends?	A good many	+.53 (528)	+.29 (250)	+.11 (41)
	Average number	−.08 (347)	−.14 (482)	−.09 (97)
	Not many	−.89 (121)	−.56 (181)	.−40 (98)

Does the satisfaction of these needs create bonds between friends, or is something else needed? We have seen that we become permanently attached to our friends only under certain conditions. Friends made among adolescents or students, or in the forces, are sometimes very long-lasting. Cousins who were childhood companions often become favourite cousins (p. 232). It looks as if the intimacy and intensity of these friendships can create a nearly permanent bond. Blood brothers, or any of the friendships which are established by a special ritual, are also very long-lasting.

However, friendship does incur costs as well as rewards. Some indication of what these costs are is provided by the rules whose breaking is commonly said to be the cause of break-up of friendship (p. 93).

Friendship can be seen as a case of approach–avoidance conflict –we are attracted to people, and also driven away. The result is that we settle down at an intermediate level of intimacy. It is like two hedgehogs trying to keep warm – if they get too close the spikes stick in. For a close friendship it is necessary to provide a high level of rewards, and also to avoid inflicting costs, which means keeping to the rules.

The benefits of friendship

Is friendship good for us in the same way that marriage is good for us? Many studies have found that those who have more friends, see them more often, or spend more time with them, are happier, in better health, and live longer. An example is given in Figure 6.

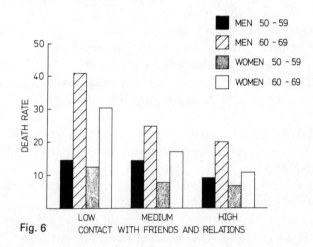

Fig. 6

The greatest effects of friendship were for the 60–69 group, for men, and for those who have a low rather than a medium number of friends. However the same people who see their friends a lot also tend to see relatives, neighbours and others a lot too. Some studies have managed to separate the effects of these different relationships statistically. Marriage has more effect on health and well-being than friends do; kin are also very important, in providing help, and workmates are good at helping with work-induced stresses. However, there are two periods of life when friends confer particular benefits. Young people, from 18 to when they get married, experience more well-being if they have more friends, because having more friends makes them feel more competent, with a consequent increase in self-esteem. In our study of 'Positive Life Events' which was mentioned briefly in Chapter 1, we found that relationships and activities with friends were very important determinants of happiness and well-being. In fact, making a new friend was rated more positively than winning a lot of money, a job promotion or pay rise, going on holiday, or buying a new house or car. And it was rated just below getting married or engaged.

Activities with friends such as friends visiting, staying with friends, going out to dinner with friends, or meeting friends at the pub were also rated as causing a great deal of happiness or well-being, far more than non-social events such as winning or watching sports, taking up a new sport or hobby or buying clothes. This is particularly true of females, who rated social and interpersonal events in general as more positive than men did.

Not only do we rate activities with friends as very positive events, but we also tend to arrange our lives so that they occur relatively often. We asked whether any of the positive life events had occurred to each of our 217 informants within the last year, and found that over 90% of people had experienced the friendship-related events (see Table 1, p 14).

Friendships may be valuable to the young in more ways than one. Bochner and colleagues[51] found that foreign students in Hawaii had two kinds of friends, Hawaiians and compatriots. They needed Hawaiian friends to show them the ropes locally, and compatriots to keep up familiar activities and topics of conversation.

Friendship becomes very important again in later life, especially for women. Friends are again associated with health and well-being.[52] Those who have no siblings describe some of their friends in terms like 'she's my old friend and would do anything for me', rather than in specific terms like 'we play bridge together', as if they are turning their friends into substitute siblings.[53] The unmarried spend far more time with their friends than the married.[54]

Can friendship substitute for marriage? It is doubtful whether friends convey benefits as great as those produced by marriage (p. 18f). Is there a need for friends in addition to marriage? Much less time is devoted to friends than to the spouse, and the level of satisfaction is less (p. 83). On the other hand, working-class wives at any rate seem to need friends as well as husbands.

It was found in an Australian study that neurotics had far fewer friends than normal controls, and that their friends did not form a network. However it was concluded that the reason for this was that neurotics were unable to make friends, rather than that they were neurotic because of the lack of friends.[55] In other research, however, it has been found that when individuals increase their level of social activity over a period of time, then their health and morale also improve. We do not really know exactly what causes what, and it is possible that health and social activity simply go together.

How does friendship help the elderly? We have discussed one important friendship activity before – acting as a confidant, which is particularly important for women and can buffer the effects of bereavement and retirement. Another is being a companion; individuals who have friends do more things – walks, shopping, going to church, joining other associations, in addition to visiting each other at home. This is still true if health, education and income are held constant. And having friends has been found to be more beneficial to health than going to church or having neighbours.[56]

These benefits are not experienced by all. Those who gain most from friendship are found to be people of low social status, or in bad health, who have no kin near by, or who are widowed. And the effects on health become more marked from 60 onwards, as Figure 6 showed. As this figure also showed, it is the people with a low, as opposed to a medium, number of friends who suffer most, which brings us to the subject of loneliness, to which we now turn.

Loneliness

This is a common and very distressing condition. A recent British survey by MORI[57] found that 24% of the population sometimes feel lonely, 4% of them every day, 8% once a week or more. Feeling lonely once a month or more is more common for:

women (18%) *v.* men (10%)
the old, 65+ (20%) and young, 15–24 (18%)
the widowed (36%) and divorced (29%)
people living alone aged 16–59 (27%), single parents (38%)
people in social classes IV and V (19%) *v.* I and II (10%)

Other studies suggest that the blind, ill or otherwise disabled are also very lonely.

The least lonely are middle-aged men with jobs, though it is interesting that they report few friends. The worst times are being ill in bed, being in a crowd of strangers, after the death of a close friend or relative, and Christmas. Lonely people have less contact with spouses, family and friends, and go to parties, pubs, dances and church less. So what do they do instead? They go to the doctor (one in five of them once a month), and they go to bingo. Some go to evening classes, where they find it easy to get into conversation with strangers. The MORI survey asked lonely people what they did when they felt lonely; the most frequent responses were:

Talk to a friend or neighbour (20%), especially among younger and middle class people;
Go for a walk (17%), especially for those living in Scotland (25%);
Watch TV (15%), especially among older and working-class people; 21% of the very lonely watch over five hours a day;
Read (15%), especially for older people;
Indoor hobby (14%), especially among women.

Other responses to feeling lonely are going to the pub (21% of men), gardening (12% of those aged 45 and over), and phoning friends (20% of younger people) or relatives (17% of older people).

Among adolescents and students loneliness is quite widespread. 10–15% say they are very lonely, and about 50% say that they often feel lonely. Those who feel lonely also feel depressed, anxious, bored, lacking in self-esteem, shy, self-conscious, and somewhat hostile to others.

It is possible to feel lonely when surrounded by friends or family, if the relationships are felt to fall short of the quality desired. It has been found that some lonely people have as many friends as the non-lonely, and are chosen as friends by others, but that there is a lower level of intimacy and self-disclosure.[58] Lonely people are aware of a discrepancy between their social attachments and what they would like; we now know that the problem is primarily that their friendships are not intimate enough.

Who are the people who feel lonely? Young people feel much more lonely than older ones. Old people are often quite well-adjusted to being alone, and the same is true of more educated people, who may be quite happy when engaged in reading, working, artistic activities, meditation, or even watching TV.[59] More women than men report feeling lonely, especially among the young.[60]

The studies just mentioned show that lonely people want more intimacy; people who are married or have similar close relationships do not feel lonely in this way. However married women who do not have jobs sometimes feel lonely in a different sense: they are not involved or integrated in purposeful, organised group activities. This second kind of belonging is associated with work-groups, and groups of friends who do things together; the satisfactions obtained are from being part of the team, cooperating in worthwhile projects, approval for one's skills and contribution, exerting influence, and definition of self.

A number of studies have documented the social skill differences which lead to loneliness, i.e. not being able to establish friendships of the desired kind. The main findings are that the lonely:

1. Engage in less self-disclosure, which in turn leads to less self-disclosure by others, and this hinders the relationship.[61]
2. Take less interest in others during interaction – ask fewer questions, refer less to the other, and continue another's topic of conversation less.[62]
3. Are less assertive, more passive.
4. Are less rewarding, like and trust others less, have a negative attitude to people.
5. Blame their interpersonal failures on an unchangeable lack of social competence in themselves, rather than on lack of effort or use of the wrong strategy, so they are easily discouraged.[63]
6. They are seen by others as lacking in self-esteem, as not being interested in other people, difficult to get to know, perhaps as having problems.[64]
7. Lonely and isolated people tend to be deficient in the sending of non-verbal signals, particularly signals of liking via face and voice.
8. Lonely and isolated people, especially in adolescence, may have an inadequate concept of what friendship involves. They do not realise that it requires concern for the other's welfare, together with loyalty and commitment.[65]

This information is invaluable in designing social skills training for lonely people, which will be taken up in Chapter 12.

The last two sections have shown that friends are a major source both of enjoyment and of health. Although friends do provide a certain amount of material help, this is not a dominant theme of friendship. The benefits of friendship come rather from being together, talking or engaging in joint leisure, enjoying each other's company. However, for these activities to proceed smoothly, common sources of friction must be avoided. The rules of friendship, which we discuss next, show how to do this.

The rules of friendship

Friendship is not governed by legal or formal rules in the way that marriage is. But if you ask people what they think friends should or should not do in relation to each other, there is a very high level of agreement. What they have in mind presumably is that if such rules are broken then a friendship is likely to break up. The following were the most important rules for friendship.

TABLE 6. Rules for Friends

1. Volunteer help in time of need.
2. Respect the friend's privacy.
3. Keep confidences.
4. Trust and confide in each other.
5. Stand up for the friend in his/her absence.
6. Don't criticise each other in public.
7. Show emotional support.
8. Look him/her in the eye during conversation.
9. Strive to make him/her happy while in each other's company.
10. Don't be jealous or critical of his/her other relationships.
11. Be tolerant of each other's friends.
12. Share news of success.
13. Ask for personal advice.
14. Don't nag.
15. Engage in joking or teasing with the friend.
16. Seek to repay debts, favours and compliments.
17. Disclose personal feelings or problems to the friend.

People also use these rules in practice in their behaviour towards different types of friends. When we asked people to describe their behaviour towards someone who is now a good friend compared to someone who was once a good friend but now is not (a 'lapsed' friend) they reported different ways of behaving[66]. With a current friend they were more likely to volunteer help, trust and confide, stand up for him/her, show emotional support, and positive regard, share news of success, disclose feelings and problems, give birthday cards and presents, look after him/her when ill, and strive to make each other happy when together. Not only do people believe that rules are important for friendship in general, but they also use many of these rules differently between friends and those who are no longer friends.

So we have rules differentiating good friends from lapsed friends. But what happens when friends do not keep to the rules?[67] We asked over 150 people to think of a specific friendship that had lapsed for some reason, because of something to do with the relationship, not just because, for example, one had moved away and they therefore did not see each other. We asked them to say to what extent failure to keep each rule had contributed to the breakdown of the relationship. Some of the rules were not seen as very important in the break-up of the friendship – for instance failing to give birthday cards, or not looking after you when ill. But certain rules were chosen by most people as contributing to the breakdown of the relationship. These are shown in Table 7.

TABLE 7. Friendship Rules and Break-up of Friendships

	moderately or very important in breaking up friendship	slightly important in breaking up friendship
Being jealous or critical of your other relationships	57%	22%
Discussing with others what was said in confidence with him/her	56%	19%
Not volunteering help in time of need	44%	23%
Not trusting or confiding in you	44%	22%
Criticising you in public	44%	21%
Not showing positive regard for you	42%	34%
Not standing up for you in your absence	39%	28%
Not being tolerant of your other friends	38%	30%
Not showing emotional support	37%	25%
Nagging you	30%	25%

Both men and women agreed on these rules, but women were much more likely than men to say that not showing positive regard or emotional support contributed to the breakdown of the friendship.

Thus we have rules that people in general believe are important to follow in friendship, rules that distinguish between good and lapsed friends in practice, and rules whose non-compliance contributes to the actual breakdown of a friendship.

These rules were in two main areas. Rules about being rewarding were important on all criteria, e.g. 'should show positive regard', and 'should volunteer help in time of need'. A second group of rules was about relations with third parties, and it was these rules that were regarded as a common cause of break-up – 'should not be jealous or critical of other relationships', 'should keep confidences', 'should not criticise in public'.

FURTHER READING

Duck, S. & Gilmour, R. (1981) *Personal Relationships vol. 2: Developing Relationships* London: Academic Press
Gottlieb, B. (1981) *Social Networks and Social Support* Beverly Hills: Sage

5

Love, Courtship and Cohabitation

Love, that 'delicious sickness', is a familiar and an extraordinary phenomenon. Most of us suffer from it at least once, but until recently psychologists have found it difficult to explain. Falling in love, being in love and being loved, even falling out of love and unrequited love affect our moods, behaviour, attitudes, and self-esteem. We noted in earlier chapters how long-term relationships affect us. In this chapter we shall examine how potent even transitory love relationships may be, and shall look closely at the how, why and when of this much sought after commodity. In other chapters we discuss liking and loving in the context of family and friendship, but in this section we shall focus on liking and loving in heterosexual attraction and partnerships.

The importance of love

Surveys of positive life events – that is, events which increase our happiness and improve our sense of well-being – have shown that love is important, but not necessarily most crucial, in what we believe makes us happy. In a survey of over 100,000 American men and women Freedman[1] found that 'being in love' was rated second to 'friends and social life' for single women and third after 'friends and social life' and 'job or primary activity' for single men, while married women thought that it was the most important, and married men ranked it second. However, in our own study of British men and women, 'falling in love' was ranked as the most important event in determining happiness or well-being for both men and women of all ages. How positively they rated 'falling in love' was unrelated to whether they had actually fallen in love within the preceding year, but did correlate with the perceived probability of it occurring in the following twelve months – that is, people who believed that it would

definitely happen to them rated the events as more positive than those
who thought that it was unlikely to happen.

In our earlier chapter on Friendship we have discussed the factors
important in forming impressions of others. These same factors also
apply to 'falling in love'. We tend to be attracted to people who:

1. show loving or liking for us or are attracted to us,
2. are similar to us,
3. are physically attractive.

Defining love

Love is a ubiquitous phenomenon. We speak of love for our children,
parents, grandparents – our 'loved ones' – and love for close friends of
the same sex. For the purposes of this chapter we have restricted love
to heterosexual relationships, but even then people make distinctions
between love and infatuation, between 'realistic' and romantic love,
and between 'real' love and everything else.

Researchers have also attempted to distinguish these concepts.
Rubin[2] has developed a scale to measure the level of romantic love,
which measures three main areas of romantic attachment.

1. Needing the other: for example: 'It would be hard for me to get on
   without X', or,
2. Caring for the other: for example: 'If X were feeling badly, my first
   duty would be to cheer him/her up', or,
3. Exclusiveness and absorption: for example: 'I feel very possessive
   towards X', or 'I feel that I can confide in X about virtually
   everything.'

So romantic love towards another person involves a high degree of
needing to be with the other person, wanting to help him or her even if
it involves self-sacrifice, and being intimately and exclusively ab-
sorbed in the other person. This is distinguished by Rubin from
liking, which represents a less exclusive respect and admiration for the
other, plus a tendency to view the other as similar to oneself. He
developed a 'liking' scale which measures such aspects as:

1. Favourable evaluation and respect for the other person: for
   example: 'I have great confidence in X's judgment', or 'X is one of
   the most likeable people I know.'
2. Perceived similarity to oneself: for example: 'When I am with X we

are almost always in the same mood', or 'X is the sort of person I myself would like to be.'

It is interesting to compare the relationship with a lover and that with a best friend. With love there is fascination, exclusivity, sexual desire and strong support.[3] It is found that people who show evidence of 'caring' are judged to be in love more than those who just 'need' the other person.[4] We can also distinguish between 'romantic' or 'passionate' love, and 'companionate love' as found in older married couples. Pope[5] defined romantic love as:

A preoccupation with another person. A deeply felt desire to be with the loved one. A feeling of incompleteness without him or her. Thinking of the loved one often, whether together or apart. Separation frequently provokes feelings of genuine despair or else tantalising anticipation of reuniting. Reunion is seen as bringing feelings of euphoric ecstasy or peace and fulfilment.

Companionate love, on the other hand, is 'friendly affection and deep attachment to someone.'[6] While we tend to assume that only young people 'fall in love', we concede that older or married couples may still 'love each other'. To some extent, we are using, in lay terms, the distinction proposed by Walster and Walster[7] between 'passionate' and 'companionate' love. Passionate love, they argue, is 'a fragile flower' and rarely lasts, while companionate love is 'a much hardier variety' and may last a lifetime. In their own and other researchers' studies there is some evidence that romantic love fades over time, to be replaced by the less passionate companionate love.

However, in three more recent studies, Walster and her colleagues come to a more optimistic conclusion. In interviews with dating couples, engaged couples and older women (aged 50 to 82) they found that reports of the amount of passionate and companionate love remain fairly high with only a slight – and equal – decline in both over time.[8]

Dating, Courtship and Falling in Love

The great majority of people, especially during the years 15–25, have affairs with members of the opposite sex. They go out together on dates, select a more permanent partner whom they will later live with or marry, and with whom at some stage they fall in love. In this section we shall discuss the stage of courtship and mate selection.

Male American students between 19 and 24 report an average of five to six affairs or romantic episodes, the women six to seven, but the number of times they say they have been in love is 1.2 and 1.3 respectively.[9] In another study 20% of males and 15% of females said that they fell in love by the fourth date, but 30% of males and 43% of females were unsure whether they were in love by the twentieth date.[10] In a recent British survey, 25% said that they fell in love with their present partner at first sight, especially older men.[11]

However love can take a number of different forms. A study of love among Australian students[12] produced the following three dimensions:

1. Desirability,
2. Love, commitment and permanence,
3. Sexuality.

It is interesting that love and sexuality belong to separate factors. Holiday affairs, one-night sex and flirtation were high on sex, low on love; platonic and religious love were the opposite. Young marriage, and marriage after twenty-five years, were high on all three factors.

Courtship can move fast or slowly. Huston et al.[13] distinguished between four types of courtship:

1. Accelerated arrested courtship, with a rapid start but later slowing, before moving to certainty.
2. Accelerated courtship, moving rapidly towards marriage in most cases.
3. Intermediate courtship, moving smoothly to a high level of commitment.
4. Prolonged courtship, with a slow, rocky ascent to marriage.

Couples were asked to estimate the probability of marriage at different times, with the results shown in Figure 1.

For example, accelerated courtship moved to certainty of marriage in a little under five months on average.

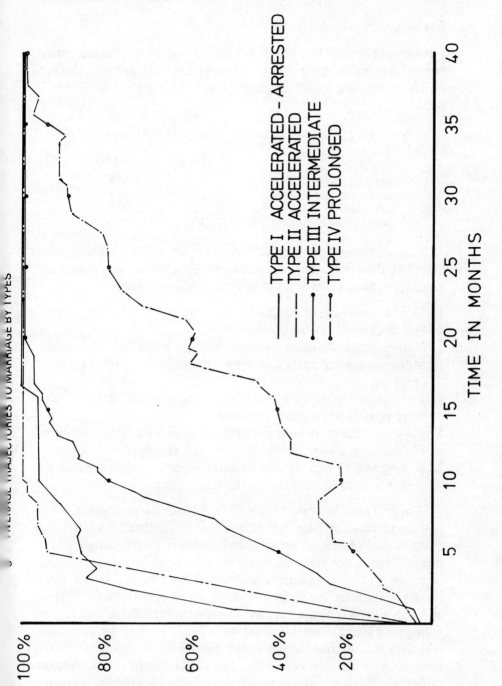

FIGURE 3. AVERAGE TRAJECTORIES TO MARRIAGE BY TYPES

TYPE I   ACCELERATED - ARRESTED
TYPE II   ACCELERATED
TYPE III INTERMEDIATE
TYPE IV   PROLONGED

TIME IN MONTHS

ESTIMATED PROBABILITY OF MARRIAGE

100%

80%

60%

40%

20%

5   10   15   20   25   30   35   40

Activities

The amount of time two people who are dating see each other varies greatly. Among students once to twice per day is the average. During courtship couples spend much of their time together, as Table 1 shows.

TABLE 1. Proportion of Leisure Time Spent with Partner.[15]

	Dating	Courtship
with partner only	35%	42%
with partner and others	13%	12%
with others only	15%	10%
alone	39%	36%

What do lovers do together? A study of 1,200 people,[16] who described their frequency of engaging in 400 activities with those they loved, produced seven areas of activity specific to love:

1. Verbal expression of affection.
2. Self disclosure: revealing intimate facts.
3. Non-material evidence of love: giving emotional and moral support, showing interest in other's activities and respect for their opinions.
4. Feelings not expressed verbally: feeling happier, more secure, more relaxed when other is around.
5. Material evidence of love: giving gifts, performing physical chores.
6. Physical expression of love: hugging and kissing.
7. Willingness to tolerate less pleasant aspects of other: tolerating demands in order to maintain the relationship.

So as well as an increase in time spent with the partner only, there is also an increase in what has been called 'affectional' activities – a combination of sexual activity and intimate conversation. Many pleasant hours are spent in this way. The level of sexual intimacy increases, in many cases up to pre-marital intercourse – known since Kinsey as PMI. In Britain 56% of young people now think that PMI is all right, and 68% would have it.[17] Another survey found that 52% of young people in Britain thought it was all right to sleep with someone you were not married to, while 36% thought it was *wrong* to marry someone you had not slept with. The remainder of course thought differently.[18] However, most PMI is between couples who are intending to marry, or who are living together. Surveys in the U.S.A.,

Canada and Germany show rather higher rates of PMI.

A recent American study for example found that the average age of first intercourse was 18 for males and 17.7 for females, most of them in a steady dating relationship. And quite a lot of them didn't like it – 25% of the girls and 12% of the boys. Those who had intercourse early were more independent and rebellious, less religious and less academic, and on less good terms with their parents.[19]

Couples who have PMI early – in the first month of going together – have been compared with those who have it late – after six months. 'Later' sex couples had higher scores on the Rubin love scale, and more felt that they were in love; they probably delayed intercourse until they felt that their relationship was sufficiently close.[20] On the other hand there seems to be no correlation between early versus late sex and permanence of the bond.

Dating and courting couples talk a great deal, with increasing degrees of self-disclosure. There is as much, or more, self-disclosure as in any other relationship. Bodily intimacy and knowledge of one another go hand in hand. Couples also engage in those joint leisure activities that may have brought them together in the first place – dancing, walking, church, tennis, etc. Couples share more practical tasks as the relationship develops.

Development

How do we progress from 'Falling in love' to more long-term emotional attachments? Heterosexual relationships can be viewed as progressing from casual dating, in which a number of different partners may be dated, through serious dating, in which there tends to be a monogamous relationship with one dating partner and some level of mutual commitment, to a longer-term contract, such as engagement, or marriage, or cohabitation.

As a couple moves through casual to steady dating there are various changes in the nature of the relationship. These include:

1. Spending more time in each other's company and being together in a wider variety of situations and settings.
2. An increase in positive feelings towards each other; there is more liking, loving and trust.
3. An increase in the expression of feelings, both positive and negative; with increased commitment, there is greater potential for the growth of both intimacy and conflict.

4. Mutual disclosure of more intimate aspects of the self, including attitudes and values about the other partner and relationship commitment.
5. An increased concern with the other's welfare; joy is caused by their joy, pain by their pain.
6. A shared sense of unity and commitment; both partners increasingly view themselves as a unit, and are treated by third parties as a couple. Associated with this increased sense of shared identity, there is a concomitant reduction in uncertainty about the future of the relationship.

Braiker and Kelley[21] have charted this progression from casual to steady dating to courtship and marriage in a group of married couples. They found that couples used four main dimensions in describing the progression of their relationship:

1. Love – references to caring, needing, attachment, and interdependence;
2. Conflict/negativity, e.g. arguments and problems;
3. Ambivalence – uncertainty or confusion in feelings about the other party; anxiety about increased commitment or loss of independence;
4. Maintenance – e.g. discussions of the relationship, disclosure, attempts to change the other's behaviour.

Fig. 2   THE DEVELOPMENT OF LOVE

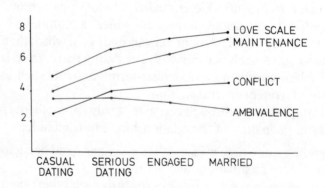

It can be seen that conflict and negativity increased especially in the period from casual to serious dating, and did not decline later. Further analysis showed that love and conflict were quite independent aspects of the relationship, so that love was compatible with conflict. In the early stages maintenance activities were associated with love, but at later stages with conflict. We shall discuss later the possible importance of conflict in developing close relationships.

In 'accelerated courtship' (see p. 99), couples move to commitment, or to certainty of marriage, in six months or less, with little conflict. 'Prolonged courtship' may take three or four years, with periods of conflict, '*Sturm und Drang*', 'it's on-it's-off'. It is quite common for couples to go through three stages: of initial excitement, disillusion and alienation, and final commitment but with a more realistic view of each other.[23]

Commitment means an intention to stick to the relationship, for better or for worse, for a long time, perhaps till death do us part. It is an essential feature of many forms of love. So it is of some importance to find out what brings about such commitment. It is enhanced by public vows and rituals, the support of friends, legal bonds, and irretrievable 'investments', especially time, money, property and the production of children.[24] It is also strengthened by private pledges of loyalty to the partner, a feeling of shared identity, and a continued balance of rewards over costs from the relationship.[25]

Mate selection

The main end-product of dating and love affairs is the choice of a more or less permanent partner out of those available. Some people 'try out' a large number of others, while some find the right person the first time. The process can be described in terms of a series of filters. The first filter a potential partner has to pass is the most easily visible – an acceptable, indeed an attractive, physical appearance. If a couple come to know each other better they will then find out if they are sufficiently similar, in background, interests and values. Finally they have to find out whether they are compatible, in terms of ideas about sex roles and other aspects of social interaction.[26] Not all couples go through this sequence. People may fall in love despite failing to pass one or more of the filters.

There is little doubt that physical attractiveness ('p.a.') is very important, especially for males choosing females, and especially at the early stages of courtship. It is easily measured, on a five-point scale:

1	2	3	4	5
not at all attractive	slightly attractive	moderately attractive	very attractive	extremely attractive

A 'computer dance' was arranged to which 750 first-year students were invited and paired off at random (though the male was always the taller). The best predictor of how much they liked one another and how often they dated afterwards was the rating of their p.a. by the experimenters.[27] On the other hand, the choice of a partner is also affected by estimates of the likelihood of being accepted: those with low self-esteem, sometimes due to low p.a., are content to opt for less attractive partners.[28]

There is widespread agreement, at least within a given culture, on which individuals are the most attractive. Winners of Miss World competitions tend to be aged twenty-one, 5 feet 8 inches tall, blonde with brown eyes, and measuring 35–24–35. An attractive face is harder to describe. The precise shape of the nose, or the position of a mole, can be important. Men vary in what they find attractive: extroverts like big breasts, quiet and religious men prefer small ones. Women like men who are 5-6 inches taller than they are, with small buttocks, slim, and with a flat stomach. Both sexes like people who are healthy and of good complexion. They are attracted by pupil dilation and other signs of sexual arousal.[29]

Women like men who are assertive and dominant. An experiment was done in which males helped blindfolded females to find their way through a maze. The girls were more attracted to their partner if he gave them firm guidance, preferably physical guidance, but only if he was also competent.[30] In another study subjects were asked to rate

TABLE 2. Desirable Attributes in a Partner, in Order of Importance [31]

In a male partner	In a female partner
1. Achievement	Physical attractiveness
2. Leadership	Erotic ability
3. Occupational ability	Affectional ability
4. Economic ability	Social ability
5. Entertaining ability	Domestic ability
6. Intellectual ability	Sartorial ability
7. Observational ability	Interpersonal understanding
8. Common sense	Art appreciation
9. Athletic ability	Moral–spiritual understanding
10. Theoretical ability	Art–creative ability

the qualities they thought more desirable in partners of each sex, with the results shown in Table 2.

A recent British survey found that looks were thought to be important by 40% of men and 23% of women. Faithfulness and personality were rated as more important by both sexes, especially having a good sense of humour, and being considerate and reliable.[32]

Many studies have shown that dating couples, like friends and married couples, tend to be similar in a number of ways. They are more similar than by chance in age, social class, religion, height, intelligence, values and beliefs, psychiatric abnormality, and in some measures of personality. They are even similar in dominance and submissiveness, and are *not* complementary, as was once supposed. On the other hand they are not *much* more similar than by chance. Typically there are rather small correlations, and some of this similarity is probably due to the couple influencing each other, for example in choice of leisure interests. Similarity is less than between friends (see p. 71f), and does not predict the future course of courtship at all well.[33] And although Jews usually choose Jews, and Catholics choose Catholics, this is not always the case. Even in Northern Ireland some marriages are between Catholics and Protestants.

Recent work with animals gives some interesting ideas on why people may choose mates similar to themselves.[34] In one experiment, Japanese quail who were reared with their siblings showed a distinct preference for first cousins of the opposite sex.[35] Animals seem to prefer mates that are similar to but slightly different from individuals familiar in early life – their immediate kin. If a similar biological principle operates in humans, then men and women would select partners similar to their own immediate kin, and therefore presumably similar to themselves since they would have shared the same upbringing and background. Biological safeguards against incest are provided, since the preference is for mates similar but *not* identical to the immediate kin. In many human societies, marriage to a first cousin is quite common,[36] possibly reflecting this biological mechanism.

Support from the social network is an important factor. It has been found that romantic involvement is greater if the relationship is supported by family and friends on both sides, and if there is strong attraction to, and frequent communication with, the partner's family and friends. The 'Romeo and Juliet effect', of parental opposition strengthening love, has also been found, but only when there is a low level of opposition from one partner's family, which is only one section of the network.[37]

Rules and skills

We have already seen that rules are important in governing relationships. Some rules are more critical in the early stages of relationship formation, while others become more important as a relationship progresses and intimacy increases.

In our Rules Study, we found the following rules endorsed as the most important ones to apply to the opposite-sex partner in the dating relationship.

TABLE 3. Rules for Dating Couples

1. Address the other by first name.
2. Respect the other's privacy.
3. Show mutual trust.
4. Be punctual.
5. Look the other person in the eye during conversation.
6. Don't criticise each other in public.
7. Stand up for the other person in his/her absence.
8. Keep confidences.
9. Show interest in each other's daily activities.
10. Be faithful to one another.
11. Share news of success.
12. Give birthday cards and presents.
13. Don't criticise him/her publicly.
14. Be tolerant of each other's friends.
15. Repay debts, favours and compliments.
16. Touch the other person intentionally.
17. Surprise each other with gifts.

When we look at the rules for young men and women (under twenty-five), we find some interesting sex differences. While both sexes believe that mutual trust, use of first name, and respecting privacy are important, young females believe that it is important to discuss intimate topics, to look each other in the eye, and to touch one another, while young men believe that it is more important to stand up for the other partner and not to criticise her in public, and to discuss more practical matters, such as news of success and daily activities.

We studied a group of forty-five young women to examine whether their reports of the extent to which they applied these rules in practice corresponded to the importance they attached to each rule. We found that, for these young women, there was a fairly close equivalence between how important they believed a rule to be and how often they reported behaving in accordance with the rule in practice. In other words, those who believed that a particular rule was very important tended to behave consistently with it, and the more highly they endorsed the rule, the more strongly their reported behaviour was in line with it. Rules 6–8 were the only cases where there was *no* strong association between how important a rule was rated by the group as a whole and how often they applied it in dating.

However, when we subdivide the group as a whole according to how often they date, it is the low-frequency daters (less than twice a month) who show the lowest consistency between the rules they believe to be important and those they actually apply to their own dating behaviour. The difference between the groups resides, not in the sorts of rules believed to be important, nor even in the actual applied rule behaviour, but in the *discrepancy* between endorsed and applied rules: low-frequency daters are less likely to practise what they preach. This may be because they have unrealistically high expectations of what is appropriate behaviour. These rules of dating relationships are somewhat similar to the rules of marriage (Chapter 6) and as we shall see in the following section, to those of cohabitation.

As a couple moves from casual to serious dating and to engagement, there is an increase in the level of love. There is also an increase in conflict and negativity from casual to serious dating, which levels off as the couple move on to engagement. And with the increase in conflict which accompanies this change in the relationship, different rules emerge to help in regulating these potential conflict areas. In our study of dating women, those involved in a single dating relationship thought that it was much more important to show the other partner unconditional positive regard, to look after him when ill, and to show an interest in his daily activities than did women involved with more than one dating partner. The single partner daters also reported applying the rules differently in practice. They were more likely to be faithful, to ask for personal advice, to show distress or anxiety in front of the other person and to show interest in the partner's daily activities.

Another rule found among groups of American teenage boys was that it was necessary to check with the group before taking a new girl out – in order to avoid fights over girls.[38] The rules about sexual behaviour for dating have been changing fast. Up to about 1939 middle-class couples in Britain followed a rule of petting, but no more.

In the 1960s surveys found that girls followed the rule of petting if seriously involved, while most of the boys had proceeded to intercourse by the age of twenty, especially if they were from the working class. Now there are no generally accepted rules about physical intimacy, though many think that intercourse is permissible for engaged or seriously committed couples.

However the skills of courtship are not completely covered by rules. In order to attract members of the opposite sex various strategies may be used – suggesting that one thinks highly of them, doing things for them, agreeing with them, and ascribing attractive characteristics to oneself, directly or indirectly – which can all be described as 'ingratiation'.[39] One study compared men who were successful and unsuccessful in dating girls. The successful ones were more fluent at saying the right thing, and quickly, and they agreed more. Their nonverbal behaviour was also different – they smiled and nodded more.[40] Non-verbal communication is one of the main ways of signalling sexual interest. Other non-verbal signals here include gaze, pupil dilation (though this is not under voluntary control), proximity and touch, and a state of bodily posture and alertness which signals a high level of arousal.[41] Physical attractiveness is to some extent under voluntary control. Attractive males have more dates and more social life, but this is mainly because they are also more assertive and socially competent. Attractive females are *not* more competent than other females: they do not need to be, since men take the initiative.[42]

Cohabitation

For many individuals, and particularly young people or divorced persons, a compromise needs to be made. On the one hand, they want to retain the autonomous and independent qualities of singlehood, while on the other hand wanting the emotional and sexual closeness and companionship of marriage. Cohabitation seems to offer this unique combination of qualities to many individuals.[43]

What was known as 'trial marriage' became popular in Sweden and Denmark in the early 1940s, and has become increasingly common in other Western countries.

About 3% of all women in Britain, 8% of single females, 18% of single females in their late twenties, and 20% of divorced women are cohabiting. Working-class women are more likely to describe themselves as 'married'. Table 4 shows that 18% of couples in their first marriage had lived together before marriage, 58% if one of them had been married before; and the numbers cohabiting have greatly increased over the last twenty years.[44]

TABLE 4. *Percentage of Couples who had Lived Together Before Marrying* [45]

| | Year of marriage | | |
	1960–1964	1971–1973	1979–1980
First marriage for both partners,			
woman aged under 20	3	4	19
20–24	2	8	15
25 and over	7	10	18
all ages	3	7	18
Previous marriage for either partner,			
all ages	26	43	58

The term 'living together' can include many different types of relationship. Cohabitation may be viewed by the couple as a temporary or casual affair, aimed at convenience or economy, without much commitment to a long-term relationship, but more often the cohabiting couple view their relationship as fairly permanent. It may be a preparation or a trial marriage – a way of seeing whether they are compatible as partners before formally marrying – or it may be an alternative to marriage, with no intention of becoming formally wed. Both of these latter types of cohabitation are long-term intimate relationships, with many features in common with marriage. There is a sense of commitment, shared responsibilities, emotional, social and economic interdependence, and also, as in marriage, interpersonal stresses and conflict.

Those who decide to live together (LTs) are different on average from those who do not. LTs are much less likely to be religiously committed, with a high proportion of atheists and agnostics. On the other hand many Catholics cohabit – they know that they can marry only once and want to be sure. And many Jews cohabit. In personality LTs are less restrained and inhibited, more independent and aggressive. Women who cohabit describe themselves as more masculine, men as more feminine. Both see themselves as more androgynous and non-traditional.

Activities

LTs engage in much the same activities as married couples, but with some interesting differences. Cohabiting couples say that they are in favour of egalitarianism, non-traditional sex roles, and are willing to carry out cross-role jobs, though in practice they are not very different from married couples. The women still do most of the housework, especially if there are children.[46] LT couples are more 'territorial': they keep to their own side of the bed, their own part of the bathroom, their own chair at the table, perhaps to symbolise a degree of separateness.[47] In other ways LTs have a lower level of commitment, a weaker dedication, to staying together than married couples have. This is not to imply that all cohabiting couples choose living together as a permanent alternative to marriage. Over 90% of cohabitors plan to marry at some time, but at an older age than non-cohabitors, and when they do wed, they produce fewer children in the first four years of marriage than married couples who had not previously cohabited. They have a wilder sex life, with more experimentation with unusual forms of sex, sometimes with other partners.

How long does it last?

We have seen that cohabitors have different degrees of commitment, though it is not always easy to classify couples in this way, and their level of commitment may change. The overall permanence of cohabitation does seem to be rather low, among students at least, who often break up at the end of the academic year, or when either or both leave college. In a study of 231 American student couples, it was found that 45% broke up over a two-year period.[48] Premarital couples who are living together in Britain have typically been together for fifteen months, and twenty-six months if one or both have been separated or divorced.

It is possible to study commitment from the expressed desire and determination to stay with the present partner. Another index is the frequency of the use of 'we' rather than 'I'. It is highest among married couples, lower among LT's, especially if they are not engaged. Commitment is greater when life with the other has been very rewarding, and also when a great deal has been 'invested' in the relationship, in terms of time, effort, money, or having children.[49] While LTs may be less committed than the married, they may also take greater care for fear of disrupting the relationship, and are mostly in the early and romantic stage.

Rules for cohabiting

People who live together have broken the traditional rules. They are radical and non-conforming in other ways too, as we have seen. However, unless they stick to *some* set of rules, their relationship is unlikely to survive. The rules we found most strongly endorsed for this relationship are as follows:

TABLE 5. Rules for Cohabiting

1. Show mutual trust.
2. Respect the other's privacy.
3. Show emotional support.
4. Address the other person by first name.
5. Be faithful to one another.
6. Share the household chores.
7. Share the costs for the house/flat.
8. Look after the other person when they are ill.
9. Share news of success with the other person.
10. Show interest in each other's daily activities.
11. Don't criticise each other when together in public.
12. Look the other person in the eye during conversation.
13. Stand up for the other person in his/her absence.
14. Be tolerant of each other's friends.
15. Ask for personal advice.
16. Keep confidences.
17. Disclose personal feelings and problems to the other person.
18. Give birthday cards and presents.
19. Talk to the other person about sex and death.
20. Don't nag.
21. Touch the other person intentionally.
22. Inform the other person about one's personal schedules.
23. Talk to the other person about religion and politics.

As we shall see in the next chapter, the rules about faithfulness, emotional support, sharing news and respecting privacy are also endorsed for husbands and wives. In fact the most important rules for cohabitors are almost identical with those of married couples. And some rules – notably trust, faithfulness and privacy – also apply to dating couples. But in addition, we have rules specific to cohabitors, which deal with the more practical affair of living together – rules about sharing household chores and costs – which are endorsed very highly. In fact quite a lot of LTs break what might seem an important rule – being faithful – and this may explain the high rate of break-up for cohabitors.

The benefits and costs of cohabiting

Living together gives a great deal of pleasure and happiness to most of those who do it. The effects are very similar to those of marriage, which will be discussed later (p. 139f); indeed some studies have found no difference at all. However in an Australian study of LTs, it was found that cohabitors had lower levels of romanticism, loving and liking than either dating couples or married couples (Table 6).

TABLE 6. Cohabitors and Others [50]

	Daters	Cohabitors	Married
Number of couples	70	96	117
Male's age	23.8	29.4	32.3
Female's age	22.6	25.6	29.5
Male's romanticism	19.5[a]	18.0[b]	18.7[ab]
Female's romanticism	19.6[a]	17.1[b]	18.2[c]
Male's love	56.7[ab]	55.7[a]	58.9[b]
Female's love	58.8[ab]	55.9[a]	59.3[b]
Male's liking	52.7[ab]	51.0[a]	54.1[b]
Female's liking	55.3[a]	51.7[b]	54.2[ab]

Note: Different superscripts (a, b) indicates a significant difference within the row ($p < 0.02$)

This table shows, in the fourth and fifth lines, that the most romantic mates were Daters, followed by the Married, and then by Cohabitors. In an American national survey it was found that LTs were much happier than those who were single, but not quite so happy as those who were married, though they were more satisfied with their sex life.[51]

Living together also provides excitement. Some people (men more than women) have a great need for excitement; a variety of sexual partners and a variety of forms of sex provide two ways to get it.

Passion and excitement are tightly – and perhaps inextricably – linked. When you're in love, it's exciting; when you experience the delight of really getting to know someone or of exploring a new sexual relationship, it's exciting. Your excitement intensifies your passion and it's easy to conclude that you're in love; the two kindle and rekindle one another.[52]

But love can also cause pain, if one person is ambivalent about the other, if he or she loves and hates at the same time, if there are rows and times of breaking it all off. They cannot quite call it off since each is attached to the other, and has become dependent on rewards from the other. Added to which, anger can produce sexual arousal.

What is the effect of cohabiting on subsequent marriage? There have been a number of careful follow-up studies, and the conclusion is that cohabiting does not make very much difference, but that LTs are a little more likely to get divorced after they marry – 36% v. 26% in one study.

Among British women now divorced or separated, 25% had lived together before marriage, compared with 12% for those still married or widowed.[53] However these divorces were not necessarily caused by the cohabitation.

Perhaps more interesting is the finding that ex-cohabitors get divorced at a higher level of marital adjustment – they have less commitment or motivation to try to make marriage work, are not prepared to put up with 'for better or worse'. Marriage is a less important part of their lives, and it is likely that they break up more amicably and with less distress.[54]

Similarly, those who have intercourse before marriage are more likely to divorce. In this country the level of pre-marital intercourse among those who later divorce has increased, but the rate among the still married has not (Table 7).

TABLE 7. Percentage Pre-marital Sex by Divorced and Married Couples [55]

	Divorced	Still married
Married before 1940	15	6
1940–1949	40	11
1950–1959	34	13
1960–1969	33	18
1970+	—	6

However, these differences may simply be due to the fact that cohabitors are different kinds of people (e.g. less conforming, less religious), rather than because of any causal effects of living together before marriage. Collett and Lamb[56] found different beliefs and expectations between couples about to marry according to whether they were cohabiting or living separately. Those who were cohabiting tended to be less romantic and less committed to the idea of marriage than those living separately. Although both sets of couples expected the impending marriage to improve their situation, those who were living apart expected greater improvement in things like how much they would love each other in a year's time, and in sexual satisfaction.

Falling Out of Love

No discussion on love and attraction would be complete without a final word on 'falling out of love'. Most of us can recall at least one broken romance from our own experience. Kirkpatrick and Caplow's early survey[57] of students found that both men and women reported, on average, two broken romances, and about half of all engagements during college years were broken. The main reasons given were mutual loss of interest – 47% of males and 38% of females give this reason. The rest were unilateral, with 32% of women breaking it off because of interest in a third party, compared to 15% of men. Women took slightly longer to 'get over' a broken romance, with 7% of males and 11% of females taking longer than one year.

Other studies have found other reasons for falling out of love: one partner has a job in another town, parents are strongly against the relationship, the female feels too dependent, there is unequal involvement, unequal costs and benefits.

'Falling out of love' and dissolution of the relationship are often mutual, but whether it is a joint decision, or determined unilaterally, the processes are similar. One of the most investigated and well-supported explanations for why relationships in general dissolve is based on the notion of the costs and benefits involved. Each individual, it is argued, has a comparison level which the difference between rewards and costs must exceed in order for the relationship to be maintained. When we are 'in love' the perceived benefits are high. As a couple becomes more interdependent, the benefits may not change, but the costs may increase. We may 'fall out of love' because this increase in the negative side of interrelatedness causes the satisfaction derived from the relationship to fall below our comparison level, particularly when we have an alternative relationship (or third party) which we anticipate will give us more rewards (or incur fewer costs).

As a relationship progresses, costs and rewards may change for a number of reasons. With increased familiarity with each other, both members of a pair will come to learn what is rewarding for the partner. Couples in long-term relationships may therefore become very adept at emitting behaviours that are rewarding to the other person, so that the increased costs of interrelatedness are balanced by a corresponding increase in rewardingness. (Conversely, the costs of dissolving that relationship become higher.)

What is rewarding for one partner may not be rewarding for another individual, and one partner's comparison level may be very different from another's. The point of dissolution occurs when one partner reaches his or her comparison level for alternatives, and this can occur however satisfied his or her partner is with the relationship. We shall examine the mechanics of relationship dissolution in more detail in later chapters, where we shall see that 'falling out of love' does not necessarily mean the dissolution of a relationship, particularly in marriage.

When there has been a high level of satisfaction the partners are more likely to try to find a solution by discussing the situation, and to wait to see if things improve, rather than leaving, ignoring the other, or seeking other sexual liaisons.[58] When the point has been reached where one partner wants to leave, there are several ways of doing it. The main choice is between open confrontation, withdrawal or avoidance, and the use of third parties. When there has been a close relationship more direct methods are used, i.e. confrontation. Ending a relationship is parallel to ending a conversation, and often contains some of the same components: confrontation summarises the changed situation, withdrawal indicates that decreased access is desired, and positive strategies are a form of continued supportiveness.[59]

The ending of love affairs is usually very distressing. A study of American women aged 17–26 found that 60% had been severely depressed at some time over love, and that 25% had considered suicide.[60] The study cited at the beginning of this section found how students had reacted to broken love affairs – dreaming or daydreaming about the lost partner, going to places associated with them, etc. (Table 8).

Sex, age and class differences

In popular literature, falling in love is a young person's prerogative.

TABLE 8. Reactions of Students to Broken Love Affairs [61]

	Males (%)	Females (%)
Frequenting places with common associations	22	10
Avoiding places with common associations	3	3
Avoiding meetings	5	5
Attempting meetings	6	4
Remembering only pleasant things	16	16
Remembering only unpleasant things	2	4
Dreaming about partner	16	11
Daydreaming	14	11
Imagining recognition	6	8
Liking or disliking people because of resemblance	6	5
Imitating mannerisms	2	2
Preserving keepsakes	7	11
Reading over old letters	7	9

We speak romantically of 'young lovers' and distinguish this from the more mundane feelings we stereotypically apply to more 'mature' couples. Older people are expected not to 'fall in love', yet we are equally suspicious of 'puppy love'.

At what age do people start 'falling in love'? An early American survey of over 1,000 college students[62] found that most had started dating at thirteen years of age. They also report their first 'infatuation' at age thirteen but their first 'love experience' did not occur, for most, till about the age of seventeen.

Girls report first falling in love five to six months earlier than boys, and they become infatuated more often. But there is much evidence to show that girls are 'cooler' (less impulsive). They are less influenced by physical appearance, they rarely fall in love with men who are younger or of lower social class, and more women than men say that they would marry without love.[63] We saw above that 43% of women, as opposed to 30% of men, are not sure whether they are in love by the twentieth date (p. 98). Girls, on average, have intercourse and engage in other intimate sexual activities at a later age than men.

Cohabitation is much more common among those over twenty-five than among younger people, though it is quite high among students, and the relationship is more stable for older couples. It is much more common among those who have been married before. On the other hand romanticism is considerably lower among LTs the older they are; this is not so with love.[64]

There are some quite interesting sex differences in cohabitation. In a study of 231 student couples, it was found that men fell in love first in most cases, while it was the women who fell out of love first. It was also found that women often initiated the separation even when they were the more involved – another case of the greater rationality of women in matters of love perhaps.[65] Other studies have found that while women have higher scores than men do for loving and liking, they have *lower* scores for romanticism.[66]

"I now pronounce you man and common law wife"

Private Eye

We shall see that girls are brought up with greater protection and restraint than boys (p. 195f). This is reinforced by the double standard of sexual morality, based on fears of pregnancy and traditionally a greater need for a permanent partner. Young men, on the other hand, are expected to be adventurous, and they have a greater interest in sexual adventure and novelty.[67]

There are no very great class differences. Schofield[68] found that working-class adolescents had intercourse rather earlier than middle-class ones; this is probably because middle-class children in Britain are more often at single sex schools, some of them at boarding schools. There are some class differences in cohabitation – middle-class couples do it more.

Personality factors have also been found, and some psychoanalysts believe that we fall in love because we need someone to help us to evaluate ourselves more favourably. Consequently people with low self-evaluations are likely to fall in love more readily. There is some experimental evidence for this. Dion and Dion[69] asked students to rate the intensity and frequency of their love experiences. They found that subjects with low self-esteem reported more intense love experiences than those with high self-esteem. So the sort of belief and attitudes we hold about ourselves may determine how readily we fall in love. The same is true about the beliefs we have about the world. Those who believe that what happens to them is determined by their own behaviour rather than being in the hands of fate, chance, or other people, were less likely to report having been in love. They also held a less idealistic view of love and they reported that their romantic love lasted longer than those who thought that external events controlled their behaviour.

Love in different cultures and historical periods

There is space here only to pick out some of the fundamental issues. Premarital sex is absolutely taboo in some cultures and a normal part of adolescent life in others. It is most controlled in those cultures in which women inherit property, especially land, and where there is advanced agriculture, so that families need to keep tighter control on sexual liaisons.[70] Often upper-class families exert greater control, because there is more property to look after.[71] In Britain the 'sexual revolution' has brought about a great increase in PMI since 1939, through the greater availability and efficiency of contraception, the greater independence of young people from their parents, and the cultural influence of Scandinavia and California, where it all started.

Love takes different forms depending on the availability of each sex. In some historical periods there has been an acute shortage of women. During the Middle Ages there was a shortage of upper-class women, due to women going into convents. This may explain the growth of chivalry and 'courtly love', found among European nobility in the early Middle Ages. This was governed by elaborate rules, and was pursued with great dedication, often with ultimate failure and distress. In parts of the American West in the 1890s there was a ratio of sixteen men to one woman, since few women had ventured West by this time. As a result there was a tradition of great courtesy and respect for women.[72]

For a long time marriages were mainly arranged by parents. This is still practised in much of India and other parts of the East. A cross-cultural study of forty-three cultures found that romantic love occurred where there was most freedom to choose a partner, and where there was more contact between young men and women, through dancing and other activities.[73] The shift to almost complete freedom to choose occurred early in the present century in the West, and the love ideology has been much strengthened by the Hollywood mythology. We have seen, however, that romantic choices are far from random and follow a long period of exploration. Women's choices in particular are fairly rational.

Cohabitation on a large scale first appeared in the modern world in Scandinavia, known as 'trial marriage', and duly shocked or intrigued those in other Western countries. California led the way with communes and various kinds of promiscuity. While 3% of people cohabit in Britain, the corresponding figure in Sweden and Denmark is about 8% and in France, 5%. The norm in Britain inclines towards trial marriage, between young couples who are seriously intending to make it last. Not only is it governed by the informal rules we have described, but the law has changed to govern it: recent rulings by the courts have given the woman rights in joint property after four years of cohabiting.

The psychology of love

Can psychology explain the phenomenon of falling in love? Obviously sex has much to do with it, and it seems very likely that there is a biological and evolutionary basis. We must bear in mind, however, that 'falling in love' occurs only in certain cultures and historical periods. What is more universal is the very strong attachment formed between a young male and an unrelated young female, usually lasting for a long time. This may have an evolutionary origin in the need to provide a stable home for rearing human children, who take longer to rear than any animal young. And there is a genetic advantage in marrying outside the family, since this will avoid inbreeding and lead to a greater diversity of offspring, some of whom will stand a chance of surviving. Finally the attachment can form very quickly. In the early millennia of the human race members of different clans would have had very brief contact and it was perhaps necessary for an attachment to form quickly.[74] However, as we have seen, people fall in love with others who are similar to themselves, though they usually find strangers more exciting than the girl or boy next door. And the phenomenon of falling in love seems to be limited to certain cultures and historical periods – arranged marriages have been more common in the world's history.

The capacity for sexual love may still be learnt during childhood. The close attachment between parents and children is a model for later sexual behaviour.

> We noted that girls tend to retain a number of baby-like features into adulthood, that they emphasise them in make-up and clothing, and that men are attracted by them. It is also clear that a lot of basic patterns of parent–child behaviour are carried over into the courting situation. Many forms of intimacy indulged in – baby-talk, hand-holding, embracing, kissing, sucking, and biting – are reminiscent of parent–child contact. In fact, a great deal of the behaviour of lovers can be viewed and understood as a return to a parent–infant style of tenderness and caring, with the two lovers taking turns in playing the roles of parent and infant.[75]

We must now take account of the extent of cultural variations in love. A theory has been put forward which combines biological factors with the importance of the love ideology. If someone is physiologically aroused, and if the situation suggests that 'love' is an appropriate label for their feelings, he or she will interpret their state as one of love.[76] Sexual arousal may be labelled in this way, but so may other emotions, such as fear. Young men who were interviewed by a girl on a dangerously swaying suspension bridge were more likely to phone her afterwards than those interviewed on an ordinary bridge.[77] Similar effects can be produced by arousal due to physical exertion which may explain the sexual excitement produced by dancing.[78]

Private Eye

We have seen that interpersonal attraction, for example to friends, is largely based on the level of rewards received from the other. How exactly is love different from this? It is partly that the rewards (i.e. those derived from sex) are more intense. Also, as two people do more things together they become more dependent on one another for a whole range of rewards. If they set up house together, if the woman becomes pregnant, the extent of their common interests increases. This is not an *exchange* of rewards, since the two have nearly identical interests, they enjoy the same rewards from their activities together. And each enjoys the gratification of the other – 'the loved one's pleasure and pain become one's own' (Spinoza).

We carried out a study of degree of altruistic concern for spouse, child between ten and fifteen, friend and workmate, using matrices in which subjects were asked to indicate how they would divide up a sum of money between self and one of the others. One of the matrices was like this.

Fig. 3   RATING SCALE FOR ALTRUISM QUESTIONNAIRE

money for your spouse	19	18	17	16	15	14	13	12	11	10	9	8	7
money for your self	1	3	5	7	9	11	13	15	17	19	21	23	25

Please fill in below the money you have chosen to give each person:

money for your spouse: ☐

money for your self: ☐

We found that greatest altruism was shown to spouse, followed by child, friend and workmate.[79]

Love is heightened if people are made aware of the rewards brought about by enjoyment of the other's company, rather than by the external benefits they produce.[80] In some sense there is a 'merger of selves' in love. There is common property, children, pride in each other's accomplishments, a shared past and future, the same books and the same thoughts.[81] Feelings of love, such as sharing, understanding, companionship, mutual support and affection, belonging, closeness, rise to a peak during engagement and the point of marriage.[82] We shall examine these in more detail in our next chapter on Marriage.

FURTHER READING

Walster, E. & Walster, G. (1978) *A New Look at Love* Reading, Mass: Addison Wesley

Wilson, G. & Nias, D. (1976) *Love's Mysteries: The Psychology of Sexual Attraction* London: Open Books

6

Marriage

Marriage is a 'holy mystery in which man and woman become one flesh
. . . that husband and wife may comfort and help one another . . . that
they may have children . . . and begin a new life together in the
community' (Church of England *Alternative Services Book*, 1980).
Marriage is quite different from all other relationships: it is a very
intense relationship, it is a *sexual* relationship, it embraces *many aspects*
of life, and it is usually intended to be *permanent*.

Despite the alleged decline in the popularity of marriage, most
people still get married. In Britain 92% of people get married. The
median (typical) age of marriage for men was 25.8 and for women 23.3
in 1981 – eighteen months later than in 1970 – see Table 1. Nearly a
third get separated or divorced, but two out of three divorcees
remarry.

TABLE 1. *Proportions Marrying at Different Ages (1981)*[1]

	under 20	20–24	25–29	30–44	45 and over
Males	8.3	42.7	23.3	16.4	9.4
Females	25.3	40.4	14.9	12.2	7.2

Median Age of Marriage for People in Different Conditions

	single	widowed	divorced	all
Males	24.1	60.4	35.8	25.8
Females	21.9	55.0	33.4	23.3

Marriage is partly a biological partnership. But it is also a socially
defined and regulated relationship, in all human societies. Getting
married, engaged, divorced are all 'rites of passage', which are usually
enacted by a priest or other official, in the presence of friends and
relations, who confirm that a change of relationship has taken place.
The swearing of oaths of loyalty, the laying on of hands, and other

aspects of the marriage ceremony, help couples to feel that they have indeed undergone a change of state, are now a united couple, and are committed to a lengthy partnership.

Marriage, like all good things, does not work unless people keep to the rules, unless certain restraints operate. We shall look at these rules later. Such rules are supported by moral and religious systems which 'sanctify' marriage, underline the importance of faithfulness, and so on. The 'love ideology' is another factor in promoting marital stability. It has been found in primitive societies that romantic love is less important in marriage where there are other important bonds, such as when the partners depend on each other for subsistence, i.e. where both contribute to the food supply.

Husband and wife roles

For a long time it was assumed that the husband should be the breadwinner, the wife the homemaker. However times are changing and about 50% of women want to have careers as well as having husbands and children, a view more widely held among younger and better educated women.[2] The question is: How far have the marital roles actually changed?

Employment In the traditional family, the husband often had a career, and was able to pursue his ambitions. The wife had to play a secondary role; if her husband was successful then she shared in the resulting benefits of increased income and greater status, but it was the husband rather than she who had the success. In addition she had to put up with his avoidance of domestic duties. If the husband was

TABLE 2. Employment Status of Married Mothers and Age of Youngest Child (1980–82)[3]

	Age of youngest child		
	0–4	5–9	10+
Percentage of wives employed			
full-time	6	13	33
part-time	21	46	38
Lone mothers			
full-time	11	21	31
part-time	13	34	29

unsuccessful there was little she could do about it – except find a job herself.

With the increased education and aspirations of women, more wives have jobs and careers than before. In Britain 60% of wives and 93% of husbands were employed in 1979; in 58% of families both were working. The majority of wives work part-time, especially when their children are young, as Table 2 shows.

We shall discuss the 'dual-career' marriage below. When women have jobs and earn money this has a considerable effect on their position in the family. In particular they do less housework, and have a greater say in decisions.

During the Depression of the 1930s, many husbands earned less or lost their jobs. The result was a large increase in the power of their wives.[4]

Housework   In most primitive societies there is a very clear division of labour: women look after children, do the cooking and preserving of food, making and repairing of clothes; men go fishing and hunting, look after animals, lumbering and mining, wood and metal work, building houses; either may look after crops. In modern societies things are not very different. An American national survey found that wives did far more housework than husbands (Table 3).

TABLE 3. Hours Per Week Spent on Housework [5]

	Employed men	Employed women	Housewives
Housework, shopping, etc.	8.1	23.5	41.9
Child care, collecting	3.3	4.6	11.3
Total	11.3	28.1	53.2

A study of forty London housewives with young children reported their doing seventy-seven hours housework a week, and 70% were dissatisfied with this. Most of them found the work monotonous, fragmented and lonely, and they resented its low status. However they appreciated their autonomy, and what they liked most was cooking, followed by shopping and washing.[6] On the other hand husbands usually do most of the home repairs, look after the car, do the heavy gardening (wives do flowers), and pay the bills. They take a hand in child-rearing, not much with babies, but more with hobbies, sports and homework for older children.[7]

Some married couples show more role segregation while others carry out the family tasks jointly. There is evidence that if each partner is closely attached to his or her kin, then they are more likely to play segregated roles. On the other hand if husband and wife have a shared social network of friends and relatives they are more likely to be complementary or to form a joint partnership, rather than be independent. There is more traditional division of labour if the parents had done this, and if the couple accept the traditional sex-role ideology. Recent studies have found that the wife does less housework when she is employed, the husband has a large income, she is well educated, and there are several children. And the unequal division of labour is slowly declining with time.[8]

Power in decision-taking In virtually all cultures, primitive and industrialised, men have had more power than women inside and outside families, though there has been a gradual rise in the power of women, and women sometimes have more power than the public relationships between the spouses suggests, especially inside the home. Each partner has certain areas where he or she is the acknowledged leader – traditionally the wife over food and children, husband over car, money, etc.

An American study tried to find out how husbands and wives took decisions in fourteen different areas. They classified them as husband clearly dominant, wife clearly dominant, equal and shared, equal and not shared decisions, as shown in Table 4.

TABLE 4. Power of Husbands and Wives [9]

	Men's reports	Women's reports
Husband dominant	10	9
Wife dominant	4	4
Most decisions shared	16	20
Equal power, most decisions not shared	70	67

However a recent English study found that although most decisions were in a sense shared, in fact husbands had much more say in some of the most important spheres – major financial decisions, and moving (usually because of his job). However in two other areas rated as very important there was more equal say – choice of house, and children's education.[10]

Many studies have found that the partner who earns the most money, has the more prestigious job, or is better educated, has the most say in decisions. However this simple principle does not always work, partly because during times of social change towards greater equality of the sexes, higher status men tend to accept these ideas first, and thus give away more power. The social skills of assertiveness and persuasiveness of each partner are also important. Better educated wives not only have power based on their education, they are also more likely to have jobs and earn money, have forward-looking husbands, *and* be socially skilled.[11]

It is found that many wives want more power than they have, and that they are happier with their marriage when they do have more power – though they don't want more than their husbands – see Table 4. Wives use different tactics from husbands to gain power – withdrawing, sulking and appealing to family unity, where husbands use more direct power strategies.[12]

A number of American studies have found that egalitarian marriages are the happiest, with husband-dominant marriages close behind. Wife-dominant marriages are on average much less happy, especially when the wife uses coercive methods of control.[13] It is also important for a happy marriage that the two partners should have similar ideas about the roles of husbands and wives.[14]

Sex roles in marriage   Sociologists have argued that there is traditionally a more general division of sex roles in the family. The wife's job is to look after the children and her husband, and to provide nurture and social support inside the home. The husband's job is to cope with the outside environment, to provide food, housing and protection, if necessary by fighting and organising others in the community. The origins of these two marital roles may be partly biological – women have a greater biological interest in looking after their children; men, in impregnating women. The social system has come to sustain these roles by tradition, law, and sex-role stereotypes.

Research on non-verbal communication has found that women are somewhat more expressive than men – they smile, look, and gesture more, and they can communicate their feelings better. They are also better at decoding the facial expressions and tones of voice of others. In the typical marriage there is an expressive wife with a rather less expressive husband. It has been found that for a happy marriage it is important for wives to be good at decoding,[15] and that in disturbed marriages husbands are poor senders and receivers of emotions to wives, via non-verbal cues. Husbands in disturbed marriages are particularly poor at sending positive messages by tone of voice.[16]

Wives are found to provide more social support for husbands than husbands provide for them.[17] Far more husbands (63%) use their spouses as their main confidant than do wives (26%) (see p. 223). And wives spend much more time looking after, and providing support for, the children. Other studies have found that for both male and female students, interaction with women friends is more rewarding than interaction with men.[18] These are probably the main reasons that marriage produces greater benefits for husbands than for wives.

Stage of marriage

We shall use stage of marriage rather than age, since it is the more important of these closely linked variables.

Honeymoon period up to birth of first child   During this period there is withdrawal from the company of friends, as Table 5 shows.

TABLE 5. *Number of Friends at Different Stages up to Marriage* [19]

occasional dating	4.13
regular dating	3.52
exclusive dating	3.07
engaged	1.51
married	1.06

At first there is a high rate of sexual activity, four to five times a week (Table 9, p. 138). The honeymoon period is a high point of marital satisfaction as Figure 1 shows.

However there are a number of problems to sort out during this period. In particular the couples have to accommodate to each other, in order to work out a satisfactory joint pattern of life. The most difficult problems tend to be over money and sex, and there may be trouble over sharing the housework, and relative influence in decision-making. Each partner has to break or weaken the ties with his or her family, to become independent of them. This is usually hardest for wives, and is very difficult if the couple are living in the home of one set of parents.[21]

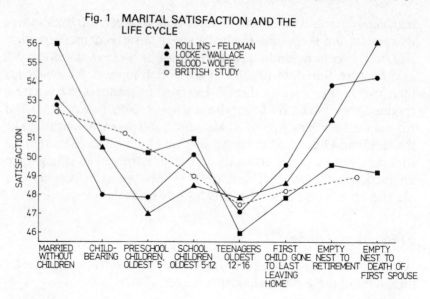

Fig. 1 MARITAL SATISFACTION AND THE LIFE CYCLE

Birth of first child to adolescence   The focus of attention and the source of the main problems is the children – their birth, illnesses, education, etc. The husband is much concerned with his career. Husband and wife have less time together, and the level of satisfaction falls (see Figure 1). The wife spends more time with the children than with her husband, and these relationships may become uppermost for her. In unsatisfactory marriages the children are the main source of satisfaction.

Adolescent children   This is the lowest point for marital satisfaction (Figure 1), mainly because of the difficulties of dealing with teenagers (p. 201f). The wife is freer of child minding, is likely to be in at least part-time work, and may find a new independence, develop new skills, interests and social attachments.

After children have left   The period of the 'empty nest' turns out to be a very happy one for most couples. The upturn in the satisfaction level in Figure 1 shows the satisfaction of those who are still married – the others have separated by now. Weak marriages may find this period a strain, since husband and wife now spend a lot more time together, and may find that they have drifted apart. They still have a common interest in their grown-up children, and usually enjoy the grand-children.

Childless marriages The level of marital happiness in childless marriages is found to be a little higher than where there are children. This is particularly true of couples who are voluntarily childless, but also for those who are undecided and who have postponed having children. In childless marriages the wife usually has a job, or career, and may earn as much as or more than her husband, so that there is greater equality. Childless wives are also more satisfied than mothers with their husbands' companionship and understanding.[22] Mothers on the other hand earn less, do more housework, and have less say in decisions, but couples with children have the satisfaction of having the children and, for some reason, live longer (p. 19). Although children appear to reduce marital satisfaction, several studies show that despite the strains of parenthood, most people say that this is overall a rewarding experience, and they believe it brings couples together.[23]

TABLE 6. *Class Differences in Marriage (England and Wales)* [25,26,27,27a]

	I	II	III(N)*	III(M)*	IV	V	Total
1. Median age of bride at marriage (1979)							
	26.0	24.0	21.6	21.2	20.4	22.0	21.7
2. Percentage first births conceived prematurely (1977)							
	6		9	18	26	43	15
3. Interval between marriage and birth of first child (months) (1981)							
	42	38	33	35	20	13	29
4. Age of mother at birth of first child (1977)							
% under 20	6	10	12	28	31	38	23
5. Number of children (1977)							
	2.26	2.18	2.02	2.37	2.40	2.74	2.33
6. Divorce rate, per 10,000 women under 55 (1971)							
	22	25	43	29	25	51	30
7. Length of marriage (1970–71)							
% divorced, whose marriages lasted less than 7 years							
wife married before 20	14	30	31	29	34	30	
20–25	10	27	23	36	37	25	
25+	15	16	26	6	20	17	

*N = non-manual; M = manual

The character of the marital bond changes after twenty-five or thirty years of marriage. Couples do more things together, there are more positive and fewer negative interactions.[24] There is less sex but more security. There is more familiarity, but less excitement. Marriage, like the partners themselves, has become quieter and duller, but also comfortable and relaxed.

Class differences in married life

The main differences between classes are summarised in Table 6. The division into classes which is now used in the British Census and many research studies is used here.

In the first place working-class people marry earlier, partly because their education is shorter. The statistics show that working-class mothers are younger at the birth of their first child, and more likely to be pregnant. Many working-class people get married because the girl is pregnant. There is a higher divorce rate for working-class couples, and they get divorced sooner. This can partly be explained by the earlier age of marriage, but as section 7 of the Table shows, working-class marriages are shorter when this has been held constant.

How about the quality of married life in different classes? Marital happiness is somewhat greater in the higher classes. One reason for this is that many working-class husbands are found to be unsatisfactory confidants. In addition working-class husbands and wives lead more separate lives – they do fewer things together. They spend less time with friends (who are usually shared), and more with kin (who are not). It has been found in an American study that marital happiness is associated with level of *education*, rather than with level of occupation. More educated people admitted to having had marital problems, and feeling inadequate as spouses, but seemed to have the skills for handling marital conflicts.[28]

Better educated people have been found to be more open with each other, less controlling, and to respect each other's feelings more.[29] On the other hand working-class wives are happier with domestic and household tasks than are middle-class wives, most of whom say they dislike them.[30]

People tend to marry others with the same social origins as themselves. This is particularly true of social class I, 42% of whom marry in the same class. Overall 30–40% marry within their class; most of the remainder marry someone from the adjacent class.

Naturally those from social class I often marry down, those from class V often marry up.

Husbands and wives may be of different classes in respect of their own careers and achievements, although there is quite a strong tendency for them to have occupational levels which are similar. For husbands in social class I, 34% of their wives have jobs in class I, 44% in class II. For husbands in class V, 89% of wives are in manual jobs, and only 0.6% in class I jobs. However there is an overall difference between the jobs of men and women. Women's work falls into two main groups: the higher group consists of teachers, nurses, social workers, etc. (Class II), and the lower group consists of clerical workers, shop assistants, etc. (Class III, Skilled non-manual); there are relatively few women in class I, and in classes IV and V, compared with men. In addition, many women work part-time, especially when their children are young, which may explain the small number of class I women. It follows that class I men often have wives of a lower occupational status, while many class IV and V men have wives at a higher level. It also follows that women whose fathers were in class I are likely to be downwardly mobile, while those whose fathers were in IV and V are more likely to be upwardly mobile, than men of the same background.[31]

What is the effect of mixed-class marriage? The main effect is that the marriage is less happy and more likely to end in divorce. An American study found the following percentages of married couples rated as having 'good' adjustment:[32]

same social class	husband higher class	wife higher class
53	35	28

Another study found that 45% of husbands were violent when the wife was better educated, as opposed to 9% when he was better educated or when they were equal.[33] If the husband is of a higher class, his wife may be very attractive, or have other desirable qualities, but she may also commit social errors, be an unsatisfactory conversationalist and prove not fully acceptable to his family and friends. It is worse when the wife is of higher social class; she may have to put up with a lower standard of living, suffer a drop in social position and see her children deprived of what she had as a child. She is also discontented if she has been socially mobile through her own career.[34]

Activities

For 60% of married couples, the most valuable aspect of marriage is doing things together.[35] But what *do* husbands and wives do together? We asked a sample of them in the Oxford area, also asking what they did together with friends, workmates and others[35a]. Certain activities were distinctive of marriage, i.e. they were more frequent for spouses than in any other of the eight relationships studied. In order of distinctiveness they were:

being in bed together
watching TV
doing domestic jobs together
playing chess or other indoor games
going for a walk
going shopping
playing tennis or squash
eating together informally
having intimate conversation
arguing, disagreeing

*"Did you know we spend
one-third of our
money sleeping?"*

(Punch)

This list of activities was found for subjects in the Oxford area; and some of them would no doubt be different in other cultures and subcultures.

These activities are very different from those shared with friends or workmates. The main difference from the activities with friends (see p. 75) is that while friends engage in eating, drinking and leisure, spouses have work to do and decisions to take. The work involved is rather like that in a small hotel, restaurant, nursery school, hospital, and market garden combined, except that there are no hours of work or payment.

Housework is mainly done by the wife, though husbands do some washing up, house-repairing, gardening and child-minding. Some of this is done jointly, though more is done in a complementary way.

Child-rearing is of course a major part of the domestic work while the children are young; most of it is done by wives, though husbands help later.

Meals are a major event in families, usually rather informal meals compared to meals with guests or in restaurants. Meals are often the only occasion on which the family meet, and one of the main occasions on which spouses meet. It is a curious fact of social life that conversation between family and friends is usually accompanied by food and drink; the same is not true of conversation at work.

The talk is about many things. Spouses report the main events of the day, work out a shared reaction to them, and in this way build a common view of the world. One partner may have problems and need information or advice. These may include more or less intimate personal problems, and then the other acts as a kind of counsellor or psychotherapist. The provision of these kinds of help and advice make up 'social support', and plays a major part in sustaining the mental health of the other. Some of the conversation is about decision-taking, problem-solving, about the innumerable matters that need to be decided. Some are large: whether to move house, change jobs, have more children; others are very minor: what to watch on TV, whether to go to the pub. Hence 'argument and disagreement' is one of the most characteristic marital activities.

If spouses often act as psychotherapists, they also act as nurses, when the other is ill, or when children are ill.

So much for work, now for leisure. We saw above that watching TV together is one of the most characteristic of marital activities. In

Britain people watch TV on average about two and a half hours per day, though they watch more in the winter. Working-class people in Britain watch about forty minutes per day more than social class I, and they watch ITV much more. People also listen to the radio about one and a half hours a day.[36] It has been found that the effect of watching TV is to reduce conversation and social activities. Although TV brings spouses together in the same room, it does so in a very low-key way, and reduces the amount of social interaction between them. Indeed one or both may be asleep, or half asleep, much of the time.

Married couples with young children, and married couples who both have jobs, may have little or no time for 'leisure' activities. In our sample, however, most subjects reported quite a high level of playing indoor and outdoor games, and going for walks. Other shared leisure activities are less distinctive of marriage, but are still important –going to the pub, going out for meals, social life with friends, and dancing. Joint social life of these kinds is important: it is a source of rewards for which the partner is instrumental, and it creates a shared social network. The more time couples spend with friends and kin, the more satisfied they are with marriage.[37]

The most characteristic marital activity of all turns out to be being in bed together – for seven or eight hours each day, most of the time asleep of course, but not all of it. We shall discuss the sexual activities of married couples below.

The more things couples do together, the higher their marital satisfaction, and vice versa[38]. The sorts of activities couples engage in may also be relevant to their marital satisfaction. We shall examine marital happiness in more detail later in this chapter, but can mention at this point that happily married couples reported enjoying similar leisure activities more than couples who subsequently divorce, in an early American study, as Table 7 shows.

Husbands and wives share many aspects of their lives, their leisure, their food, their good and bad habits; they are in a real sense 'one flesh'. As a result they share a similar state of health and length of life. There is an astonishing similarity of length of life for spouses, as a function of husband's occupation. Table 8 shows 'standardised mortality ratios': these are numbers of people aged 15–64 in a given group, who died in relation to the whole adult population of the same age composition. So a figure of 200 means that twice as many died as expected, and the expectation of life is correspondingly shorter.

TABLE 7. Activities enjoyed by partners in happy and unhappy marriages[39]

| | | Partner Enjoying Activity | | |
| | | Husband | Wife | |
Activity	Both	only	only	Neither
Listening to the radio				
Happily married couples	90%	3%*	6%**	2%*
Subsequently divorced couples	75	9*	12**	8*
Music				
Happily married couples	89	4*	1**	4**
Subsequently divorced couples	75	10*	22**	10**
Reading				
Happily married couples	72	9	12**	—
Subsequently divorced couples	46	20	38**	—
Cinema				
Happily married couples	68	—	5	17*
Subsequently divorced couples	72	—	13	7*
Parties				
Happily married couples	57	1	4*	24**
Subsequently divorced couples	46	7	11*	45**
Sports				
Happily married couples	54	20*	3**	22**
Subsequently divorced couples	36	35*	15**	32**
Playing cards				
Happily married couples	39	8	—	36*
Subsequently divorced couples	45	21	—	24*
Dancing				
Happily married couples	25	2	7	45*
Subsequently divorced couples	38	9	21	24*
Drinking				
Happily married couples	7	10	1*	42
Subsequently divorced couples	19	38	8*	28
Gambling				
Happily married couples	2	10**	—	—
Subsequently divorced couples	3	40**	—	—

*Reported by husband
**Reported by wife
Unstarred percentages are averages for husbands' and wives' reports combined. 'Neither'
column means that both partners were 'indifferent' to the activity.

It can be seen that the mortality rate of wives depends a lot on their husband's occupation. The most likely explanation is that each occupation produces a level of stress, and a way of life which affects wives, directly or indirectly, as much as their spouses.

TABLE 8. Mortality Ratios for Men and Married Women for Different Occupations of Husbands[40]

	Men	Women
Foremen	47	61
Sales managers	70	72
Clergymen	76	76
Personnel managers	80	80
Doctors	81	92
Commercial travellers	88	85
Accountants	88	89
Police	109	109
Butchers	109	116
Nurses (male)	112	114
Railway guards	121	125
Garage proprietors	140	142
Dock labourers	140	145
Tailors	140	145
Coal miners	141	164
Armed forces	147	150
Publicans	155	139
Fishermen	171	177
Sailors	233	186
Bricklayers, labourers	273	241
Electrical engineers	317	295

Sex

Is sex the magic ingredient which binds most husbands and wives together for so many years? Biologically sex is a central feature of marriage: it leads to children, and it is one of the factors attracting the male to the female, so that he will look after her and the children. Traditionally all sexual behaviour was supposed to occur within marriage, but there has been a great increase during recent years in sex outside marriage.

TABLE 9. Frequency of Intercourse per month after marriage [41]

Months		
	1–2	17.2
	3–6	13.4
	7–12	11.6
Years	2	9.5
	6–10	9.4
	15–20	9.4
	21–25	6.8
	26+	4.8

The rate of sexual activity among newly-weds is very high, over four times a week, but this falls sharply during the first two months, and then declines more slowly (Table 9).

However there are wide individual differences; many women have difficulty reaching orgasm, and 10% never have one. Freedman[42] found that 50% of men and 30% of women, married or unmarried, were moderately or very dissatisfied with their sex lives, though there was a very high general level of satisfaction with marriage. There are differences between the sexes in the desire for sexual activity: husbands say they want it more than wives. Many wives state that they have intercourse more often than they want, many husbands claim they would like more than they get – when their wives complain of 'headaches', etc. It has been found that the frequency of intercourse is more a function of the wife's age than of the husband's – the effects can be separated statistically. This is probably because the wife's androgen level falls with increasing age, thus reducing her desire and sexual responsiveness.[43] The sexual satisfaction of husbands is related to the strength of their wives' sex drive, but the wives' sexual satisfaction is not affected similarly.[44]

"Well, if you must know, it's 35% natural headache, 65% man-made ennui."

(Punch)

Many studies have found an association between sexual satisfaction and marital happiness. But does sexual satisfaction lead to marital satisfaction or vice versa? There is some evidence that for men sexual satisfaction leads to marital satisfaction, while for women the reverse is true. That is to say, for men sex leads to love, for women love leads to sex.[45] For women sex and love are closely linked, while for men sex can occur without love, and often does. The biological interest of females is to have a mate around who is a permanent source of support and protection for her and her children, so love is of primary importance. The male biological interest is in propagating his genes, which he can do by sex without love.

Is sex the magic ingredient of marriage? It appears to be more important to husbands, but half of them report being sexually dissatisfied after marriage, and many of their wives don't have orgasms much of the time. However, most people agree that sex is very important – though not as important as love. While the two can be separated, it looks as if the combination of the two is what married couples need.

Marital satisfaction

We showed in Chapter 2 that married people are, on average, happier and in better mental and physical health than the single, widowed or divorced. And for those who are married there is a close relation between overall happiness and marital happiness, especially for women.[46] In other words happiness is dependent for most people on marital happiness.

How is marital satisfaction or happiness measured? It can be assessed by asking a whole battery of questions, or just one question as in, for example, a British survey by Mark Abrams which produced the following results:

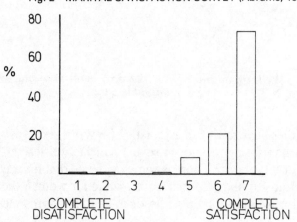

Fig. 2   MARITAL SATISFACTION SURVEY (Abrams, 1972)

This survey shows that most people claim to be happily married. Do these results exaggerate the happiness of marriages? Of course many of those who are *not* happily married nowadays part company, so these surveys are of those who are still together. And they may be lying, but other questions such as 'Have you ever wished you had married someone else?', or 'Has the thought of getting divorced ever crossed your mind?' produce very similar answers. However among all these 'happy' marriages there are probably quite a lot which are fairly dull and 'devitalised', without a great deal of mutual involvement.

Marital happiness or satisfaction is a single dimension, and a number of questionnaire scales have been constructed to measure it. However, there are two partly independent aspects of marital satisfaction, 1. happiness, experience of affection, support and understanding, and 2. frequency of arguments and rows, mutual criticism, specific problems.[48] Marital happiness can be predicted surprisingly well from frequency of intercourse minus frequency of rows (defined as one partner storming out of the room).[49] It can be predicted better from the total frequency of positive activities minus frequency of arguments and other negative events.

In one of our own studies we found three factors of positive satisfaction and one of conflict. The spouse was by far the highest source of all three kinds of satisfaction, and also of both kinds of conflict. In this and other studies it was found that high levels of satisfaction and conflict can occur together in marriage, and are quite compatible with one another (Figure 3, p 144).

Marital satisfaction depends on a number of features of social interaction between husband and wife, the main ones being:

1. Pleasing verbal acts, e.g. compliments, and fewer negative ones, especially criticisms. In disturbed marriages it is common for a negative act from one partner to be reciprocated by a negative act from the other.
2. Pleasing non-verbal acts, e.g. a kiss, a present, helpful behaviour, and fewer negative ones, e.g. grunts of disagreement, unhelpful acts around the house.
3. Enjoyable sex life.
4. A lot of time spent together, e.g. in leisure activities.
5. Agreement over finances.
6. A problem-solving approach to matters to be decided.[50]
7. As we showed in Chapter 2, the benefits from marriage depend on

there being a close relationship, where each acts as confidant for the other.

A great deal of careful research lies behind this list, and it provides a guide to some of the skills needed for successful marriage.

Abrams asked people to state what they believe the main determinants are of happy and unhappy marriages.

TABLE 10. Reported Determinants of Happy and Unhappy Marriages [51]

Happy marriages	Percentage of people
tolerance	35%
absence of money worries	31%
love and affection	26%
understanding	26%
Unhappy marriages	
financial problems	47%
unfaithfulness	24%
drink and gambling	20%

Women, elderly people and middle-class respondents tended to think that tolerance was particularly important for a happy marriage, while more men than women believed that absence of money worries was important. Love and affection and understanding were cited as more important by 16 to 29-year-olds than other age groups. Everyone agreed that financial problems were major determinants of unhappy marriages. More 45 to 49-year-olds thought that unfaithfulness was important than any other age group, while more working-class respondents and the elderly thought drink and gambling more important than the others did.

Other kinds of research have examined factors which make happy and unhappy marriages. One of these is whether the other partner fits the expected role, whatever that is, Curiously, it makes more difference to the marital satisfaction of both that the husband's role expectations are met. And wives do in fact conform more to their husband's role expectations than vice versa. Marital happiness can be predicted from a number of factors, the lack of which also predict divorce, and will be listed in the next chapter (p. 160f).

Wives are somewhat less satisfied with marriage than their husbands, and seem to have more to complain about. As we have seen in

Chapter 2, married men are in far better physical and mental health than single men, but the benefits for married women are much smaller (p. 18f). When women marry they have a greater adjustment to make, which is a serious source of stress. They are often isolated at home, doing boring housework, and have less say in decisions. They are happier if they have jobs, and if they have an equal voice in decisions.[52]

Positive rewards, sex, companionship, etc., are very important in marriage. And predictions of marital satisfaction can be improved by subtracting the frequency of negative interactions. On the other hand, as we shall see below, conflict probably plays a positive role in the development of close relationships. Couples who split up often suffer a great deal in health and mental health (p. 15f); perhaps they have failed to estimate correctly the costs involved in dissolving the relationship. The main criticism of the exchange theory point of view is that in a close relationship each person becomes concerned for the welfare of the other – it is enjoyable to see them happy, so the rewards and costs of *both* partners are taken into account. Those couples who are most concerned about getting rewards themselves tend to be the least happily married.

A further extension of exchange theory is necessary. Marriage, as we have seen is an all-embracing union of two people in many ways. A little community is created, usually containing shared children, a shared home, and an interdependent way of life. This produces many kinds of satisfaction and ties both partners into this community, where each is dependent on the other for many things.

Marital conflict

One of the central features of marriage is the high level of conflict that occurs in it. 'Marriage inevitably involves conflicts'.[53] In an American national survey of marital violence, 28% of spouses had experienced physical aggression from their partners, and 16% suffered chronic and severe abuse.[54] Other studies estimate rates up to 60% for family abuse, and this can include very severe violence. Half to three-quarters of all homicide victims are intimately acquainted with their killer,[55] and this is predominantly the spouse or other close family member. Physical aggression is often used by husbands to enforce their demands and as a response to the wife making demands. Interference by third parties often increases the violence.[56] Alcohol is involved in many of these incidents and they generally follow arguments.[57] Neither is domestic violence limited to married partners. The rate of violence among cohabiting couples is at least as high.[58]

In unhappy marriages verbal or physical rows occur daily; in happy marriages such rows take place weekly or less. In our study of sources

Fig. 3   RELATIONSHIPS PLOTTED ON TWO
          DIMENSIONS OF CONFLICT

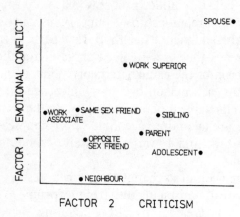

FACTOR   2   CRITICISM

TABLE 11. Why Rows Start[60]

	Total %
Little arguments which grow	27
Disagreements over how to treat kids	26
Budgeting for expenses and bills	15
Feeling he doesn't appreciate me	15
Visiting in-laws	14
Housekeeping money	11
Him not helping in house	10
Deciding what TV programme to watch	9
His being jealous of other men	9
Wife wanting to get a job	8
Wife being jealous of other women	6
What to do in leisure time	6
Unsatisfactory sex life	5
His not taking an interest in wife's life	4
Temperamentally incompatible	4
Wife not taking enough interest in his work	1
None of these	14

of satisfaction and conflict we found that the spouse was the greatest source of all three areas of satisfaction, but the spouse was also the greatest source of conflict (Figure 3).

The main areas of conflict are over money (husband not earning enough, wife spending too much), sex, affection (e.g. husband's lack of), nagging (especially by wife), how to handle the children. In one survey, people stated that conflicts occurred for the reasons listed in Table 11.

There are characteristic patterns of interaction in disturbed marriages, between couples in conflict. There is a high rate of *negative* communications, especially *non-verbal* ones, and these are often reciprocated.[61] These cycles of negative acts, often escalating into rows, take a standard, ritualised form in each unhappy marriage.

Evidently a high level of satisfaction with one's spouse is compatible with a high level of conflict. This is confirmed by a number of studies which have found two statistically independent dimensions of positive and negative interactions or experiences in marriage.[62] Nevertheless overall marital satisfaction is diminished by such conflicts or negative interaction.

We think it is worth emphasising the fact that marital conflict is so common; it is likely that some couples break up because they had not expected such conflict, or because they do not know how to deal with it.

It may be necessary to face up to conflicts, rather than avoiding the issues involved. There is more conflict in the early years, when there are many matters to be settled. It has been argued that couples should work through these conflicts, but in a spirit of openness, flexibility, and willingness to concede and to be changed if necessary.[63] In addition, facing up to a conflict can help each partner to see the other's point of view.[64]

There are a number of features of marriage that make conflict so common.

1. Living at very close quarters means that agreements have to be made over a wide range of issues, some of them very important, like moving house and changing jobs.

2. Husband and wife nearly always play different marital roles, which give them different points of view on many issues; for example he is more concerned with money and the condition of the house, she is more concerned with the happiness of its occupants.

3. The two spouses are from different homes and backgrounds, and as

a result have different ideas on many matters, including how husbands and wives should behave.

4. There is a high level of emotional involvement with each other; as a result it is easy to become upset by the other's behaviour.

5. Minor irritations, when repeated many times, can grow into major sources of annoyance.

How can marital conflicts best be coped with? One way is to put up with the other's behaviour, for example do the neglected jobs yourself, or to change one's own behaviour. Other couples avoid confrontation, but tensions may build up, and the opportunity to proceed to a better relationship through facing the conflict is lost. It is interesting that in distressed marriages people think that the causes of negative spouse behaviour are global rather than specific.[65] It is best to try to solve particular problems by discussion.[66] A number of techniques for doing this have been devised, such as negotiating a new exchange of rewards; these will be discussed later in the book (p. 302f).

Rules of marriage

Marriage is already governed by rules of law, which require in Britain that the husband shall support his wife, and that she will look after the house, care for the children, and feed the family. There is a rather precise requirement that intercourse shall occur at least once, to consummate the marriage, but more generally that the couple shall maintain a mutually tolerable sexual relationship, and be faithful to one another.[67]

In Chapter 3 we discussed the general rules which apply to many relationships. Now we turn to the particular rules we have found to be most important for marriage. While the same number of rules were regarded as important for both husbands and wives, their order of importance tended to be different. The most important rules for husbands and wives are shown in Table 12.

Rules about emotional support, faithfulness and sharing news of success are very important for both husbands and wives to follow. So are rules about respecting privacy, using first name, giving birthday cards and presents, and creating a harmonious home atmosphere.

The general rules that apply to most relationships are of two main kinds. Some are about providing rewards ('should be emotionally supportive'). Others are about avoiding inflicting costs, which are in danger of occurring in any relationship ('respect privacy', 'keep

TABLE 12. Rules for Both Spouses

1. Show emotional support.
2. Share news of success.
3. Be faithful.
4. Create a harmonious home atmosphere.
5. Respect the other partner's privacy.
6. Address the partner by first name.
7. Keep confidences.
8. Engage in sexual activity with the other partner.
9. Give birthday cards and presents.
10. Stand up for the other person in his/her absence.
11. Talk to the partner about sex and death.
12. Disclose personal feelings and problems to the partner.
13. Inform the partner about one's personal schedule.
14. Be tolerant of each other's friends.
15. Don't criticise the partner publicly.
16. Ask for personal advice.
17. Talk to the partner about religion and politics.
18. Look the partner in the eye during conversation.
19. Discuss personal financial matters with the other partner.
20. Touch the other person intentionally.
21. Engage in joking or teasing with the partner.
22. Show affection for one another in public.
23. Ask the partner for material help.
24. Show distress or anxiety in front of the partner.
25. Repay debts and favours, and compliments.

Additional Rules for the Husband

1. Look after the family when the wife is unwell.
2. Show an interest in the wife's daily activities.
3. Be responsible for household repair and maintenance.
4. Offer to pay for the partner when going out together.

Additional Rules for the Wife

1. Show anger in front of the partner.
2. Don't nag.

confidences'). Then there are a number of rules that apply in all close relationships – with family and friends as well as marriage – that one should talk about intimate topics, disclose feelings, touch, ask for advice, joke and tease. These rules are a kind of recipe for maintaining intimacy.

Finally there are rules that apply *only* to marriage (and to a lesser extent, to cohabitation and dating) – be faithful, show affection in public, and create a harmonious home atmosphere. These are rules for keeping up a high level of affection. Other rules are solutions to common marital problems, for example, be tolerant of the other's friends. One rule applies to husbands only: pay the bill when out together. One particularly applies to wives: don't avoid showing anger in front of the partner.

In a second study, we asked married couples to complete the same questionnaire and we also asked each partner to rate the quality of their relationship, from 'perfect' to 'unsatisfactory', and we found that those men and women who rated their relationship as 'perfect' thought that several rules were more important than those who rated their marriage as less than perfect. The main difference was for the rule about emotional support, but only for the wife. In other words, men and women with 'perfect' marital relationships think it is more important for wives to be emotionally supportive than men and women reporting good, but not 'perfect' marriages. And when we asked these people how they actually behaved in practice, those men and women who believed they had perfect relationships said that they showed their partner emotional support more often than husbands and wives with less perfect relationships reported doing. There were no major differences in how important both groups believed this rule to be for husbands. But there was a greater expectation for husbands to show unconditional positive regard. Men and women who reported perfect relationships believed that it is more important for husbands to show the wife unconditional positive regard than did couples in less perfect relationships. They also reported showing unconditional positive regard more often in practice.

Perhaps, then, it is these rules about emotional support and regard that are the major ingredient of a good marriage. We shall look more closely at whether rules about marriage differentiate between married and ex-married people in our next chapter.

Our samples all stressed the importance of faithfulness in marriage. A MORI survey[68] found that two-thirds of their sample thought that extramarital sex was wrong, though this was not rated as very important.

Extramarital love

Our society is based, in the legal and normative sense, on monogamous long-term relationships. As such, it tends to be in the minority, since many more societies (albeit not Western ones) tend towards polygamy. One survey has shown that only 15% of 185 different societies restrict sexual liaisons to single mateships.[69]

But does society practise what it preaches? Apparently not, since surveys have shown that a high proportion of married individuals have extramarital relations at some time in their lives. For example, the classic Kinsey studies of over 16,000 Americans in the late 1940s to early 1950s found that 50% of males and 26% of females had extramarital affairs by the age of forty. Hunt[70] later found the same frequency for men as did Kinsey, but 24% of his young wives were now having extramarital affairs compared to only 8% of Kinsey's young married women.

While our behaviour is becoming more permissive, our attitudes tend not to change. Extramarital affairs are still seen as 'wrong', and, as we have seen, people still endorse faithfulness as a rule for marriage. Glenn and Weaver[71] examined sexual attitudes in two large-scale surveys of over 1,500 subjects in 1972 and 1978. They found that while attitudes to premarital, and even homosexual, relations were becoming more permissive, attitudes to extramarital sex remained fairly constant (and in general, unfavourable). Their figures are given below:

TABLE 13. Attitudes to Sex Outside Marriage [72]

	1972	*1978*
Pre-marital sex:		
always wrong	36.6	29.3
almost always wrong	11.8	11.7
wrong only sometimes	24.3	20.3
not wrong at all	27.3	38.7
Extra-marital sex:		
always wrong	69.6	73.0
almost always wrong	14.8	13.6
wrong only sometimes	11.6	10.1
not wrong at all	4.1	3.2
Homosexuality:		
always wrong	74.3	71.9
almost always wrong	6.7	5.8
wrong only sometimes	7.8	7.5
not wrong at all	11.2	14.9

A British survey found that 62% of men and 51% of women thought that extramarital sex was morally wrong.[73]

The factors that lead to a person approving of extramarital affairs were teased apart in a study by Reiss and colleagues.[74] They found that extramarital permissiveness is predicted by two main variables – premarital sexual permissiveness and marital (un)happiness. Both kinds of sexual permissiveness are predicted by (more) education and (less) religiosity.

It can be seen from Figure 4 that sexual permissiveness also depends on political liberality, marital satisfaction (low), emphasis on the pleasurable aspects of sexuality, and other variables.

Fig. 4 A MODEL OF EXTRAMARITAL PERMISSIVENESS

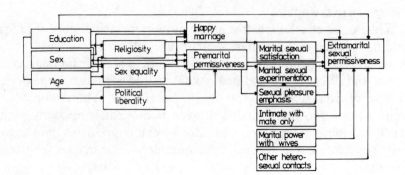

This model gives us some understanding of the factors in extramarital sexual permissiveness, but little additional information on extramarital 'love' – that is, in terms of this chapter, the extramarital *relationship*. Reiss *et al.* go on to describe different types of extramarital sexual relations, depending on three factors:

1. Whether the relationship is acceptable to both spouses;
2. Whether it is based on a love or pleasure emphasis;
3. Whether the marriage itself is 'happy' or 'unhappy'.

These can be viewed in Fig. 5 which shows the relationships between eight types of extramarital affairs. So, for example, Types 1 and 3 emphasise love, Type 1 is where both spouses accept the extramarital affair, 1A is in a happy marriage.

It is argued that types 3 and 4 – that is non-acceptable relations – are most common, with type 4 (the pleasure emphasis) more predominant for males, and type 3 (the love emphasis) more common for females. They estimate that types 1 and 2 account for less than 10% of

TYPES OF MARRIAGE AND EXTRAMARITAL SEX

Fig. 5

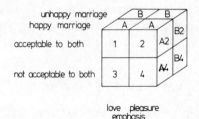

love   pleasure
emphasis

extramarital sex. Bell's survey[77] presents some additional information which can be added to their model. He found that females rating their own marriage as poor are more likely to engage in extramarital affairs. This implies that, at least for women, it may be important to look at the B3 cube in the figure. And in terms of our discussion of extramarital love, this is perhaps the most important cube: extramarital sex in a love relationship, especially when sought in order to compensate for unhappy marital relations. Evidently 'love' occurs inside and outside marriage, and the initial processes of love and attraction operate in the same way for extramarital attractions as for premarital ones. It is the costs and benefits that vary between these types of relationships.

TABLE 14. Effect of Extra-Marital Sex on Divorce [79]

Question		Major Effect	Moderate Effect	Minor Effect	No Effect At All
Did *your* extra-marital sex have any importance in causing your divorce?	(Women)	14%	15%	10%	61%
	(Men)	18%	9%	12%	61%
Did your *spouse's* extra-marital sex have any importance in causing your divorce?	(Women)	27%	49%	24%	0%
	(Men)	51%	32%	17%	0%

Do extramarital affairs disrupt marriages? Certainly those who get divorced are much more likely to have had extramarital affairs than those who have continued to be married – but they may have had the affairs *because* of the failure of the marriage. In one British survey only 12% said that they would consider ending their marriages if they discovered that their spouse had been unfaithful.[78] But an American study found that extramarital sex was regarded as a cause of divorce by many people (Table 14).

Cultural and historical variations in marriage

We can add some further information to the earlier notes on variations in love (p. 118f). The nuclear family – husband, wife and their children – is found in some form in almost all cultures and historical periods. Primitive men bought wives for camels or other goods, or exchanged them between families. It has been common for a man to have more than one wife (i.e. polygamy) as in Muslim countries (up to four wives), the Mormons at one time, and in some primitive societies. In Hong Kong husbands may have a concubine as well as a wife. In India most marriages are still arranged by the families; the couple scarcely see one another before the wedding, which is an elaborate and dramatic affair. There is a very low divorce rate in India, perhaps because of the high degree of family support for marriages. It has been found in Japan that in arranged marriages husbands were happier, while in love marriages wives were. However, the degree of support from the two families was a more important factor.[80] Two recent attempts to abolish the nuclear family have been in Russia and in the Israeli kibbutzim; however in both places there has been a return to a pattern of family life very similar to that elsewhere.

In Europe there has been monogamy for a long time, but the nature of marriage has changed a lot in other ways, especially since the growth of industrial society.
1. Families have become smaller – fewer children, and fewer other relatives.
2. Some of the traditional functions of the family have been removed –educating children, and the house as a place of work, for example. It has been argued that a smaller nuclear family 'fits' industrialised society better than a larger family – there is greater geographic mobility, greater social mobility between classes, and less need for protection, educational funds, or finding jobs for relatives, all of

which are still found in African families.[81] However children when
young still need to be cared for and socialised; women, while
producing and rearing young children, need economic and other
forms of support.

3. We have seen that there has been pressure from women for greater
equality in marriage: for more say in decisions, for husbands to share
domestic tasks, and for women to be able to have careers. This change
is still taking place, and one outcome is the 'dual-career family', which
is discussed below.

4. There is greater emphasis on marriage for love, and a greater
emphasis on companionship, shared leisure, spouses acting as confidants and if necessary psychotherapists.

However, marriage has been criticised from various points of view:
it doesn't work for the 30% or so whose marriages break up, it is unfair
on women, it is unfair on men (who have to support one or more
women for life), it is too closed, restricting, and emotionally
demanding. As a result some people are trying out alternatives to
marriage. We have already discussed one, cohabitation, though this
usually leads to marriage.

Another alternative is 'open marriage', or 'swinging'. Studies of
samples of swinging couples in the U.S.A. have found that the
husband usually wants to start it, the wife to stop it. Those involved
have typically been salesmen and small businessmen in California and
large cities. The point of greatest interest to us is that quite strict rules
have often grown up among groups of swingers. For example, another
couple is involved only once, emotional involvement should be
avoided, singles are not allowed, parties are anonymous, careful
rituals of first meeting are followed, at which other couples are sized
up. The main purposes of these rules is to preserve the marriages of
those taking part, and to prevent extramarital affairs.[82] However it is
reported that there has now been a shift away from these rules in the
U.S.A. There is some evidence that swinging couples are as happily
married as non-swingers, or more so; the divorce rate is not known.[83]

On the other hand life in communes has been found to be stressful,
and in some there is a very high rate of breakup of couples.[84] There is
ready availability of alternative partners, and perhaps a lack of rules to
preserve relationships.

Dual-career couples These are couples in which 'both heads of
household pursue careers and at the same time maintain a family life

together'.[85] The main difficulties arise when there are children. The idea is that both partners should pursue their careers with equal commitment, and that the husband should accept his share of the domestic work. It is the end-product of the move towards egalitarianism in marriage, and it is estimated that there were one million such couples in the U.S.A. in 1977, most of them professional couples. The gains are clear: the wife can pursue her career, and the family income is enormous.

Mothers who also have jobs are usually found to be happier and in better psychological health than those without: they enjoy the social life at work and the recognition of their competence rather than the money, and they have greater self-esteem. But their physical health may suffer: they are more prone to heart attacks, for example. Their husbands, however, tend to be more depressed, anxious, ill and lacking in self-esteem.[86] Mothers who work experience conflict of roles, and guilt over neglecting their children, especially if they have more children, and if they are very committed to their jobs; they have more conflict of this kind than their husbands.[87]

The costs are fairly obvious too. There is great overload, home life is 'frantic' and stressful, and there must be reliable domestic help. It is difficult for both spouses to find jobs in the same town, and their geographical mobility is greatly reduced. There is a weaker social network since they have less time for social life with friends, or with each other. When both partners have jobs there are additional strains on the marriage. The more wives earn, the more marital disruption there is likely to be, possibly because of competition between the spouses.[88]

It is usually found that dual-career couples are often not fully egalitarian: the husband takes more decisions, and it is his job that dictates where they shall live, while she does more of the housework and subordinates her career. In terms of job success dual-career husbands do as well as, or better than, other husbands, their wives do not do so well, are often underemployed, do not do as well as other women, and are dissatisfied with their careers.[89]

The dual-career family is obviously here to stay, and it is clear that it is producing a lot of problems, as well as a lot of satisfaction, though mainly for women. It looks as if some new rules or skills or family arrangements are needed to make it work more smoothly. One scheme which some have adopted is taking it in turns, over longish periods of time, for his or her career to take precedence.

The psychological basis of the marital bond

Despite the high divorce rate there clearly *are* very strong marital bonds for most couples. Marriage lasts a long time, longer than the relationship with most friends or workmates, for example. Great distress and ill-health are caused by the ending of marriage through bereavement or divorce, again far more than is caused by loss of friends. And for the great majority there is a strong sense of commitment, an assumption that the marriage will last for ever.

We discussed the biological and evolutionary origins of love earlier (p. 120), and the same considerations apply to marriage. It seems likely that a form of attachment takes place during the early months of marriage, comparable to early parent–child interaction. As we have seen, there is a very high rate of sexual intercourse during the first two months, and a withdrawal from the company of friends. This period of intense social and sexual interaction, living at close quarters with intimate disclosure, may provide a special form of attachment between spouses.

There is certainly exchange of rewards throughout married life. The division of labour in marriage can be seen as producing an exchange of rewards between spouses. She does the cooking and housework; in exchange he is the provider, and does heavy jobs. Other rewards are more symmetrical: sex, affection, and companionship. Some of these rewards, and not only the sexual ones, are very intense; we saw earlier that marriage provides higher levels of satisfaction of all kinds than any other relationship. Since married couples co-operate so closely, the other partner becomes instrumental in many forms of satisfaction. This will be greater the more things they do together, such as sharing leisure.[90] As in the earlier stages of love, a strong empathy develops, in which each is concerned with the rewards received by the other.

The closely shared life leads to other kinds of bonding. Hours of conversation and disclosure lead to a shared cognitive world, a joint construction of social reality. The shared past and future, adventures, children, produce a sense of shared identity.[91]

Finally there are external supports. The home is the framework for shared daily life. The children, relatives, shared friends, constitute a powerful shared social network. Shared property and finances make marriage into a small business which also binds the partners together[92]. We shall see, in the following chapter, what happens when this shared life is disrupted by separation or divorce.

FURTHER READING

Blood, B. & Blood, M. (1978) *Marriage* (3rd edn) New York: Free Press
Leslie, G. (1980) *Marriage in a Changing World* New York: Wiley

7

Divorce

Divorce is the most acute problem in the whole field of social relationships at the present time. The levels of separation and divorce have greatly increased in most countries, causing a very great deal of distress, both to the couples concerned, and to their children and relatives.

In the last chapter we described the nature of marriage and outlined the activities and functions of marital relationships. We saw that marriage is an all-embracing and comprehensive personal relationship. Married couples are usually financially, materially, emotionally and sexually involved over a long span of time. As a result of this intense and prolonged interdependence the scope for conflict is high. The majority of married couples resolve this conflict and remain together, but the spiralling divorce rate in most Western countries shows that many fail to do so.

While it is possible to have a total breakdown of the marital relationship – emotional, sexual, and economic bonds – within a formally intact marriage, and even to have both partners living independently in the same house, a breakdown is more likely to involve permanent separation, and typically a formal dissolution of the marriage contract – divorce. In this chapter we shall examine marital breakdown and look more closely at the causes of marital dissolution, and the processes involved.

The costs of divorce are high, both for the individual and for society. These include economic costs. From the individual's point of view there is division of property, payment of maintenance, single-parent support of children, and many other costs. From society's stance, there is a massive expenditure of time and resources on legal battles. Although the majority of divorces in England and Wales are not contested, 67% of civil legal aid is spent on matrimonial cases: on issues of property division, maintenance, and child custody.

But psychological costs may be even more damaging. Children can become unwilling victims, and many studies have documented the adverse effects of marital separation on them. There is also, however, evidence that continuing an unhappy marriage may be more disturbing for children than actual separation of the parents.

"He identifies with the sausages."

(Punch)

Incidence

In the 1850s, there were only 3 divorces per year in England and Wales. In 1979 there were 129,000. Between 1970 and 1980 the divorce rate in England and Wales doubled for those over twenty-five and trebled for those under twenty-five.[1] The growth in recent years is shown in Figure 1. There are now twelve divorces per year for every thousand existing marriages, and it is estimated that in Britain about one marriage in three now ends in divorce. In the U.S.A. the rate of divorce is still higher.

Fig. 1   DIVORCE RATE PER 1000 EXISTING MARRIAGES[2]

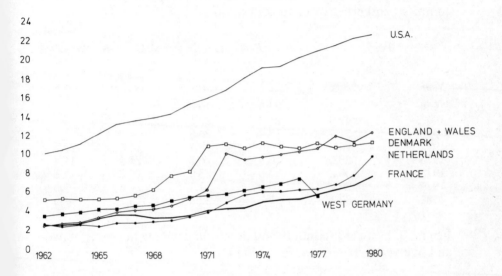

When the divorce rate was much lower, there were unhappy marriages, many of which ended in separation. Has the number of broken marriages actually increased? It has not grown as much as the higher rates of divorce suggest, but numbers of social security applications indicate that there has been a real increase in broken marriages.[3]

There are several reasons for the increases in the divorce rate. A number of changes in the law in most countries have made divorce progressively easier. The 1969 Divorce Reform Act in Britain became law in 1971, and produced the sharp rise in divorces shown in Figure 1. Under this new law divorce could be obtained when the spouses have lived apart for two years if both consented, or after five years' separation if one did not consent. This led to a sudden backlog of five-year divorces, but the higher level was then maintained. Legal aid has also become more readily available, and may have contributed to the rise in working-class divorces.[4] In addition the age of consent was reduced from twenty-one to eighteen in 1969, thus making early marriage easier – and early marriages tend to be the least successful.

Grounds for divorce

Up to 1971 the grounds given for divorce were those accepted by the law – adultery, desertion and cruelty. Of these adultery was the most common, and cruelty overtook desertion.

TABLE 1. Percentage Distribution of Petitions for Divorce by Grounds, 1964–1981[5]

Year	Adultery	Desertion	Cruelty	2 years + consent	5 years
1964	46.2	24.5	19.3	—	—
1967	47.3	21.2	23.0	—	—
1970	51.7	17.4	24.8	—	—
1971	24.8	10.3	18.7	14.6	27.2
1973	28.0	6.6	26.5	21.0	14.4
1975	30.2	4.6	25.9	26.0	11.8
1979	29.2	3.0	31.1	26.8	9.3
1981	30.1	2.2	33.5	25.2	7.5

From 1971 onwards adultery and desertion declined in favour of two- and five-year separations (see Table 1).

Fig. 2   COMPLAINTS BY 600 COUPLES ABOUT THEIR MARRIAGE

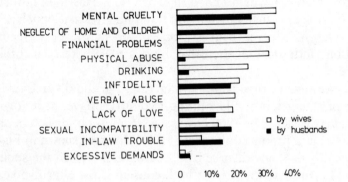

The proportion of divorce petitions filed by wives increased from 41% in 1900 to 71% in 1981. Wives, especially younger working-class wives, complained more often of cruelty, while most husbands used desertion as grounds for divorce. Older people used cruelty less and desertion more.

A recent survey asked people which was the single thing most likely to break up a marriage. The most common reply was unfaithfulness (35%), followed by lack of respect for each other, violence, growing apart, and drink.[6]

A study of 600 divorce applications in Cleveland, Ohio, produced the above set of reasons given for breakdown.

There are some interesting sex differences, which will be discussed below.

Here are the most common complaints of couples who were seeking marital therapy, and from non-distressed couples selected as a comparison group and not undertaking therapy. The requests most commonly made for changes in the partner's behaviour were:

TABLE 2. *Most Frequent Requests for Changes in Partner's Behaviour*[8]

Distressed Group

Wives about husbands	*Husbands about wives*
1. Express emotions more clearly	1. Express emotions more clearly
2. Give appreciation to spouse	2. Give appreciation to spouse
3. Attend to spouse	3. Initiate having sex
4. Arguing	4. Arguing
5. Start interesting conversations	5. Attend to his sexual needs

Non-Distressed Group

1. Give appreciation to spouse	1. Express emotions more clearly
2. Express emotions more clearly	2. Initiate having sex
3. Initiate having sex	3. Attend to his sexual needs
4. Start interesting conversation	4. Keep house clean
5. Go out	5. Start interesting conversations

The types of criticism were similar for both distressed and non-distressed couples and appeared to differ only in frequency or severity. For example, 86% of distressed wives wanted change in the husband's expression of emotions, compared to 38% of non-distressed wives. The figures for husbands are 79% and 31% respectively for this item. However, arguing ranks among the top five for both husbands and wives in the distressed group only. We shall show that couples who divorce are more likely to break up even during the pre-marital courtship phase, so that the presence of conflict and less successful ways of negotiating it predate the marriage itself. And the level of conflict can be extreme, resulting in some cases in severe physical violence. In 1981, 34% of divorces granted to women in this country were granted on the grounds of cruelty.

In Chapter 6 we noted that satisfaction and conflict occur together in marriage and may be compatible with a happy marital relationship. Some level of marital conflict is inevitable. Marriage, as a long-term and intimate relationship, requires a deep meshing of two separate individuals' aims and wants. As such the scope for interpersonal conflict is increased even further.

The failure to fulfil personal needs in the marital relationship is a second area of difficulty. Both marriage and the family are undergoing marked changes in their role in society. As Blood[9] noted:

Today's family specializes as never before in personal relationships. The 'lost' functions of the family have been taken over by specialized economic, political, educational, and religious institutions. What remains is an opportunity for families to specialise in an area where no other social institution can. Perhaps in the past marriage was not a personal relationship. Now, however, this is the essence of marriage . . . expectations for marriage have risen. We are no longer satisfied with the perfunctory functional relations that were once the rule. We hope to continue indefinitely the intense personal involvement we experience when love is new.

The same sentiments are found in the comments of married people

TABLE 3. Aspects of Life That Gave Greatest Happiness

Married Men	Married Women
1. Personal growth	1. Being in love
2. Being in love	2. Marriage
3. Marriage	3. Partner's happiness
4. Job or primary activity	4. Sex life
5. Partner's happiness	5. Recognition, success
6. Sex life	6. Personal growth
7. Recognition, success	7. Job or primary activity
8. Friends and social life	8. Friends and social life
9. Being a parent	9. Health
10. Finances	10. Being a parent

themselves. Freedman[10] in a survey of over 100,000 people asked them to rate those aspects of their lives that gave greatest happiness. He found that they were ranked as shown in Table 3.

Personal growth and being in love, marriage and the partner's happiness rank higher than the traditional functions of marriage and the family – being a parent and sex, and for men, the provision of finances. Men and women aspire to personal fulfilment and growth, which marriage, still our most intense and permanent long-term relationship, is increasingly expected to provide. Marriages may therefore become vulnerable, not through any overt conflict, but simply because the relationship fails to meet one or both partners' expectations for personal fulfilment. These expectations may be fulfilled elsewhere, in extramarital relationships for example. In 1978 23% of divorces granted to wives and 39% of those granted to husbands were on grounds of adultery.

Class, sex and age

Social class Recent statistics in Britain show that the highest divorce rates are for class III (non-manual) – shop assistants and clerical workers; and class V – unskilled workers.[11] Divorces per 10,000 married women aged under 55 in each social class were:

I	II	III(N)	III(M)	IV	V
22	25	43	29	25	51

Middle-class divorces also occur rather later in life than working-class ones – as a result of the earlier working-class marriages.

One explanation for the lower rate of divorce among middle-class people may be that more property is involved; there is more to lose, and other family members are involved. This fits the finding that blacks in the U.S.A., who are mostly poorer than whites, have a divorce rate of two and a half times that of whites.[12] It is also found that better educated people are more happily married (p. 132).

There is evidence from survey data that similarity of social class between partners is important. For example, Thornes and Collard[13] found a tendency for marriages ending in divorce to have wives with higher-status occupations than their husbands at the time of marriage. It was better if they were in the same grade of occupation. However, similarity or dissimilarity in education was not important.

The pattern of complaints is different in different classes.

Working-class and less educated couples complain more of physical and psychological abuse, sex problems, infidelity, drinking, non-support, being out too much with the boys or girls. Middle-class and more educated couples complain more of changes in interests or values, gender role conflict, no sense of family life, lack of communication or understanding, overcommitment to work.[14]

Sex differences Is divorce unfair to women, or is marriage, for that matter? Women certainly think that they get a worse deal. A recent MORI Survey[15] found that 42% of women thought that men get the most out of marriage, 7% thought women did, 38% that both profited equally. In Chapter 2 we found that women benefit from marriage less than men in terms of health and mental health. Seventy-three per cent of divorce petitions in England and Wales are made by wives.

The figure on p. 161 showed some of the differences in the pattern of complaints. Other studies have confirmed that women complain more often about personality problems, authority, drinking, being out with the boys, sex problems, non-support and money management. Husbands complain more about relatives.[16]

The process of coping with divorce is rather different too. Wives are more sensitive to things going wrong with the marriage, and spot it earlier. They discuss it more with the children and friends, receive more social support, and work it through better.[17]

The outcome pattern is different; but it is not clear who comes out worst. The wife usually receives custody of the children, but has greater financial problems, and is usually less well equipped to find a good job. The husband usually loses the children, and has to support two establishments, but is in a better position to marry again, for older couples. His health and mental health are more affected during the years of separation.

Age at marriage It has long been known that early marriages are more likely to end in divorce, especially if both bride and groom are under twenty. However part of the reason is that the wife is often pregnant in early marriages, and this is a factor predicting divorce. Early marriages are less at risk if children are delayed until later.[18] In England and Wales the chance of divorce is twice as high for teenage spouses as for those aged between twenty and twenty-four at marriage.[19] In 1982, 13% of divorces involved couples where the husband was under twenty at the time of the marriage, and 37%

involved teenage brides.[20]

Other factors predicting divorce

We now turn to a number of causes of divorce which are not necessarily known to those involved, but which can be demonstrated from research findings. These are the factors that predispose couples to have unhappy marriages and get divorced.

Length of marriage   Most divorces take place quite early in marriage, and marital breakdown often occurs long before this. In a recent British study,[21] 38% of marriages ending in divorce lasted less than four years, 24% lasted five to nine years, 28% lasted ten to twenty years and the remaining 10% over twenty years. In fact the median, or most typical, duration is 2.9 years, which can be regarded as the 'danger period'. In the U.S.A. many couples separate in the first year.

In a British survey more than one-third of the divorced sample claimed that the serious marital problems leading to divorce started within the first year of marriage.[22]

TABLE 4. *Year of Marriage and the Start of the Marital Problems of the Divorced*

	All Divorced n=520 %	Divorced Women n=336 %	Divorced Men n=184 %
By 1st anniversary	37	44	23
2nd	15	15	15
3rd	9	10	8
4th	7	6	8
5th	5	5	5
6th	6	5	7
7th	5	4	8
8th	3	2	4
9th	2	1	3
10th	3	1	5
11th	3	1	4
12th	1	1	2
13th	1	1	1
14th	1	1	—
15th+	4	3	8
Mean duration of marital 'happiness'	3.87 yrs	3.27 yrs	4.98 yrs

It is also found that the first year of marriage is a particularly vulnerable period for teenage brides, especially for those pregnant before marriage.

The pattern of complaints is somewhat different at different lengths of marriage. Those who divorce early complain more about relatives and sex problems; those who divorce late complain more about changes of interests or values, and the lack of a family sense.[23]

Many of these 'at-risk' factors are not independent. For example, the association between divorce and the duration of courtship may be largely a function of pre-marital pregnancy, in the sense that pre-marital pregnancy would inevitably curtail the length of the courtship period. Similarly, there will be confounding effects of age, social class and education. Taken in combination, those most at risk are teenage marriages in social classes V and III (non-manual) in which there is a pre-marital pregnancy.

Yet it is not only new marriages that are vulnerable. Thirty-eight per cent of all divorces in England and Wales occur in marriages which have lasted for ten years or more. Jack Dominian[24] suggests that there are three phases of marital breakdown. The first occurs within the initial five years of marriage because the basic affective bond of 'social, emotional, sexual, and spiritual ties' has not been firmly established. During this phase, he claims, the marriage is vulnerable to problems of communication, conflict, and expression of affection between partners, as well as to practical difficulties such as finances, accommodation, sharing of household tasks, and other practical aspects of adjustment.

The second phase occurs in the middle years of marriage, between the ages of about thirty and fifty, and usually during the period when children are growing up. The major contributing factors during this period are, he states, changes at the personality level. Both partners are becoming more emotionally independent and establishing their individuality and identity, and improving their self-esteem. Breakdown of the relationship can occur for two reasons: either the realisation that there has never been an affective bond, or, more commonly, the erosion of an established bond through the social, emotional and psychological changes brought about by this growth of the self.

The third phase begins at about fifty years of age, after children have left home, till the death of one spouse. Some marriages will break down at this stage because the affective bond has already been disrupted at the second phase, but the partners have remained together while children were growing up. More common, however, is the recognition that there never has been a basic emotional bond. And,

TABLE 5. Length of Tolerance of Marital Differences [25]

Problems started	Less than 5 yrs n=186 %	5–9 yrs n=104 %	10–14 yrs n=101 %	15–19 yrs n=64 %	20 yrs + n=60 %
By 1st anniversary	58	24	19	28	30
2nd	19	15	12	10	10
3rd	10	13	7	5	7
4th	7	10	6	5	3
5th	6	5	6	3	3
6th	—	16	9	3	3
7th	—	12	10	3	2
8th	—	3	3	13	—
9th	—	2	6	2	2
10th	—	—	10	3	2
11th	—	—	8	3	5
12th	—	—	3	—	3
13th	—	—	2	5	2
14th	—	—	—	5	—
15th+	—	—	—	11	28
Mean period before the start of the problems	1.4 yrs	3.3 yrs	5.2 yrs	5.8 yrs	7.9 yrs

TABLE 6. Conflict and the Duration of Courtship [26]

Duration of Courtship:	Divorced n=520 %	Married n=570 %
Less than 6 months	6	1
6 but not less than 12 months	14	7
1 year but not less than 2 years	39	34
2 years	41	57

Number of pre-marital break-ups for those reporting at least one	n=149 %	n=106 %
1	49	70
2	23	18
3 or more	27	11

in some cases, there have been continuing problems which have never been resolved, and which date back to lack of adjustment in the very early years of marriage. However, the couple has continued to tolerate these difficulties in some cases for many years as Thornes and Collard's figures show (Table 5).

Length and tranquillity of courtship   The longer the courtship, the more likely the marriage is to be successful (up to two years of courtship at any rate). (Table 6)

It is not only the length of the courtship period that is important, but also its level of conflict and conflict resolution. Divorced couples reported far more pre-marital break-ups with their eventual spouse than do those continuing married in Thornes and Collard's British survey.

Having children   In a British survey with over 1,000 divorced and married interviewees, pre-marital pregnancy was far higher among couples who eventually divorced than for those who continued married, especially for teenage brides.[27] Among the divorced couples 32% of the wives were pregnant at marriage, 47% among those married under twenty. Of those still married only 19% of the wives were pregnant at marriage.

It has often been reported that childless couples have a higher divorce rate. However there are few children in most divorcing families – because most divorces occur early in the marriage. But if couples who have been together for the same number of years are compared, the childless couples are *not* more likely to be divorced.[28] In the last chapter we showed that married couples are *less* happy during the years the children are at home.

Religious affiliation   There is a much lower divorce rate among church-goers, especially Catholics, though marital breakdown tends to involve desertion and separation without divorce for Catholics. However church-attenders also report being more happily married. Perhaps the religious ceremony increases commitment. Perhaps it helps if a couple belongs to a group together where the ideals of love and family life are prominent. And marriages do better where both share the same religious ideas.[29]

Similarity of background, values and interests   This is an important predictor of marital happiness and successful marriage. Differences of race, class or nationality impose an additional source of conflict, as do differences of politics or values. Similar interests will bring a couple together in their leisure time, provide rewarding experiences in each other's company, and a shared social network.

Personality   A number of aspects of individual personality have been found to be linked to the probability of divorce. The main personality and background variables are:
1. Mental disorder (the most important): there is a clear relationship between the mental ill-health of one partner, and low marital satisfaction, complaints, etc., from both;[30] mental disorder is accepted as grounds for divorce.
2. Excessive ambition (with marriage and family relegated to second place).
3. Divorced parents (presumably providing a model).
4. Bad health.

The process and stages of divorce

Breakdown may start with a series of rows or crises, which are unresolved, and become increasingly serious. The precipitating events may be extra-marital liaisons, drunkenness, violence, or financial troubles.[31] The level of rewards in relation to costs falls. It also depends on the opportunities and temptations to become involved with other partners, though, as we have seen, extra-marital inter-course is itself partly a product of marital dissatisfaction. However when either partner works in a mixed-sex organisation, or takes part alone in mixed-sex leisure, other partners are more readily available. It was found in one study that the perceived availability of another and 'better' partner predicted marital break-up more than did marital unhappiness.[32]

Divorce may be precipitated if the couple have to live apart for a time for work reasons, or through delays in moving house. If either has somewhere else to sleep, such as a room in college, or with mother, there is less pressure to achieve reconciliation after a row.[33]

One partner usually decides first that the marriage is probably ending, or that he or she would like to change partners, and initiates a period of separation. This may be quite unexpected for the other partner. A study of fifty-eight divorced people showed the different forms this break took.[34] In 57% of cases one partner deserted, while in 24% one forced the other to leave. In 5% of cases there was a joint decision, and 14% failed to reunite after separation for other reasons.

The separation may be seen as temporary and it may prove to be so. In any case there is still the possibility of reconciliation until a divorce is granted, which is likely to take at least two years. But the marital bond does not consist only of rewards and costs. There is a joint way of life to dismantle, a social network to withdraw from, and an attachment to the spouse to be broken.

The joint way of life   Separation involves the disruption of a whole way of life, which was shared with spouse and children, in the family home. This means the ending of countless routines, many of them very enjoyable. It means new problems – for the wife dealing with children and coping financially, for the husband looking after himself domestically, and for one of them setting up a new establishment.

Loss of the social network   Much of a couple's social life is shared, most of it with other couples. They will be shocked and disapproving, and a large proportion of the network will be lost by each partner. In one study 42% of friends were lost after separation.[35]

Ending the attachment   Even though the costs of the marital relationship are high, a strong attachment may remain, based on experiences in the earlier and happier years together. It has been found that as many as 25% of divorced couples feel high attachment, 18% moderate and only 16% no attachment to their former spouses. Attachment is particularly strong if the divorce was recent and if the other had requested it. Males were more attached than females, either because wives usually petition for divorces, or because of their more rapid accommodation to the situation.[36] Empathetic concern for the partner may also remain after separation, even after divorce and remarriage. Previous partners often want to continue to see one another, inventing excuses to do so, such as calling to collect things left behind. 'There are continued feelings of warmth and caring for each other, in spite of the fact that they cannot succeed in living together in a marriage relationship.'[37]

Another sign of this continuing attachment is the high rate of pregnancy and childbirth during the period of separation. An American study found that 11% of a sample of divorcing women gave birth between separation and divorce, and another 14% between divorce and remarriage, most of those in question being under twenty-five.[38] Many of these are probably 'last chance' pregnancies, in an effort to keep the marriage intact.

Both partners will have a great deal of time after the separation to think about it all, and to work out why it happened. They may engage in endless rumination to work out an explanation, partly to understand, but partly to justify and to protect themselves from painful acknowledgement of failure. The complex and confused story is packaged into a simplified plot with a beginning, a middle and an end.[39]

The rewards and costs of divorce

The rewards *may* be considerable – the chance of a happier second marriage. What is the likelihood of this? As we shall see below, about two-thirds of divorcees in Britain marry again, the exact proportion depending on age and sex. For those who do marry, the chance of divorce is greater than in first marriages (p. 179). So a certain proportion of divorcees, rather less than half, end up happily remarried, the rest becoming either single or unhappily remarried.

The costs are the distress experienced during the period of conflict and in the early months and years of separation. In Chapter 2 we reviewed the difference in happiness and health of the divorced or separated and the married. The chances of dying were over three times as great for divorced women, compared with married women, and over twice as great for divorced compared with married men (p. 15). The causes of death which were higher for the divorced or separated include TB, cirrhosis of the liver, pneumonia, breast cancer, cancer of the mouth and throat, diabetes, strokes, and coronaries. Some of these are due to bad health habits – more smoking and drinking. The levels of depression and other mental illness are far higher for the divorced and separated, but this is partly a *cause* of divorce, as well as a consequence. The suicide rate is two to four times as high for the divorced compared with the married.

The separated and divorced are less happy than other groups, but this does not do justice to the intensity of suffering often experienced in the early months of separation. They are depressed, anxious, lacking in self-esteem. They often feel very lonely – the house is empty, and they have lost most of their social network outside the home. They feel outside society, or inferior members of it. They may feel unreal, that life is meaningless, they lose the motivation to do anything. There is no one to share ideas with.[40] The exact duration of this depressed and disturbed state is not known. The state of well-being has certainly improved within three or four years after the separation in most cases.[41]

Separation brings with it financial costs. The joint property has to be divided into two, so both spouses may have to live in smaller houses. And it is much more expensive to finance two separate establishments. Many of the poorest families in the country are single-parent families.

There is often a further cost for ex-husbands: usually the children live with their mother, so that father sees very much less of them, and can become a rather remote kind of uncle.

The effects of divorce on children

In 1982 163,000 children under sixteen were involved in the divorce of their parents, compared to 71,000 in 1970; most became members of one-parent families, usually with their mothers; many later had to cope with step-parents and step-siblings. By age sixteen one in three American and one in five British children will have experienced family disruption by divorce. Seven per cent of all five-year-olds in England and Wales and 21% in the USA will have been involved in parental divorce.[42] Many children will experience this more than once. An American survey found that 37% of children re-experienced family disruption after becoming step-children. Nearly as many children had experienced two or more family transitions as one, and almost one-fifth of those who became step-children had at least three changes of family. It was concluded that one child in ten will experience three or more family transitions before reaching eighteen years of age.[43]

Is it better for the children if the parents stay living together in an unhappy marriage, or get divorced? According to some studies the children suffer more in an unhappy home (Table 7).

On the other hand: divorce has a more disturbing effect on children than death of a parent; homes which are broken without conflict do not have such a great effect; the effects of parental conflict are greater than the effects of separation. However, separation where the child ceases to see much of a parent is also distressing. The reasons that conflict and divorce are harmful for children include the loss of an

TABLE 7. Effect on Children (15–18-year-old boys and girls) of Parental Unhappiness or Divorce [44]

| Child's Characteristic | Marital Status of Parents | | Unhappy/ Divorced Ratio |
	Unhappy %	Divorced or Separated %	
Disagrees with mother about values	47	26	1.81
Feels rejected by father	69	40	1.73
Psychosomatic illness	50	31	1.61
Disagrees with father about values	53	34	1.56
Rejects father	55	37	1.49
Feels rejected by mother	55	44	1.25
Delinquency	48	39	1.23
Rejects mother	42	35	1.20
Number of cases	112	115	

attachment, the loss of a model for imitation, and poor and inconsistent discipline.[45]

Divorce produces several kinds of disturbance in children but especially:

delinquency (twice as high as for intact marriages, while loss of a parent by bereavement has no effect)
aggression, disobedience, conduct problems
depression and anxiety
enuresis

Divorce has a more disruptive effect on boys than on girls: for boys in single-parent families, separated from father, there is less identification with the masculine sex role, taking the form of more dependency, less aggressiveness and a lower preference for masculine activities, especially if the separation occurred before the age of five. For girls differences do not appear until adolescence, and take the form of difficulty in establishing relationships with the opposite sex. Both sexes are more likely to form unstable marriages. Things go better for a child of divorced parents if it retains a very good relationship with one parent, if family relationships are improved rather than otherwise by the divorce,[46] and if the child is of a calm temperament and high IQ, and not predisposed to crime or psychopathology.[47] Many of the studies showing disruptive effects of divorce on children are based on 'disturbed samples', that is, children who are being treated for some sort of problem. When more 'normal' groups of children are compared, there is less evidence of divorce affecting children's self-esteem or behaviour.[48]

It is best for the children if they are given detailed explanations of what is happening, if they continue to see both parents, and if the latter have joint custody. Unfortunately this does not often happen. There is often little contact with the outside parent, especially if this is the father. In America, less than a third of these children have more than monthly contact with their fathers, and less than one-sixth have weekly contact. However, if it is the mother, nearly one-third see the outside parent weekly. Thirty-six per cent had no contact within the last five years with the father and 7% with the mother, and a further 17 and 7% had no contact for more than a year. There is more contact if neither divorced parent remarries. If both remarry, 11% of children have weekly contact; if neither remarry, the figure is 49%.[49]

Coping with divorce

Close interpersonal relationships, including marriage, have been described in this book as buffers against stress. In divorce or separation not only is this buffer removed, but the process itself is highly stressful, leaving the individual doubly vulnerable. Different sources of social support are needed and various studies have shown that divorcees with close and supportive family and friendship networks cope better with their changed status, both as individuals and as single parents.[50] It has been found, for example, that post-divorce stress is negatively correlated with the level of support and social involvement reported for both sexes – that is, high stress is found in those who have low support and little social involvement, and high support is associated with low stress.[51]

It is found that successfully adjusted and poorly adjusted female divorcees have different types of social network.[52] Although both groups reported similar interrelationships existing six months before the divorce, after divorce the successfully adjusted group had slightly larger networks which were less dense (or interconnected) and contained a lower proportion of kin to non-kin than the networks of unadjusted women. Low-density networks may be more effective because they allow:

1. Access to a larger diversity of role partners;
2. Greater openness to change because they comprise two-person

TABLE 8. Type of Relationship [52a]

Type of Difficulty	Kin	Friends	Acquaintances	Neighbours	Religious	Self-Help	Legal	Professional
1. Financial or material help	X	X						
2. Practical help on money, e.g. how to pay bills								
3. Practical help around the home or garden	X							
4. Help with employment, e.g. finding or changing job								
5. With transport								
6. Help with child-minding and children								
7. Shared leisure activities	X	X	X					
8. Shared social life, e.g. someone to go out with	X	XXX						
9. Holidays, e.g. someone to go with	X	X						
10. For advice on the divorce or separation	X	X					XXX	
11. For advice on personal matters	X	X						
12. For talking over problems to do with divorce or separation	X	X					X	
13. For talking over other sorts of problems	X	XXX						
14. Emotional support	X	XXX						
15. Providing companionship at home	XXX	X						
16. Providing companionship outside of home	X	XXX	X					
17. Providing affection	XXX	X						

Key: XXX Reported the *most* helpful for this problem by more than half the women.
     X Reported helpful for this problem by more than half the women.

rather than group relationships;

3. More chance of finding partners whose needs and interests are complementary to the changing needs and interests of the divorcee.

In one of our studies[52a] we asked women who had been divorced or separated within the previous four years to rank how helpful they had found a number of different social and professional relationships in dealing with seventeen problem areas in the six months immediately following their separation. We found that certain relationships were particularly helpful for specific difficulties, but overall, friends were rated more helpful than kin. (Table 8)

Friends were considered the most helpful source by more than half the women in our sample for providing companionship outside the home and for social life, but also for discussing problems and emotional support. Family, including own children, were most helpful for providing companionship inside the home and for providing affection.

Wives may have to start earning their living, and many prepare for this by re-entering education or taking training courses. Education and taking on a job lead to financial security, and they also lead to personal growth and increased self-confidence, as well as taking the mind off other problems, and permitting the acquisition of a new social network.

Establishing independent lifestyles and new relationships after divorce may be difficult, because the process, though legally culminated, has not been fully worked through by the individual. Hagestad and Smyer[53] emphasise the importance of time in coming to terms with divorce and separation. They describe two types of divorce – the orderly and the disorderly. In orderly divorces there has been a gradual dissolution of the marital relationship before the legal decree. The individual has withdrawn emotionally and detached him- or herself from the role of spouse before the formal dissolution. In these terms, the individual has experienced psychological and interpersonal divorce prior to the legal one. In disorderly divorce there is an incomplete ending for several possible reasons:

1. There is still an emotional attachment to the partner;
2. There is a continued attachment to the role of wife or husband;
3. There are still shared routines of everyday life.

In their study of ninety-three mid-life divorces, Hagestad and Smyer found that one-third were of this type. They describe a typology of disorderly divorce based on combinations of these three factors:

Type A: 'Divorced in name only' – couples are still living together, are still emotionally involved with each other and attached to the spouse role.

Type B: 'I wish it hadn't happened' – there is still emotional and role attachment but the couple is no longer living together.

Type C: 'I've got you under my skin' – there is emotional attachment to the other person but no role attachment or shared living arrangement.

Type D: 'Common-law arrangement' – couple emotionally involved with each other who live together after the divorce but have no attachment to the spouse role.

Type E: 'Why not be room-mates?' – shared living accommodation but no emotional or spouse role attachment.

Type F: 'Married status has its advantages' – individuals with no emotional bond who don't live together but are still attached to the role of husband or wife.

Type G: 'Business as usual' – shared living arrangements but without emotional involvement or role attachment.

Because these divorces are all 'incomplete endings', individuals in these seven types would have greater difficulty beginning new relationships and developing autonomous lifestyles than couples who have undergone 'orderly' divorce.[54]

It has been found that adjustment after separation is related to characteristics of the married lifestyle. The strongest contribution to adjustment is the existence of separate social activities and leisure interests during marriage. For older men, adjustment is related more to willingness to share domestic tasks and traditional female tasks during the marriage. Deviation from such traditional marital norms predicts better adjustment later. This may be because the adoption of responsibilities of the opposite sex role results in a broadening of the individual's competence.

Similar results have been obtained for newly separated women. Adjustment was easier for those with non-traditional sex role orientations, without dependent children, who had played an active role in the decision to separate.[55] The best post-divorce adjustment by males was by men who had established social lives independent of the marriage.[56]

It appears that successful adjustment after separation or divorce for both men and women is associated with:

1. Social support network;
2. Time for 'orderly' withdrawal from the relationship;
3. Flexibility in adopting opposite sex role demands;
4. Independent leisure or social activities.

Remarriage

It has been found that the most important factor in recovery from the
feelings of depression, anxiety, loss of self-confidence, etc., following
separation is establishing a satisfactory heterosexual relationship,[57]
though it makes no difference whether people are married or not.[58]
Many divorcees have another go at marriage – 'the triumph of hope
over experience'. The proportions of the divorced who do marry again
are highest in the U.S.A. and have been increasing in recent years
(Figure 3).

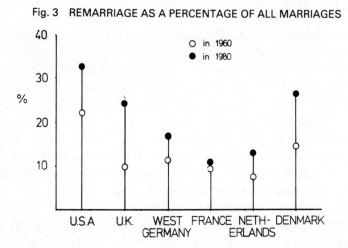

Fig. 3 REMARRIAGE AS A PERCENTAGE OF ALL MARRIAGES

This figure shows that about a quarter of all marriages in Britain are
remarriages. In 1970 only 8% of all marriages in England and Wales
involved the remarriage of a divorcee, and in 3%, both partners had
been married previously. In 1980 these figures were 22% and 11%. In
other words, one in nine marriages are remarriages for both bride and
groom.[60] About two-thirds of divorcees in Britain eventually remarry,
80% in the U.S.A. Most marry others who have never been married,
and only 30% marry other divorcees. Younger divorcees are more
likely to marry; men remarry more than women; older women find it

more difficult; children are only a minor handicap.[61] Most remarry in a civil rather than religious ceremony, and this is particularly true for divorced women.[62] More divorced men remarry in religious ceremonies, possibly because they are more likely to marry someone who has never been married before, while women are more likely to remarry another divorcee than men are.

The interval between divorce and remarriage is typically 2.8 years, though in the U.S.A. 45% remarry in the first year.[63] To this must be added the interval between separation and divorce, making a total unmarried interval which is rather longer.

How happy are second marriages? They are not on average as happy as first marriages, especially for women.[64] The likelihood of divorce is greater in second marriages than in first marriages, and even higher in third or later ones.

Fig. 4   PROBABILITY OF DIVORCE BY MARRIAGE ORDER[55]

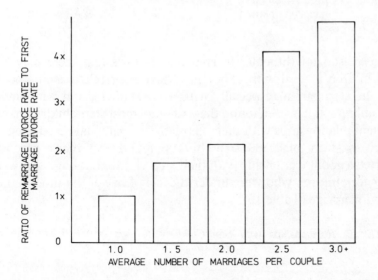

It can be seen that when both partners are on their third marriage, the divorce rate is four and a half times as high as for first marriages, and the chance of divorce is estimated at 90%. And they do not last so long: in the U.S.A. the period from second marriage to divorce is typically

1.7 years compared with 4.9 years for first marriages.[66] In England and Wales, remarriages of the previously divorced which again end in divorce fail much more quickly than those of first marrieds, and those of the widowed last the longest. Remarriages of the divorced last about half as long, on average, as marriages for those who were previously single. In fact, the chance of a divorced male's remarriage ending in divorce is one and half times greater than that of previously single men of the same age. For divorced women, it is two times greater.[67]

However the happily remarried are just as happy as happily married people in first marriages, and much better off than those who are divorced but not remarried, as the depression scores given in Table 9 show.

TABLE 9. *Depression, by Marital Status, Success and Race* [68]

Per Cent Depressed	White	Black
Happily married	7%	4%
Unhappily married	32%	22%
Separated	27%	19%
Divorced	18%	10%
Happily remarried	10%	5%
Unhappily remarried	32%	24%

One reason for difficulty in later marriages is that there may be step-children to deal with. They may have poor relationships both with the step-parent (especially with a step-father), and with their step-siblings. It has been found that although most step-children have excellent relationships with their step-fathers, many have a poor one. A British study of 1,583 step-children found that many parents reported a good relationship with their step-children, though this was better for children who were under the age of five at the time of the second marriage (Table 10).

TABLE 10. *Relationships with Step-Children by Age of Child at Time of Remarriage* [69]

		Age of child		
		0–4	5–11	12+
Satisfaction with relationship	high	75%	53%	40%
	low	4%	11%	21%

It is found that relations inside families with step-children are improved if a new child is born to the marriage.

The paternal grandparents, aunts and uncles also see less of a child who lives with his/her mother. Whereas 72% saw the child regularly during the first marriage, this fell to 33% after divorce, and 29% after remarriage.[70]

Rules

Up to 1971 divorces were granted if one partner could be shown to have broken the rules. It was assumed that there was a 'guilty party' who had engaged in adultery, desertion or cruelty. The new law reflected changing ideas about divorce by granting a divorce if a marriage has simply broken down.

Nevertheless the cause of marital breakdown may be that one or both partners have broken rules. However, the rules which may be important go far beyond adultery, desertion or cruelty. In the last chapter we listed the rules individuals believed should be followed by husbands and wives. In a second study we asked married couples which rules they believed should apply as well as which rules he/she actually followed in their own marriage.

In a third study we asked separated and divorced women which rules they believed should apply for the husband and the wife. We also asked which rules they had followed in their own marriages in the year immediately before the separation or divorce. We found there were very few significant differences between the rules women in our previous married sample and those in the current group believed should apply to either spouse. However there were more differences in how these rules were actually applied by the two groups in the preceding or final year of their marriage. Separated and divorced women were more likely during the year before parting than currently married women to:

1. Avoid asking the other person for material help.
2. Avoid asking the other person for personal advice.
3. Avoid intentionally touching the other person.
4. Avoid discussing personal financial matters with the other person.
5. Avoid talking to the other person about sex and death.
6. Avoid joking or teasing with the other person.
7. Avoid showing distress or anxiety in front of the other person.

The are also less likely than married women to:

1. Share news of success with the other person.
2. Stand up for the other person in their absence.
3. Feel free to take up as much of the other's time as desired.
4. Show unconditional positive regard to the other person.
5. Avoid criticising the other person publicly.
6. Be faithful to the husband.
7. Seek to repay debts, favours or compliments no matter how small.

It appears that even before actual separation the two partners are showing poor communication and reduced intimacy and support for each other. They are in fact breaking the rules they believe husbands and wives should be applying to one another. They are gradually distancing themselves from the relationship by failing to apply these rules. We shall see in Chapter 12 how changing such behaviour may be useful in marital therapy.

Should divorce be made easier?

Divorce has already become very much easier in most countries, as we have seen. The result has been a colossal increase in divorce rates during the twentieth century. Although some of this simply replaces separations and desertions which were without legal recognition, there is evidence that the rate of break-up of marriages has really increased. The view of marriage has also changed; it is coming to be seen more as a civil contract than as a religious affair with binding vows, whose breaking is a form of moral failure.

There is a difference between countries. In France after the Revolution in 1791, and in Sweden from 1915, marriage became a civil contract, with easier divorces, while in other Catholic countries there is still a religious concept of marriage, and divorce is more difficult. However, public opinion polls have shown that most people are in favour of easier divorce – 60% in an Italian referendum in 1974. The divorce rate is very high in Japan and the Arab countries. However both cultures contain strong family systems, and divorce has been interpreted as a 'change of personnel'.[71]

It seems that there is 'a high degree of support for the liberalisation of divorce laws (or a relative indifference to the process), and an apparent lack of widespread public anxiety about divorce trends, and it would seem that our family system is in course of transformation, with frequent divorce as a normal feature of the new scene.'[72]

If this trend were to continue, the entire institution of marriage could gradually fade away in favour of more transient relationships. But we have seen that 92% of people choose to get married at some point, some of them more than once. Clearly people are not disillusioned with the institution of marriage. We have seen that marriage provides the greatest satisfaction, and benefits to health and mental health, of any relationship. We have also seen the costs of divorce, in terms of increased death rate, from illness and suicide, and increased mental disorder rate, up to the time of remarriage for the two-thirds who do remarry. And we have seen the costs to children, the loss of contact with fathers, the difficult relations with step-parents and step-siblings.

It is possible that many marital break-ups could be avoided. Perhaps some couples are simply not prepared for bad periods. Perhaps some do not realise that conflict and argument are a normal part of marriage. Some may not know the rules. Some may lack the social skills needed to sustain this relationship. We shall describe forms of training and therapy in Chapter 12.

FURTHER READING

Chester, R. (1977) *Divorce in Europe* Leiden: Nijhoff
Hart, N. (1976) *When Marriage Ends* London: Tavistock
Thornes, B. & Collard, J. (1979) *Who Divorces?* London: Routledge & Kegan
   Paul

8

Parents and Children

In all societies the helpless infant, getting his food by nursing at his mother's breast and having digested it, freely evacuating the waste products, exploring his genitals, biting and kicking at will, must be changed into a responsible adult, obeying the rules of his society.[1]

In this chapter we deal with relationships between parents and children until the children leave home. Relationships with children when they are grown up we discuss in Chapter 9 under Kinship. We shall see that the bond between parents and children is very strong, so that the relationship survives, in most cases, until the death of the parent. This is also the first social relationship the child enters, and is in some ways the foundation for all others.

We shall try to explore how this powerful attachment is formed, how parents socialise their children, the changing character of the relationship during childhood, and the skills parents need.

The size and shape of families

We think of families as normally consisting of two parents and one or more children. Indeed the average number of children in British families is 2.33, though working-class families continue to be the largest, while class III (non-manual) are the smallest (see Table 1). The majority of families with four or more children are in social classes IV and V.

Working-class mothers are younger than middle-class ones – 38% have their first child when they are under twenty. Over a quarter of their first-borns were conceived before marriage. Fourteen per cent of all live births in England and Wales in 1982 were illegitimate, more than double the proportion in 1961. About one-third of these were to mothers aged under twenty, and this is the first time (at least in the recent past) that illegitimate births outnumbered legitimate births in

TABLE 1. Social Class and Birth of Children [2]

	I	II	III(N)	III(M)	IV	V
Average number of children to women in first marriages (15 to 19 years completed) (1971)	2.26	2.18	2.02	2.37	2.40	2.74
(10 to 14 years completed)	2.23	2.13	2.00	2.31	2.32	2.62
Age of mother at birth of first child (% under 20)	6	10	12	28	31	38
Percentage first children conceived pre-maritally (1977)		6	9	18		26
Social class of adopters		33	17	32	12	2
Social class of foster parents	3	15	44		24	14

this age group.[3]

However families vary greatly in their composition, as the following analysis of American families shows:

TABLE 2. Family Types, U.S.A. 1970

Family type	% distribution
Nuclear family (with children)	
single workers	30
dual workers	14
Nuclear dyad (without children)	
single workers	4
dual workers	11
Single parent	13
Reconstituted (remarried nuclear)	15
Other traditional	
e.g. three generational, bilateral or extended kin	5
'Experimental' marriages and families	
(including unmarried couple and child)	8

The British family has not yet changed as much as this, but we should consider briefly the main variations.

Married couples About 92% of people in Britain marry, but about 13% of wives do not have children. Some of them adopt, others take in foster children. Middle-class couples are more likely to adopt, i.e. they adopt illegitimate working-class children; working-class couples are more likely to take in foster children (Table 1).

Many marriages are now second or later marriages for one or both partners, and may contain step-children from previous marriages.

While the husband is usually the main earner, over 40% of wives are employed, many of them full time, and over 7% of wives earn more than their husbands.

Single-parent families Mainly as a result of divorce, about 9% of families have only one parent, the mother in most cases. These families usually have only one child. This is the main alternative to the traditional family, and is becoming increasingly common.

Communes and institutions In the U.S.A. about 6% of children are reared in communes, consisting of a number of adults, usually not married. The number in Britain is probably lower than this. In addition there are children in care or in orphanages, again being reared by a number of adults.

Activities of parents and children

These activities are of interest, though they are very familiar, since they go a long way towards defining the whole relationship, and they make a great contrast with the activities characteristic of other relationships. The most extensive British data here are provided by John and Elizabeth Newson in their studies of 700 children in Nottingham at the ages of one, four and seven.[4]

Feeding This is one of the main things that parents do for their children. Infants are first fed at the breast, though only 51% were breastfed at all in 1975, and only half of those for more than a month. Feeding, whether by breast or bottle, takes up a great deal of time in the early months. By the age of four children are having normal meals, but a lot of them have feeding problems, not eating what they are given or leaving food on the plate, and efforts are made to enforce proper behaviour at meals. During middle childhood mealtimes are an enjoyable family occasion; during adolescence they may be the only time parents and children meet, and can be the occasion for major rows.

Supervision Much parental work consists of supervising, or attempting to supervise, the children's activities. Infants have to be dressed, changed, bathed and undressed, settled in pram, cot or playpen, persuaded to go to sleep and constantly attended to. By the age of one, most mothers have started toilet training, with a high rate of failure at this point; they are preventing children from playing with their genitals (especially working-class mothers); and 62% of mothers smack their child regularly.

During childhood, they have to be given toys, books, paper, etc., set to play indoors or out, or with friends, taken and fetched from school, and kept clean. At seven, 30% of girls and 15% of boys are fetched from school, and there is a high level of what the Newsons call 'chaperonage', i.e. keeping a pretty close eye on where they are and what they are doing. For adolescents supervision is more difficult, but parents try to make sure that they go to school and do their homework, come home at a reasonable hour, and keep away from bad company. This is easier said than done.

Conversation   Mothers talk a great deal to infants, at first a rather one-way conversation, but in which the infant takes an increasing part and thereby learns to talk. Parents read to young children; there is talk during meals; children ask many questions to which they may or may not receive adequate answers; and they like to report what has happened at school and on other outings. In early adolescence the amount of conversation falls off, as children prefer to talk to their peer group. They become expert at non-communication:

>   Parent: 'Where have you been?'
>   Adolescent: 'Out.'
>   Parent: 'What did you do?'
>   Adolescent: 'Nothing.'

Showing affection and enjoying each other's company   Mothers of infants spend a great deal of time in physical contact with them; later this occurs particularly at bathtime, bedtime, and while reading to them. At the age of four most children demand to be cuddled and kissed, and 95% of mothers enjoy doing this; 66% of mothers have four-year-olds in their bed if they cannot sleep; 66% take part enthusiastically in children's play. There is a high level of bodily contact with parents during the early years, and children still cling to their mothers or keep close to them when in strange places or when meeting strange people.

At age seven children and parents still enjoy each other's company and display a lot of affection, especially mothers and daughters. Daughters are at home more, and mothers enjoy doing their hair and dressing them up. Boys on the other hand are more likely to share interests with their fathers, and spend time together, for example playing trains or going to football. During adolescence physical contact and displays of affection are sharply reduced, though affection may be expressed indirectly by parents showing concern, interest and approval, and giving presents, while the family may come together more on holidays.

Helping Parents do a great deal for infants and four-year-olds, but the children cannot do much in return. By the age of seven most children are expected to tidy up their toys, either alone or with mother. Only 18% of children do regular household chores, such as washing up, more boys than girls, and more in middle-class homes. A further 53% earn money from their parents for doing jobs. Adolescents are not always very helpful around the house, and may be accused of 'treating it like a hotel', though some contribute to the family income.

In these basic activities shared by parents and children we can see the roots of activities in other relationships in later life – meals as the focus of encounters in close relationships; mothers and daughters sharing intimacy, father and sons having joint interests, reflected in the pattern of male and female friendships. Bodily contact is seen later mainly in sexual relationships; supervision is found mainly in working relationships; conversation and helping are central to all relationships.

Satisfaction and conflicts

Children are a great source of satisfaction to their parents. Our study of satisfaction in different relationships found that they fell below spouse, but at much the same level as siblings and close friends, in this respect (Fig. p. 83). An American national survey obtained detailed information about the value of children as seen by parents and non-parents (Table 3).

Each of these headings contained a number of more specific items.

Primary group ties and affection, i.e. providing love and companionship, is the most frequently given value of children, especially for

TABLE 3. *The Value of Children* (percentage of sample)[5]

	Women		Men	
	Parents	Non-parents	Parents	Non-parents
Advantages of children				
Primary group ties and affection	66	64	60	52
Stimulation and fun	61	41	55	35
Expansion of the self	36	34	32	32
Adult status and social identity	23	14	20	7
Achievement, competence and				
creativity	11	14	9	21
Morality	7	6	6	2
Economic utility	5	8	8	10
Help expected from sons/daughters				
Give part of their salary when				
they begin working	28/28	18/18		
Contribute money in family				
emergencies	72/72	65/63		
Support you financially when				
you grow old	11/10	9/9		
Help around the house	86/92	88/91		

women, for those of less education, and for racial minority groups.

Stimulation and fun, including pleasure from watching children grow, is next, especially for women, for parents as opposed to non-parents, and for parents of very young children.

Expansion of the self includes having a purpose in life, learning experiences and self-fulfilment, and was higher for the Jews and the non-religious. The authors of the survey suggest that for these groups children are the main source of immortality.

Adult status and social identity includes a feeling of having something useful to do, feeling adult and more mature. This was particularly strong for less educated women. It was found that having children is the most important factor in feeling adult and mature.

Achievement, competence and creativity, especially from creating a human being, were reported by many, especially the better educated, perhaps because of their greater concern with achievement.

Morality included becoming less selfish, a better person, leading a more settled life, and was mentioned most by men.

Economic utility includes security in old age and help with household chores. This was a much less important value, though it was considerably greater among blacks and those in rural areas. The lower part of Table 3 shows that many people expect financial help and help around the house from their children, either now or in the parent's old age. It was found that those people who stressed *Adult status, Morality* and *Economic utility* wanted to have larger families than those who did not.

We now turn to the negative side – the *costs* of children for parents. Our study showed that children are a major source of conflict as well as of satisfaction. Studies of marital satisfaction show that satisfaction is greatest before couples have children, and after they have left home. The two worst patches are stage III, when there are pre-school children, and stage V, when there are teenagers. Stage IV, children 5–12, is the happiest of the years with children in the house (see Figure on page 130).

If these results suggest that children are mainly a cost rather than a reward for parents, it is worth noting that people who have children do at any rate live longer.[6]

Children can however be a great source of stress to their parents. At the pre-school period mothers often become exhausted and depressed, while some husbands turn to drink. Violence, such as 'baby-battering', is the most extreme response. This is most likely to occur with mothers who are under twenty, have several young children in the home and also lack child-rearing skills. For example, they may use too much physical punishment, which makes the children more aggressive. Violent mothers also have weak social networks, with little help or support from husbands, relatives or neighbours.[7] It has been found that depression is common among working-class mothers in London, if their youngest child was under six, if they did not have jobs, and if their husbands were not supportive.[8] The second bad patch can be when the children are adolescents; these problems will be discussed below.

We turn to the satisfactions and costs for *children*. Children are of course fed, housed, clothed, protected, given pocket money, and so on by their parents, so there is a great deal on the positive side. The Newsons found marked physical display of affection by mothers of four-year-olds, while at seven hugs, cuddles and kisses were given by 87% of mothers, and displays of affection by 75% of children. Many mothers scored high on child-centredness, i.e. they showed a very positive and sympathetic attitude to their children, gave them special places to keep their things and allowed their friends to come and play. Many parents shared some interest with their children, especially fathers with sons. Nearly all parents gave their seven-year-olds pocket money, and often paid extra sums for doing jobs; the poorer the families, the *more* pocket money they gave.

The negative side for children is based mainly on the parents' responsibility to discipline and to restrain them from dangerous or anti-social activities. The Newsons found that most mothers smacked their children regularly, at one, four, and seven, boys more than girls (Table 4), and working-class mothers more than middle-class ones (Table 6).

TABLE 4. *Frequency of Smacking by Mothers (percentages)* [9]

		once a week or more	once a day or more
1-year olds (frequency not reported)		62	
4-year-olds		68	7
7 year-olds	boys	41	11
	girls	25	6

Twenty-four per cent of mothers sometimes used withdrawal of love as a threat, 22% threatened to bring in external authorities like policemen or teachers. In extreme cases the level of punishment or deprivation becomes so high that the child runs away from home. This is most common among sixteen-year-olds, of both sexes, though they are usually away for less than three days. Some are really pushed out by their parents, while most run away to get out of what is seen as a bad situation. Those most likely to run away are children who are alienated from parents and school, who feel rejected by their parents, or who have a great desire to engage in prohibited activities like sex and drugs. [10]

The origins of the parent–child bond

We shall see in the next chapter that the bonds between parents and children (and between siblings) are very long-lasting, indeed they are virtually permanent. The better the relationship with either parent, especially the mother, the happier the person is as a child or adolescent, and the less likely he or she is to seek therapy or consider suicide as an adult. However, there is no overall relationship with adult happiness.[11] There is often a bad patch in this relationship, during adolescence; we have seen that marital satisfaction is very low at this point, and that some adolescents run away from home. Nevertheless this is nearly always a short-term problem, and affectionate relationships are soon resumed again. When does this powerful bond between parents and children form, and how?

We shall discuss later the 'selfish gene' theory that parents look after children because they share the parents' genes (p. 227). However these theories do not affect the attachments of children, who become bonded to the people who look after them most, even if they are foster parents or nannies or au pair girls. But, children who live in residential homes until age three or four later fail to form strong attachments to foster parents, and a number of studies suggest that bonding takes place in the first three years of life.

There is evidence that the first week of life is a sensitive period, especially for mothers, who become particularly attentive to their babies if they have a lot of contact with them during the first week. However, this is a relatively small effect, and interaction during later parts of the first year is more important. Infants are innately responsive to female voices and to face-like objects at about the distance of the mother's face during feeding. Mothers do not seem to need to be told how to interact with babies either. During the first year they develop simple repetitive patterns of interaction, consisting of looking, smiling and vocalising; they are normally responsive to crying, which is a signal for attention, they imitate the child's noises, and play simple games like peek-a-boo. Mother and baby seem to respond to one another for the sake of responding.

Babies develop an attachment to their mother, especially during the period seven to ten months, when they object to being separated from her, want her to be near, and try very hard to get her attention. From about seven months they want their mother rather than anyone else.[12]

In studies by Ainsworth and others attachment was measured by the child's seeking physical contact, or proximity with the mother in a strange situation, crying, and other protests at separation from mother. 'Secure' attachment was most common, consisting of willingness to explore in a strange environment while mother was present, and little crying until a second period of separation. A second group showed acute distress at separation, and would not leave their mothers to explore – 'mal-attachment'; a third group showed very weak attachment. Ainsworth found that secure attachment takes place when the mother is sensitive to the infant's crying and other signals. The nature of attachment behaviour changes as the child grows older: at twelve months it needs bodily contact, at two years old proximity, at five looking, smiling and talking are enough to reduce anxiety.[13] Securely attached infants compared to anxiously attached children show better problem-solving ability and quality of play at two years, better peer competence at three and a half, and more curiosity and resiliency at pre-school age.[14]

The conditions for attachment to take place include the sensitivity to infant demands mentioned above; feeding is probably important, though attachments are also formed with those who play with the child; bodily contact, looking, smiling, and other social stimulation affect it.

The child gradually becomes more independent, but the early attachment to parents and siblings is probably the basis for the life-long relationships with these close kin (p. 227).

The effects of attachment, especially of secure attachment, are that the child is able to use the mother as a 'secure base' for exploring strange places and people, is able to spend more time away from mother, and so becomes free from her, attends more to her and is able to learn from her, and to engage in more complex social interaction both with her and with others. Meanwhile the mother is more affectionate and responsive to the child.

We have spoken of the mother as the primary attachment figure, which she normally is. However, infants will be attached to whoever looks after them most, as well as to other members of the family. The attachment to father usually occurs at the same time as that to mother, though it is not so strong.[15] However, a secure attachment to the father can compensate for an insecure attachment to the mother, but is not as effective as a secure attachment to the mother only. Both are inferior to a secure attachment with both parents.[16]

Sons and daughters

Boys and girls have different relationships with their parents. In an American survey, 80% of men said that they had good relationships with their mothers but only 45% were close to their fathers. For women, the figures are more equal, with 62% close to their mothers and 57% to their fathers.[17] There is evidence that the quality of parent–child interaction is more important in the psychological functioning of sons than daughters.[18] The differences between the sexes are at least partly due to the different ways boys and girls are treated. Studies of hermaphrodites show that they turn into 'males' or 'females' depending on how they were labelled and treated in the first three or four years of life.[19] In rare cases a child who was anatomically male has been reared as a girl, and developed feminine characteristics as a result. What do parents do differently to boys and girls? Moss[20] and others have found clear, though not very large, differences in the treatment of babies during the early months. Mothers look, smile and vocalise more with girls, while they touch and hold boys more. This is partly in response to innate features of boys and girls – boys are stronger, girls are more reactive to touch (so don't need so much), and more responsive to faces.

By thirteen months girls are already more dependent on the mother, and when they are four and five there is much more pressure on girls to be obedient, responsible and nurturant, while boys are encouraged to be self-reliant and to strive for achievement. While this difference has been found in a number of cultures, it is greatest in primitive societies which hunt large animals.[21]

Boys and girls are trained in the forms of behaviour thought to be appropriate for their sex. There are almost certainly some biological differences: for example, males of all species are typically more aggressive than females. However, parental handling develops such differences much further. Parents have a very clear idea of what boys and girls should be like, though this varies somewhat with the needs of society. As Roger Brown puts it:

> In the United States a *real* boy climbs trees, disdains girls, dirties his knees, plays with soldiers, and takes blue for his favorite color. A real girl dresses dolls, jumps rope, plays hopscotch, and takes pink for her favorite color. When they go to school, real girls like English and music and 'auditorium'; real boys smoke pipes, drink beer, and

major in engineering or physics; the girls chew Juicy Fruit gum,
drink cherry Cokes, and major in fine arts. The real boy matures
into a 'man's man' who plays poker, goes hunting, drinks brandy,
and dies in the war; the real girl becomes a 'feminine' woman who
loves children, embroiders handkerchiefs, drinks weak tea, and
'succumbs' to consumption.[22]

Parents reward or punish their children in order to train them in the
right sex role. In addition they use much more physical punishment
with boys, as the survey of seven-year-olds by the Newsons[23] showed.
Nearly twice as many parents used corporal punishment on boys as on
girls, and they were more likely to use an implement (see Table 4).

It has been found that girls are expected to be physically affectionate, to develop close interpersonal relations, and are encouraged to
talk about their troubles. Boys, on the other hand, are allowed greater
freedom to go about on their own, for example to roam in the street,
come home from school alone, and are expected to be self-reliant, to
compete and achieve, and to control their feelings. This adds up to a
closer and more dependent role for daughters, a more independent
one for sons.

English parents diverge more in their handling of boys and girls
than parents in some other countries. In addition to punishing boys

"Personally, I feel he rather over-disciplines his children"

Private Eye

more, greater demands for achievement are made of boys, while girls receive more nurture.[24]

Babies are primarily attached to, and dependent on, the mother, unless someone else has taken over as caretaker. As the child grows older the father plays an increasingly important role. According to Freud, children between about three and five go through a period of increased love for the opposite-sex parent, combined with jealousy of, and hostility towards, the same-sex parent. The 'Oedipus complex' has been the object of a great deal of research. Anthropological studies have found that there is often hostility not to the father, but to the mother's brother; this happens when the mother's brother is the main disciplinarian and the father a cheerful older playmate – which suggests that any hostility of boys to fathers is not due to sexual jealousy but to dislike of being spanked.

However a number of studies suggest that sons do become sexually attracted to their mothers during socialisation, and that this affects their later choice of a spouse. In those primitive societies where the son sleeps with the mother for a period after birth (presumably to prevent father from procreating more children too soon), there are particularly unpleasant initiation rites for sons at adolescence.[25].

The interest of girls in fathers may be different. The feminine sex role requires girls to be pleasing to others, and so more social feedback is needed; it is found that fathers are a necessary factor in the development of femininity. For both boys and girls it seems to be normal and necessary for there to be some kind of attachment with the opposite-sex parent, but of a kind which does not involve taking that parent as a model.

Children take the same-sex parent as a model, and this is one of the main sources of gender identity, the conscience, and achievement strivings. Most children take this parent as one of their main guides to behaviour. In homes where the mother is dominant, it has been found that boys and girls imitate her more and identify with her, thus disrupting the usual pattern with dominant fathers.[26] Boys brought up without a father are consistently found to be less aggressive and less masculine, though some of them later develop an exaggerated masculinity, perhaps as a protest against the femininity of the home, perhaps using other models from outside the home.

It used to be believed that children *identify* with a parent, that is, take him or her as a model for all kinds of behaviour, attempt to duplicate their behaviour, attitudes and values. However, it is found that children imitate their parents in some respects but not in others: there is not enough consistency to support the idea of unitary identification. Children imitate the behaviour of their parents, and that of other possible models under certain definite conditions – when the model is warm and rewarding, when the model is powerful, i.e. able to control rewards, when he or she is similar to the model, and is of the same sex. Under some conditions the same-sex parent is the model, but often not. If the older child in a family identifies with one parent, the second child will often identify with the other parent, regardless of sex. The son–mother, daughter–father pattern is quite common, and is found in normal samples. The function of this 'split identification' may be the avoidance of sibling rivalry.[27]

Relations with mothers and fathers

We saw in Chapter 6 that fathers are mainly concerned with earning a living and dealing with the world outside the home, while mothers look after the children and home. However, fathers have always been important inside the home as well, and there is a general trend in the modern world for fathers to do more domestically and in particular to have more to do with the children. In a small proportion of families the roles are reversed, and it is the wife who goes out to work, while in a larger proportion of cases husband and wife both have jobs and share the housework and the child-minding.

It is now normal for fathers to be present at the birth of their children, and experts like Spock are recommending in their books that fathers should do their share of playing with the baby and other aspects of baby-care. For example, in 1959 43% of fathers had never changed a nappy, while in 1979 only 11% had not done so.[28] Although the mother is usually the main caretaker of the babies, in nearly a third of cases she is not, and in most of these cases it is the father instead. Most infants have an attachment to their father by the time they are eighteen months, and often by one year.[29] A MORI poll[30] found that 76% of the fathers of children under five played with them every day or most days. However, this is the main thing that fathers do for small children; they are much less likely to do the following (every day or most days):

put them to bed	34%
bath them	16%
change their nappies	15%
dress them	14%
prepare their meals	9%

This pattern has been found elsewhere: while fathers *play* with young children, mothers are mainly concerned with caretaking.[31]

When the Newsons' children were seven, more of them felt closer to their mothers (see Table 5), both boys and girls – no evidence here of an Oedipal preference for the opposite-sex parent. And more shared an interest with the *same*-sex parent.

TABLE 5. Fathers v. Mothers (When Child is 7)[32]

		boys	girls
Child's closeness to parents:	closer to mother	39	42
	closer to father	21	18
Child shares an interest with a parent:	with mother	33	49
	with father	68	40
father participates a lot		50	31
mother is child-centred		29	35
who smacks most?	mother	76	82
	father	12	8

It can be seen that fathers spent more time with boys, while mothers were more rewarding to girls. If we turn to discipline, fathers smack boys more than girls, while for mothers there is no significant difference.

Adolescents see their fathers as more authoritarian than their mothers, regard their fathers as stricter and more aggressive, while mothers are seen as more emotionally supportive, affectionate and protective. However, authoritarian fathers were seen as fairer than similar mothers, and permissive mothers were regarded more favourably than permissive fathers.[33]

The commonest kind of family after those where there are two parents is the family with a mother but no father. Comparisons of children in these two kinds of family can tell us something about the effects of the normal relationship with father – though it is important to hold other variables constant, such as the standard of living. Other studies have compared the impact within intact families of different kinds of father.

The effects of the father's absence, or of ineffective fathers, are mainly found among boys. For example, the development of a masculine sex role in boys, i.e. feelings of masculinity, together with appropriate patterns of behaviour, is impaired by the father's absence. This is especially so if a father leaves before the boy is five or six, but there is little or no effect if there is a step-father and if mother encourages masculinity. Within intact families masculinity develops more when the father has a warm relationship with his son, is seen as a powerful decision-maker and competent, and when he has masculine interests and encourages the same in his son. Daughters become more feminine if fathers are nurturant, and accept and reward their femininity.

The development of morality and self-control is affected much more by mothers than by fathers. However for boys, when there is a bad relationship with father, or when the father is absent, moral development is weaker, and delinquency somewhat more likely. The most important 'father' skill is affection, sharing joint leisure, with boys, and avoiding discipline that is too harsh.

Academic achievement is affected most by fathers. Children from homes without fathers do worse at school-work, but especially at arithmetic. In intact families, children do better at school-work when father takes an active part in looking after them. The presence and involvement of fathers affects the educational achievement of girls as well as of boys, possibly more than that of boys. On the other hand, too much parental interference can have a negative effect, and the father's role may be to enable the child to have enough independence.

Social competence is greatest when children have a warm relationship with both parents, and the parents with each other. Relations between parents are particularly important for the parent–child relationship. There is a strong association between the amount of negative affect expressed between parents and the amount of such affect directed at the young child. The mother's relations with her wider social network are also important to the parent–child bond. Mothers with low social support are more likely to have poor infant–mother attachment.[34] Mothers are more likely to abuse or neglect their children if they are isolated from their peer social networks.[35]

Children who have no father do not get on so well with the peer group, and adolescent girls do not get on as well with the opposite sex. Children from intact homes get on better with the peer group when fathers are nurturant and actively involved. The absence of a father does not have much effect on self-confidence, since maternal warmth is sufficient.[36]

Now that mothers are increasingly going out to work, the effects of mother and father are becoming more symmetrical. What are the consequences of partial maternal absence? Many studies have been made of this issue, and the upshot is: there is little evidence that children suffer emotional deprivation, but the children are supervised less well and are more likely to be delinquent. The mother is often happier, though she may experience guilt and stress through having too much to do, and she provides a better adult role model, especially for her daughters.[37] These findings have strengthened moves to provide adequate day-care facilities for working mothers.

Adolescence – a period of changing relationships

The relationship with children undergoes a major change, and sometimes a temporary breakdown, during adolescence. The child feels increasing urges to break out of a childish, dependent form of attachment to the parents, to one of greater independence and equality. This is less of a problem in primitive cultures where nothing changes very much, but more of a problem in our own where historical changes create a 'generation gap' between the ideas and interests of parents and children.

We have seen that the period when the children are adolescents is a bad time for parents (Fig. 1, p. 130); it is often a bad time for the children too: self-esteem is lower, and self-consciousness greater at twelve and thirteen than either before or after.

For most adolescents there is some degree of rebellion, if only to establish that they are separate individuals in their own right. For some there is a more serious rebellion, and rejection of the parents, though this is usually temporary. Rebellion often takes the form of rejecting parental restraints on smoking, drinking, sex, or late nights, of adopting different views on religion or politics, or merely a different preference in music, clothes or hair. Rebellion is particularly acute among children who are socially mobile, or who have become attached to a deviate peer group; in developing countries adolescents often reject the traditional ways of their parents in favour of modern ideas. On the other hand, recent American surveys[38] have found that:

88% of teenagers had a lot of respect for their parents as people;
75% shared their parents' values and ideals;
57% said that they got on well with their parents and enjoyed their company;
about a third had difficulty in communicating with their parents;
about 25% thought there was a large generation gap;
4% did not enjoy spending time with their parents.

These surveys suggest that there is a problem of communication or values for 25–30% of adolescents and their parents, but that serious conflict is fairly rare. The nature of these conflicts was explored further by Coleman[39] in a study in London, using a projective method, in which subjects completed sentences ('When a boy is with his parents . . .') and wrote stories about pictures. Negative themes were produced by over 90% of adolescents, on the subject of parents, but the contents were different for boys and girls. Boys reported feelings of frustration – 'When a boy is with his parents . . . he is usually chained up.' Girls on the other hand reported not feeling themselves when with their parents – 'When a girl is with her parents . . . she is not herself . . . she has to behave differently . . . she becomes like them.' (Fig. 1).

Fig. 1   PERCENTAGE OF BOYS AND GIRLS EXPRESSING NEGATIVE THEMES ON A SENTENCE COMPLETION TASK CONCERNING PARENTAL RELATIONSHIPS[40]

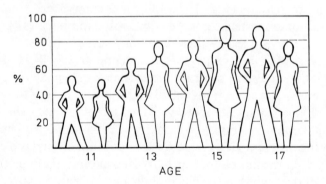

For boys the problem was frustration at restraints, demands for greater freedom. This is less important for most girls, because, as we have seen, girls were socialised more strongly during childhood to be dependent and obedient, while boys were trained more to be independent. On the other hand boys, as well as girls, have a lot of ambivalence during adolescence: while fighting for more independence they also need parental help and support, and may switch back suddenly into a more dependent relationship.

Does the peer group have more influence than parents? Some spheres of behaviour are affected more by one, some by the other. Activities which are important to the peer group are most influenced by it, for example such leisure activities as tastes in music, dancing and sport, but also sometimes drugs and delinquency. The parents however have more impact on educational and career plans.[41]

In primitive societies the transition from childhood to adult status is marked by dramatic ceremonies, 'rites of passage'. As for marriage and graduation, these ceremonies make public the change in status of those concerned, and give them social and dramatic support for a change in their condition. In modern societies there are no such ceremonies for adolescents; certain birthdays are the nearest equivalent, since different legal rights are acquired at each point – to drink, drive a car, vote, leave school, marry, and so on. This long-drawn-out process is matched by similar inconsistencies in the ways that parents and other adults treat the young. Adolescents are going through a number of changes in role, with increasing independence from parents, entering employment, leaving home, getting married. These are major changes, and entail discontinuities with the life of childhood.

During adolescence, young people have to take a number of important decisions about education and career. They also have to decide what kind of person to be. The heightened concern with these issues has been called the 'identity crisis'. The individual needs to achieve a self-image or an identity, which incorporates his or her actual abilities, interests and past experiences, and provides a basis for self-esteem. He also wants it to be distinctive, to some extent different from that of his parents and family. The process of establishing an independent identity is partly done by attachment to peer groups, and conforming to their ideals and values, rather than to those of the parents. There has been a great increase in the power of the adolescent peer group over the last forty years, and it now helps to assert the teenager's independence of parental control by powerful social norms about clothes, pop music, sex, and sometimes drugs.

Sometimes peer groups act as useful sources of information and social skills. Sometimes they are sources of delinquency and other kinds of deviance. They usually keep adolescents apart from parents and the rest of the adult world. Bronfenbrenner wrote, as chairman of a White House committee on children:[42] 'By isolating our children from the rest of society, we abandon them to a world devoid of adults and ruled by the destructive impulses and compelling pressures both of the age-segregated peer group and the aggressive and exploitive television screen, we leave our children bereft of standards and support and our own lives impoverished and corrupted.'

While the parents were often taken as models for imitation in middle childhood, they may be positively avoided as models during adolescence. On the other hand we saw above that the majority of adolescents share parental ideals and values, and many do take their parents as models. Even if parents are out of date in their tastes in music and clothes, they have nevertheless succeeded in mastering the adult tasks of establishing a family and earning a living. Adolescents are more likely to take their parents as models during their quest for independence and maturity if they have a warm relationship with them, and if the parents are visibly competent in their work – including mothers too.[43]

Class differences in parent–child relations

Parents of different social classes are fairly similar in the ways they treat their children – they all want their children to be healthy, happy, and well-behaved. However there are a number of quite striking differences, which have consequences for later personality development. These are partly because middle-class parents are the first to read the new books, and to start the new fashions. They were the first to read Spock, the first to adopt feeding infants on demand, and to be permissive about infant sexuality. And as we saw above (Table 1), working-class families often have more children, start when the mother is younger, the first child is more often conceived premaritally, and there are more illegitimate children.

Parents in different social classes appear to love or reject their children at much the same rates, as shown by displays of physical affection, or taking children into their bed. On the other hand, middle-class parents talk more to their children; in the early months middle-class mothers vocalise more to their infants, and later they read more stories to them; middle-class parents initiate more inter-action, talk to their children more, play more games with them, watch, help and teach more. Middle-class parents are more rewarding in a number of ways, they are more responsive to requests, and make more use of praise, but provide *less* pocket money.

Middle-class parents are more permissive in regard to early sex play, early aggression, toilet training failures. The Newsons found that working-class mothers smack their children more when they are four, and use more physical punishment when they are seven, and they do it to enforce obedience, or because the child has struck its mother. Many studies show that working-class parents make greater use of power and coercion, backed by physical punishment and threats of more to come. The aim is to produce obedience and conformity, children who are neat and clean. Middle-class parents, on the other hand, do it more by talking, by persuasion and explanation, with the aim of developing self-control, consideration for others, children who are happy and healthy and on good terms with their parents. Working-class parents are less tolerant with young children, of aggressive behaviour, early sexuality, and lying; they are more moralistic about these forms of behaviour. But later on it is middle-class parents who are more concerned with their children's behaviour outside the home (See Table 6).

TABLE 6. Social Class and Discipline[44]

	I & II	III(N)	III(M)	IV	V
smacks once a week to once a day (at 4)	61	68	70	66	79
frequent use of corporal punishment (at 7)	21	27	34	31	40

Working-class fathers are at home less, and are less available to spend time with their children; they are stricter and punish more than mothers do. Middle-class fathers establish a warmer relationship with their children, and are more likely to share an interest with them.

There is greater pressure for educational achievement on the part of middle-class parents. As well as talking more to their children, the parents answer questions more fully, teach them more, encourage them to tackle intellectual tasks, and reward performance.

Historical variations in parent–child relationships

There have been very great changes in the relationship between parents and children. Up to the middle of the eighteenth century children had a hard time of it: many of them died in childhood, they were often severely beaten, many were sent to other families for training or service, and there was often a very distant relationship with their own parents. Plumb[45] suggests that from about 1740 things greatly improved for children in Britain: they lived longer, their families were better off, and more books were available for education. Childhood became recognised as a definite period of life, between infancy and adulthood. By the early nineteenth century, however, parents became stricter, less permissive, and were confident that they could socialise children into the right kind of adults; religious ideas were important, the child's evil dispositions must be overcome with threats of religious punishment, and with emphasis on duty and conscience.[46]

In the present century the ideas of psychologists have had a great effect on parent–child relations, via popular baby-books and women's magazines, first affecting middle-class parents, and then the rest of society. Early behaviourism was passed on via Truby King, with what now seems a very authoritarian approach, in which children were to be trained in self-control and obedience and ignored when they cried, with a particularly tough line on early sexuality and thumb-sucking. Freud and his followers, like Susan Isaacs and John Bowlby, on the other hand, persuaded people that children have legitimate needs, which should be met, that they should be given plenty of attention, and that they need a close relationship with their mother.

Spock's book *Baby and Child Care* was published in 1946, sold 20 million copies, and advocated an extreme permissiveness, and what has been called the 'fun morality' – it was now correct to have fun with baby. American studies have found that there was a shift towards permissiveness which reached its height in that country in 1950. There has been a shift away from permissiveness since then, and the latest fashion is to take more account of the needs of parents as well, with some move away from permissiveness, and an emphasis on the role of the father.[47]

Meanwhile, just as childhood appeared as a special time of life in the early nineteenth century, so adolescence emerged as a period between childhood and adulthood in the twentieth century. 'Teenagers' appeared for the first time as a special group, with their own clothes and tastes, during World War II, and postwar parents had to work out how to handle them. The sexual revolution and the drug scene created particularly acute problems for parents of adolescents in the 1960s, but relationships seem to have improved since that time, and there is less talk of 'rebellion', 'generation gap' and 'identity crisis'.

Cultural variations

We now turn to cultural variations in parent–child relations. One important difference is in the size of the household in which children are reared: for us it is typically one to two adults and two to three children, while in Third World countries it is at least twice as great, and families live in groups round courtyards, so there are more adults and more children all together. Some of these play an important role in child rearing, such as grandparents and sometimes the mother's brother. European and American mothers breastfeed less and begin weaning and toilet training earlier than in the Third World, while Western mothers spend a lot more time on the care of their infants, and are the main person looking after them.

A comparison was made of child rearing in England, Germany and the U.S.A. The English families differed from American and German families, in being:

higher on	*lower on*
physical punishment	nurture
nagging and scolding	protectiveness
indulgence (letting off lightly)	achievement demands
	discipline by explanation
	punishment by love withdrawal
	close surveillance
	giving jobs round the house

The English sample consisted of 713 children from the top forms of primary schools in Surrey, from both industrial and residential suburbs, and their families were studied in 1964. The English parents treated boys and girls more differently than either the German or American parents.[48]

There are great variations in the way aggression is handled during childhood. It has been found that American parents are less restrictive than parents in Third World countries. Very little aggression is permitted by children among peasant communities or those living in crowded courtyards, but with urbanisation, aggression is encouraged more, as has happened in the Lebanon. Aggression is also encouraged in those tribes that are constantly at war with their neighbours and need a supply of aggressive young men.[49]

Achievement motivation has been shown by McClelland to be one of the factors behind economic growth, and in turn to be produced by certain parent–child relations. Studies in a number of cultures have shown that subsequent achievement motivation is greatest if there is training for independence at around the age of eight, rather than earlier or later, and if fathers are not too powerful or authoritarian. This pattern of child rearing, in turn, occurs more often under Protestantism; hence its link with capitalism.[50]

A number of studies have compared parent–child relations under different social and economic conditions. In agricultural communities which store food and keep animals, more pressures are placed on the children to be obedient and responsible – this kind of behaviour is needed for effective co-operation in the farm work. In primitive societies which require strength, for example for hunting large animals, the boys and girls are reared rather differently.[51] In most primitive communities, the children are treated like small adults; they do not play, but learn adult roles when quite young, mainly by imitation.

Parental skills and rules

To begin with, there are legal rules, giving rights as well as duties, governing the relations between parents and children. They can be summarised as follows:[52]

1. The right to decide where and with whom the child shall live and associate,
2. The right to determine education, and the duty to educate,

3. The right to chastise reasonably,
4. The right and duty to protect and maintain the child,
5. The right to manage the child's property (though, probably, not the right to make a claim to the services of the child),
6. The right to apply for a passport for the child,
7. The right to consent or refuse consent to medical treatment for the child,
8. The right to give or refuse consent to adoption,
9. The right to give or refuse consent to the marriage of a child of between sixteen and eighteen years,
10. The right to conduct or defend litigation on the child's behalf,
11. The right to succeed to the child's property on his death intestate.

We have seen that there have been fluctuating fashions in parent behaviour in the history of our own country, some variations with social class, and rather greater differences between cultures. The more recent changes in parental skills have been stimulated by psychological research; and as this body of knowledge expands, the better the guidance that can be offered to parents. It is now possible to indicate the acceptable limits of parental behaviour, outside which the children are likely to suffer now or in the future. Inside those limits it is also possible to say what effects different styles of child rearing will have on the personality of the child.

The most important dimension along which parents are found to vary is that of *acceptance–rejection*. Accepting parents love their children, spend a lot of time with them, their interaction with the children is warm and rewarding, rather than critical or hostile, and they have a high opinion of the children. There is a definite lower limit here: if parents reject their children, the children are *more* likely to be:

delinquent
aggressive
neurotic
schizophrenic

They are *less* likely to develop:

friendly, socially skilled behaviour
a conscience, concern for others
cooperative behaviour

These effects are strong; for example the Gluecks[53] found that 60% of a large sample of delinquents had been rejected by their fathers, as compared with 19% in a non-delinquent control group. It is now recognised that such effects are partly because parents reject children who have become delinquent. However, a review of studies on the causes of delinquency found that parental management techniques, such as supervision and discipline, were the main predictors of delinquency, followed by the child's conduct problems, parental and family criminality, and poor academic performance by the child.[54]

There may be an upper limit too: if the relationship is too close or overprotective the child may have difficulty becoming independent during adolescence, may develop too strong a conscience, with anxiety and guilt feelings, and if too close to the opposite-sex parent, become homosexual.

Parents are also responsible for controlling their children, so that they are not a danger to themselves or a nuisance to others, and for training them in the rules of behaviour shared in their community. We have seen that *permissiveness v. strictness* is one of the main dimensions along which fashions have shifted backwards and forwards. We can indicate the limits here: if parents are too permissive, the children will be a nuisance in the home and outside, and will grow up wild and uncontrollable. If parents are too strict, the children are more likely to be badly behaved outside the home, hostile, rebellious and delinquent. It has come to be accepted that there is no need to make so much fuss as previous generations did about thumb-sucking and playing with the genitals.

More important perhaps are the skills that are most effective in controlling children, and in teaching and internalising the rules of society. Studies have been carried out examining the success of different parental skills in producing internalisation of the rules of society, as evidenced by strength of guilt feelings, resistance to temptation, and confession and acceptance of blame after transgression. The child-rearing techniques that are most successful are:

affection
verbal explanation and appeals pointing out consequences for others.

The child-rearing techniques that are *not* successful are:

physical punishment, deprivation and threat
love-withdrawal, ignoring, rejecting or isolating the child.[55]

Parental behaviour varies along other dimensions besides the two discussed here, for example in stimulating different degrees of creativity or achievement motivation. However no other dimensions affect the relationships with children so profoundly, or provide such clear evidence of the existence of rules.

We turn now to the parental skills needed for dealing with adolescents. We have seen that this is a period many parents and many children find difficult. The secret lies in continuing those skills that were successful for younger children – warmth, control, and reasonable explanation. The parent now has less power; the child, more; and it is necessary for the child to participate more in decisions concerning him or her. It has been found that parents attempt only moderate levels of control with adolescent children, with mothers somewhat more controlling than fathers. The most frequent type of control is giving a command together with a reason, then unqualified commands, and then persuasion, although behavioural compliance by children is not especially great. Children complied more with high or moderate control, but in the case of mothers, moderate attempts were the most successful and high levels of control the *least* successful.[56] Research carried out by Elder[57] and others has compared the effects of different parental styles during this period.

1. Democratic supervision is most successful. Here the adolescent contributes freely to discussion of matters relevant to him, and may make his own decisions. However the final decision has to be approved by his or her parents. This style is better than permissive, egalitarian, or authoritarian styles, in that it is seen as more fair, less rejecting, and results in greater independence and confidence for the child. The main points of disagreement are often such things as hair styles and time of coming home. Parents need to set limits, but to bear in mind that things might have changed since they were young.

TABLE 7. Effects of Different Parental Skills on Adolescents [58]

		Autocratic	Democratic	Permissive
Parental behaviour seen as	*mother*	55	86	80
good and reasonable	*father*	51	85	75
Felt unwanted	*mother*	42	11	11
	father	40	8	11
Confident and independent				
Frequent explanations		29	45	50
Infrequent explanations		30	32	33

TABLE 8. Rules for Parents and Adolescent Children

Rules for Parents

1. Respect the child's privacy.
2. Give guidance to the child and an example.
3. Show affection for the child.
4. Encourage the child's ideas.
5. Respect the child's own views.
6. Show emotional support.
7. Don't engage in sexual activity with the child.
8. Keep confidences.
9. Don't be overly possessive.
10. Treat the child as a responsible adult.
11. Share news of success.
12. Look the child in the eye during conversation.
13. Address the child by first name.
14. Give birthday cards and presents.
15. Stand up for the child in his/her absence.
16. Talk to the child about sex and death.
17. Talk to the child about religion and politics.
18. Be responsible for rules of respectable behaviour.
19. Seek to repay debts, favours and compliments.
20. Don't be critical of the child's choice of friends.

Rules for Adolescents

1. Respect the parent's privacy.
2. Keep confidences.
3. Don't engage in sexual activity with the other.
4. Share news of success with the other.
5. Be considerate of parent's rights, e.g. noise level, use of telephone and TV.
6. Be polite to parents, particularly in company.
7. Stand up for the other in their absence.
8. Give birthday cards and presents.
9. Look the other in the eye during conversation.
10. Talk about sex and death with parents.
11. Bring friends home.
12. Talk about religion and politics with parents.
13. Ask for personal advice.
14. Repay debts, favours and compliments.
15. Inform parents of personal schedules.
16. Respect parent's values even if old-fashioned.
17. Don't criticise parents in public.
18. Confide in parents.
19. Disclose personal problems and feelings to parents.
20. Accept parental direction in general.

2. Warm, rewarding, parental behaviour again has a variety of favourable consequences, including the better achievement of an independent identity, self-confidence, and self-esteem.

3. Explaining the reasons for rules and for parental expectations, has similar effects.

Comparisons of the behaviour of the families of normal as compared with disturbed adolescents in laboratory discussions shows that they differ in a number of other respects. In the families of normals there were more jokes and laughter, more co-operation, more information-sharing, and more agreement, though they could also disagree in a friendly way.[59]

In our own study of rules, the twenty most strongly endorsed rules for parents of adolescents, and for the adolescent children, are shown in Table 8.

FURTHER READING

Pilling, D. & Pringle, M. (1978) *Controversial Issues in Child Development* London: Elek

Rapoport, R., Rapoport, R. N., Strelitz, Z. & Kew, S. (1977) *Fathers, Mothers and Others* London: Routledge & Kegan Paul

9

Kinship

Relatives are a perishing nuisance. The more I have to do with
relations the better I like my dog. I don't have anything to do with
them. They're no use to me, except Alice.[1]

In primitive and developing countries like Africa, India and the
Middle East, kinship is extremely important. It is the main form of
social organisation, and gives everyone a place in society. In Western
countries kinship is much less prominent, but nevertheless many
kinship links are kept up. By kinship we mean relationships with
blood relatives and in-laws outside the nuclear family, consisting of
parents and children before they have left home. People feel closest to
kin, in the following order:

parents and adult children
brothers and sisters (siblings)
grandparents
aunts and uncles
cousins
in-laws

Most people have living kin. Among those over sixty-five, about
80% have children, 80% have siblings, 75% have grandchildren, and
4% have living parents, while only 50% of women of sixty-five have
husbands.[2] Quite a number of adults live with kin, while over 90% of
the rest see some kin at least monthly.

A survey in Toronto found that 50% of the strongest ties outside the
home were to kin.[3] We shall see that the first two kin relationships on
the list above – between parents and adult children, and between
siblings, are kept up most strongly, and that kin are very useful in old
age.

We shall make some use of earlier studies, such as that of Shanas,
Townsend *et al.*,[4] of 2,500 people over sixty-five in Britain, and that of

Firth *et al.*[5] on middle-class families in London, and a number of large-scale American studies, such as those carried out by Adams[6] in Greensborough, North Carolina, and Hill *et al.*[7] on three generations of families in Minneapolis.

Living with or near kin

In primitive societies there are definite rules about living near the husband's family, or less commonly near the wife's. In our society there are no rules of residence quite as explicit as that. It is assumed that children will leave home when they reach the age of eighteen or so, and most of them do, often moving away to another town. Figure 1 shows that many people over sixty-five live with kin, while many of the widowed and divorced live with their children – either a married daughter or an unmarried child. Those who have never married often live with a sibling.

Fig. 1   PERCENTAGE OF PEOPLE OVER 65 LIVING WITH KIN (UK)

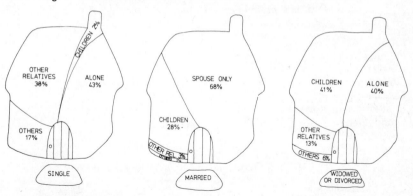

When the parents become older they want to be near their children, though preferably in their own home. When widowed, divorced, or infirm, fathers in particular are likely to move in with one of the children, usually a married daughter. The reason is probably that while it is reasonable to ask a daughter to perform intimate help, this could be more difficult for a daughter-in-law. While there is no rule about living near a parental home, in fact most people do live in the same part of the country as their parents and other kin, e.g. London, N.W. Scotland. If the husband's and wife's families are in different parts there is quite a strong preference for living near the wife's people. The parent–daughter link proves stronger than the parent – son link.[9] There is a trend for more middle-aged women to share a household with an older relative the older they themselves are. In an American study[10] 16.6% of 55 to 59-year-olds were living with an older relative, compared to 5.5% of women between the ages of 40 to 44 years. Most old people who are living in institutions are those who have never married or are widowed and have no children.

Most of those who do not live with one of their kin live quite close by. In the same study cited in Figure 1, 27% of married people lived within ten minutes of their nearest child, 46% within thirty minutes' travel time.[11]

Frequency of contact

Frequency of contact with different kin is shown in Table 1, which is based on a number of large-scale American surveys.

TABLE 1. Frequency of Contact with Kin (U.S.A.) [12]

	weekly	monthly	
Parents	45	94	
Children	70	—	[10]
Siblings	20	54	
Cousins	5	20	[11]
(best-known cousins)		27	
Grandparents	10	50	[12]

TABLE 2. Frequency of Contact with Parents [13]

| | Feel close to parents | |
	to both	to neither
At least once a week	26%	7%
2–3 times per month	54%	26%
Less than once a month	20%	67%

| | Share values with parents | |
	with both	with neither
At least once a week	30%	7%
2–3 times per month	54%	19%
Less than once a month	16%	74%

It can be seen that contact between parents and adult children is the most frequent. It is particularly high if they feel close and share similar values (Table 2).

The British survey of over-65s found that 69% of them had seen a child 'today' or 'yesterday', and another 17% in the previous week. Frequency of contact is also affected by distance: the further apart kin live, the less often they meet. However the effect of distance is much less on the closer relationships of parent–child and between siblings, than for other kin. In Britain kin see each other a great deal if they live really close (under three miles), but less if they are much further apart than this. Contact is often maintained by female kin rather than men, and women have been described as 'kinkeepers', in charge of maintaining contact with both their own and in-law relations.[14]

Similar results are obtained for siblings. About 95% of them keep in touch with each other; the frequency of contact falls off quite rapidly with distance, rather more so than for parents. In an American study, for siblings who lived over 250 miles away, 60% met once a year or less.[15] Contact between siblings is partly dependent on contact with the parents, since siblings often meet at the parental home; they usually meet less after the parents have died.

Many families in Britain take joint holidays. Young families may stay with relatives for economic reasons, or look after the children while their parents go on holiday; the children are sent for a holiday with kin, or groups simply share holiday accommodation. While much of this is to save money, it must also reflect positive links between those concerned.

Family gatherings Kin gather together on social occasions, when it is felt necessary to invite them and they feel a duty to come. Weddings and christenings require some kin to play special roles – to give the bride away, as bridesmaids, godparents, and witnesses. A large proportion of the family turn up, especially to weddings, where the parents of the couple being married rarely fail to attend. Kin also come to funerals, which often turn into cheerful family parties; those attending provide social support for those bereaved, but also gain a sense of family solidarity. Birthdays, especially eighteenth and twenty-first birthdays, and silver and other wedding anniversaries, celebrations of achievements and the arrival from or departure abroad, are other occasions for family gatherings. These may also happen at Christmas, or other religious festivals, or holidays.

Christmas in particular is widely recognised as a family occasion, and gifts are exchanged (see Figure 2). The main Christmas guests are again parents and siblings. And the gatherings typically take place at the home of grandparents; it is their daughters and their families who are most likely to come.

These family occasions are of great interest. There seems to be an obligation to come and presumably to enter into the spirit of the occasion, but there are usually no actual duties to perform, apart from some of the jobs at weddings and christenings. Simply being there is what is required. Perhaps this indicates social support for the network of kin. Perhaps those attending also gain a feeling of belonging and support. We shall see later how valuable that support can be.

Kinship networks   Kinship is more than a number of pair bondings between individuals. If A is linked to B, C and D, the latter are often also linked, and this affects A's relationship with them. The kind of linkage often used here is 'knowing and interacting with', though it may also be useful to assess more intimate linkages than this. Much research has focused on the effect of networks on married couples. It is found that if they belong to segregated male and female networks they are more likely to have traditional marital roles (see p. 127). And the more a married couple, or indeed any two people, are both linked to the same individuals in the network, the less easily broken is their relationship. Also they will be more dependent on, and constrained by, the network group. When A and B are both linked to C, A and B depend on each other for keeping up their links with C, so each is dependent on the other.

The obligation to help kin

Many studies have shown that people are willing to provide major help for kin, but would be less willing to ask for, or to provide, similar help from friends or neighbours. People feel a sense of obligation to help their kin, especially their own children and aged parents. There appears to be a set of widely shared rules – that one should help kin when help is needed, especially in close relationships, and that contributions should be shared out, for example between children for an aged parent. These rules lead to strong feelings of moral responsibility.[16]

Much of this help is domestic, and mainly carried out by women –

such as helping with the family when the wife is ill or having a baby, or domestic help with elderly parents. A survey[17] found that time spent by middle-aged daughters in helping their elderly mothers averaged 8.6 hours per week. If the daughters and mothers shared a household, they gave eight times more help than if they lived apart (28.5 and 3.5 hours per week respectively). Married women averaged 6 hours compared to 19 for widowed, divorced or single daughters, and working women spent half as much time as non-employed daughters (6 versus 12 hours). The sorts of help provided are shown in Table 3.

TABLE 3. Percentage of Middle-Aged Daughters Providing Help to Their Elderly Mothers [18]

Type of Help		Percentage
Instrumental services:	Food shopping	34.2
	Travel	28.0
	Laundry	23.0
	Meal preparation	20.5
	Housework	19.9
Personal care services:	Bathing	10.6
	Taking medication	8.7
	Dressing	5.0
	Getting around the house	3.7
Confidant		60.9

Some help consists of money or goods, especially in the case of working-class families who may have periods of economic hardship. The amounts of help found in a study of 100 families in three generations during different kinds of crisis is shown in Table 4.

The table shows a high level of help between parents and married children in both directions, though parents give more in three

TABLE 4. Help Given and Received by Kin (U.S.A.)[19]

		Parents	Married children	Grandparents
Economic	given	41	34	26
	received	17	49	34
Household	given	47	33	21
management	received	23	25	52
Child care	given	50	34	16
	received	23	78	0
Illness	given	21	47	32
	received	21	18	61

spheres. Even grandparents give a lot, though they receive more than they give. How much people provide help depends on their financial and physical capacity to provide it, and on the state of need of the other. When the parents are of higher social status than their sons (and therefore presumably more prosperous) they give their sons more than they get in return, and vice versa.

Siblings sometimes help one another too, though the amount of help is less than that between parents and children. There is not the strong obligation to provide help that there is for parents and children, though help is greater between those pairs of siblings who form a close relationship. Sometimes brothers are involved in family businesses together, and here the kinship bond is felt to be very important. However, in these cases they often keep their social lives apart, and feel a need to do so.

Most Christmas presents are given to close kin. Caplow (see Figure 2) carried out a study of several thousand Christmas presents in 'Middletown' U.S.A., and found that nearly all presents other than 'token' ones (under 5 dollars) were to kin; children under eighteen received seven times as many as they gave, and three times as many presents were given to younger people than older; females gave 84% of all presents, but men gave most of the large ones; in-laws were treated the same as their spouses, and presents were put on display. Some of the results are shown in Figure 2.

Fig. 2 CHRISTMAS PRESENTS AND KIN (USA)[20]

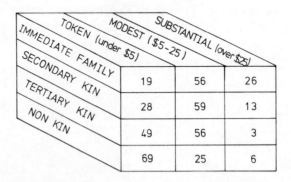

	TOKEN (under $5)	MODEST ($5–25)	SUBSTANTIAL (over $25)
IMMEDIATE FAMILY	19	56	26
SECONDARY KIN	28	59	13
TERTIARY KIN	49	56	3
NON KIN	69	25	6

In Britain, in middle-class families, a common form of financial help is to contribute to the cost of school fees. Public school fees are very high for young parents to pay, and the grandparents may help. They may see this as an investment in the future of a child, they may want him or her to go to the school one of them went to, or they may want to pay for a school with a religious connection, e.g. Jewish or Catholic. This means that the grandparents have an influence over the child's education. More generally kin are often interested in, and consulted about, educational matters.[21] This happens in other cultures too; in Africa, for example, relatives will contribute to the costs of sending a member of the family to be educated abroad.

Kin also take an interest in, and may provide help in, choosing a career and finding a job, or coming to terms with not having one. The most direct example of this is a family business in which a member of the family is given a job, or even becomes a partner. In other cases parents or other kin know about a certain career and can provide information on how to get into it, introductions, or information about vacancies. Kin may simply influence a young member of the family by encouraging him in a particular direction. The study in London found that about 25% of children were influenced by kin in choosing a career.

All this help from parents might be experienced as meddling, or keeping children dependent. In fact the more such help is received the greater the marital satisfaction, and the greater the expected number of children – perhaps reflecting an increasing feeling of security.

There is also an obligation simply to visit relatives, to 'keep in touch'. What actually happens consists in part of keeping up with the family news, but also of providing social support, acting as a confidant. In working-class families in particular the husband is often an unsatisfactory person for the wife to discuss her troubles with; this has been found in Britain, the U.S.A., and Japan. As a result wives turn to friends and kin; in the case of working-class wives it is likely to be kin, typically her mother or a sister.

Does help have to be reciprocated, as exchange theory would lead us to expect? Between siblings it is reciprocated, partly because they face similar problems during the same period. Parents help children when they are young much more than vice versa; later there is a lot of two-way traffic. When the parents become old the direction of help is reversed, though grandparents often make themselves useful, for example by baby-sitting. Overall however, the parents do more for their children, and also eventually pass on their property if they have any. But they know that the children in turn will do the same for their children, who share 25% of grandparental genes and carry on the family group, thus guaranteeing immortality either through the genes or through social influence.

On the other hand kin keep a sharp eye on the help being provided by other kin, for example in the case of siblings looking after elderly parents. There is often a sense of grievance that the others are not doing enough, or are not doing enough in relation to their resources. So the sense of obligation towards kin is relative to the contribution of others, as well as to possible exchanges of rewards with the recipient.

We showed earlier that social support of different kinds, including close contacts with kin, led to longer life (p. 18). Frequent social interaction with kin is associated with good health and mental health, and with happiness. This is presumably a product of the various kinds of help and social support discussed above. On the other hand the effects of social support from kin are much weaker than the effects of a satisfactory marriage. The two groups most benefiting from kin are working-class wives (whose husbands fail to act as confidants), and the widowed, who need the company of their children or siblings.

Relatives can also be unsupportive, as the example on p. 214 illustrated.

Inheritance

In earlier periods of human society inheritance played a very important role in life. Typically the eldest son became the new head of the family and controlled the family lands. In our own society property is usually divided equally among the children.

A study of middle-class families in London found that one-third of them had inherited money or houses from parents, usually fairly modest amounts, and two-thirds had inherited furniture or other family possessions. Keeping up the family house or 'estates' happens mainly among farmers nowadays. The same study found that family disputes about unfair wills occurred in about one-fifth of families, because it is sometimes very difficult to decide what is fair.[22]

Class, sex and age

The effects of social class We have noted some of the variations of kinship with social class already. Working-class people, in Britain and elsewhere, are less geographically mobile and live quite close to their kin, and are part of a well-connected network of kin. Relationships between mothers and daughters and between sisters are particularly close, and these pairs of kin may see each other every day, or several times a week. Working-class young people are likely to marry someone from the same neighbourhood, and to settle down in it. Middle-class couples are more likely to marry outside the neighbourhood, as a result of meeting at college or at work, and to settle down at a distance from the parental homes. In the studies of families in London it was found that more of the married children in Bethnal Green lived with or very near their parents than those in predominantly middle-class Woodford.[23]

TABLE 5. Proximity of Nearest Married Child to People Below and Above Pension Age, in Woodford and Bethnal Green (people with at least one married child)[24]

	Woodford		Bethnal Green	
	People below pension age	People above pension age	People below pension age	People above pension age
Same dwelling	10%	23%	24%	21%
Within five minutes	6%	17%	23%	32%
Elsewhere in same borough	21%	22%	10%	8%
Outside borough	63%	38%	43%	39%
Number	119	109	146	131

Working-class husbands and wives spend much of their time in same-sex groupings – the wife with her mother and sisters, the husband with his workmates, or friends at club or pub. An American study showed this very clearly (see Table 6).

TABLE 6. Confidants of Working-Class Men and Women [25]

	Husbands	Wives
none	10	4
spouse	63	26
kin	16	69
pub, etc.	10	0

Other studies have shown that the closest confidants of working-class wives are mainly kin. The reason that working-class men are poor confidants is partly that working-class marriages are less close, more role segregated, and partly perhaps because these husbands lack the necessary skills for acting in the confidant role – which may be regarded as a rather feminine skill.

We also saw above that in middle-class families there is more transmission of wealth by inheritance, and that middle-class grand-parents sometimes pay school fees.

We turn now to class differences *within* the family. One feature of the small nuclear family is that it can rise or fall as a unit in the class system. Sometimes one member does better or worse in the occupa-tional system than another member; what effect does this have? The general result is that it leads to strains within the family, and reduced interaction between those concerned. We have discussed husband – wife strains of this kind elsewhere (p. 133). When children do better than their father, there is some pride in their accomplishment, combined with a reduced level of contact. The mother–daughter relation is affected least, the father–son relation most. In a study in London of middle-class adults, mobile daughters saw nearly as much of their mothers as socially stable daughters, but socially mobile sons saw much less of their fathers.[26] Mothers and daughters are still playing similar roles whether they are mobile or not, while mobile sons are doing quite different jobs from their fathers. Studies in the East End of London found that working-class families felt less happy than middle-class families about daughters who had gone up in the world.

When children are downwardly mobile, however, there is a feeling of disappointment on both sides. For the London middle-class families the frequencies of seeing their families in the last week were:

downwardly mobile	41%
upwardly mobile	60%
non-mobile	70%

When one sibling is upwardly mobile this has more effect on sibling contact than it has on parent–child relations. In an American study frequency of meeting outside the home fell by 42%. However the effect is most marked for two brothers, least for two sisters: 59% of the brothers felt less close, in cases of different mobility, compared with 23% for sisters, while 61% of sisters where one had been mobile felt *more* close than earlier.[27] The explanations for these strains is that siblings naturally compare themselves with one another, since they have very similar chances in life. Again, the closeness of the bonds between female kin enables them to withstand these strains.

Sex differences Women are more involved in most aspects of kinship than men. They play a major role in rearing children, and as a result have closer ties with them. In particular they form closer links with their daughters; in one study 62% of married women felt close, or very close, to their mothers, only 34% to their fathers. Daughters are socialised to be dependent and obedient more than boys (p. 195f). In addition most women have the common experiences and interests of child rearing and domestic work, whereas men usually have different jobs. When daughters are grown up a special bond is created by their children, and maternal help with housekeeping and child-minding is very useful. Except on farms and similar enterprises, sons are not able to help their fathers in the same way. Females are more active in giving Christmas presents, writing letters, and generally keeping in contact with kin – though it remains to be seen how far these female roles are changing. There can also be links in the male line where sons, and sometimes grandsons, are all doctors, or share some other occupation, take on the family house, business, or farm, and have a similar life-style.

We have seen already that sisters form close relationships and help each other a good deal. And we have seen that wives are better confidants than are husbands, and that working-class wives in particular turn to female kin for this purpose. Working-class women make fewer friends though they see more of their neighbours, so that their close social contacts are more based on kin than is the case for middle-class women. The links between women, such as mother–daughter and sister–sister, are so strong that the family has been described as a 'female trades union'.

Sometimes a male is regarded as 'the head of the family', though this role may carry few duties. And male kin are likely to make the decisions about giving money and are the ones who can help their relatives to get jobs.

The effects of age Concern with kin varies greatly with stage in the life-cycle. The years of least interest are twenty to thirty; in one study 59% of single people of this age included no kin in their six closest relationships. However concern with kin increases rapidly with age after this period.

Kinship takes different forms at different points in the life cycle. In

Chapter 8 we discussed parent–child relations as far as adolescence. In this chapter we mentioned that parents do quite a lot for their children when the grandchildren appear – helping with baby-sitting and domestic jobs and helping financially. The children are an obstacle to friendships, but they are a focus of interaction between kin – because kin are always very interested in the development of the new members of their family. When the original parents retire, and become disengaged from other social institutions, and when their friends die off, they become increasingly dependent on their kin. When they are widowed they are likely to live with one of their children, usually a daughter, to live near their children and see them frequently (Figure 1).

Finally, when the parents have died, the links between their children become weaker, and a new head of the family takes over.

The relationships between parents and adult children

This is a bond which is kept up, over many years in nearly all cases. Parents and their adult children keep in touch despite geographical separation, social mobility or the passage of time, despite disagreements over basic values. American surveys have found no decline at all in frequency of these contacts over time.[28] The main form of contact consists of home visits; these are different from social life with friends, in that the main purpose is finding out about each other's well-being and general news, and expressing positive concern. Large areas of life are excluded, and the talk is not necessarily very intimate. Those who live at a greater distance keep in touch by telephone and letter. There is more tangible help than in any other relationship apart from marriage, and there are family gatherings at Christmas and other times.

There is a strong tendency for relations to be closer with mothers than with fathers. The mother–daughter link is especially strong in the working class, and mothers here are more like friends, and are closely involved in their daughters' domestic and social lives. Daughters typically describe their relationships with their mothers as rewarding, especially if they are married and childless.[29]

Parents and their grown-up children usually feel affection for each other, and enjoy each other's company. They also feel an obligation to help one another. The amounts of each component were found in an American study (Table 7).

TABLE 7. Enjoyment and Obligation in Relations With Parents [30]

	Enjoyment only	Obligation only	Both
close to both parents	46	3	50
close to neither	12	38	24

The feeling of obligation is stronger when a parent is widowed. And these feelings of obligation are stronger for working-class people – who are more often in need of help.

In our study of sources of satisfaction in relationships we found that parents were seen as a major source of instrumental help, and rather less a source of emotional satisfaction (p. 83). Strong feelings are involved, most but not all of them positive, especially of parents towards children. Children come to have a sense of duty and positive concern towards their parents. However, more children stay in touch because they enjoy it than for a sense of duty.

The basis of parental concern for their children is not difficult to explain. One theory is the 'selfish gene' doctrine: that we are motivated to promote the welfare of our own genes and of those who carry them. Our own children share 50% of our genes, and parents are directly responsible for looking after them. In addition the early years in the family develop great intimacy and bodily closeness, and may have effects rather like conditioning or 'imprinting' in animals – a permanent attachment is formed with the other. The concern of children for their parents could not be accounted for by selfish genes. The shared intimacy may have created the bond for them too, and a real concern for, and perhaps empathy with, their parents, with widespread social expectations that obligations to parents shall be met.

It looks as if there are important social rules governing this relationship – one should keep in touch, show positive concern, and be prepared to provide tangible help.

The relationship between siblings

This is one of the strongest kinship bonds, second only to the parent–child link. It is part of a network, in that siblings often meet at the parental home, and are linked to other siblings. Most siblings see one another regularly, and feel close to each other; this varies from intense loyalty and very frequent contact, to losing touch in a minority of cases. Overall the frequency of contact does not fall off with time, though for some individuals it does, for example as a result of moving house.[31] There is some evidence for a U-shaped trend, with lower frequencies of meeting during middle adulthood. It is a very long-lasting relationship, for most people the most long-lasting. In old age about a third of unmarried people live with a sibling.

The range of activities with siblings is quite different from those with friends, who are liked to about the same degree. As with other kin, the main activities are visiting, chatting, and keeping up with the family news, turning up at Christmas and other family gatherings, and providing help, though less than is given to parents.

Clarke and Allen[32] have found that a special pattern of emotions was associated with siblings for females, as shown in Table 8. There is

TABLE 8. Emotional Reactions to Siblings on a Scale of 1 to 7[33]

	siblings	friends	husband	workmate
warm	5.6	5.5	6.5	3.7
responsible for other	4.3	3.4	5.4	2.6
rivalry	4.2	2.5	2.3	3.8

TABLE 9. Rules for Brother or Sister of Similar Age

1. Address him/her by first name.
2. Respect his/her privacy.
3. Show emotional support.
4. Be supportive in matters outside the family.
5. Be willing to advise the other.
6. Give birthday cards and presents.
7. Don't be jealous of the other.
8. Be willing to listen to the other's advice.
9. Keep confidences.
10. Should not interfere in the other's social relationships.
11. Share news of success.
12. Stand up for the other in their absence.
13. Don't be over-protective.
14. Treat the other as a friend.
15. Look him/her in the eye during conversation.
16. Help him/her get on with your own friends.
17. Don't criticise him/her in public.
18. Ask for personal advice.

a high level of warmth, together with feelings of responsibility and rivalry.

There are certain rules and obligations for siblings. There is some obligation to help if needed, but a greater obligation to keep in touch. The rules we have found to be most strongly endorsed are as in Table 9.

What is the nature of attachment between siblings? In our study of the sources of satisfaction (p. 83), we found that siblings scored fairly high on instrumental help (but lower than parents or spouses) and high on emotional support. But what explains the very long-lasting attachment here? Again the 'selfish gene' theory may apply, though siblings do not have the responsibility for each other that parents have for their children. For infants, the older siblings are the main people to whom they become attached, apart from the parents. There is a strong feeling of shared identity, which has a realistic basis in shared name, family and physical characteristics, and there is a long period of great intimacy, often involving shared bedroom, or even bed. In later life most adults feel that they have always been close to their siblings, and there is a strong sense of family unity and sibling solidarity. Siblings feel particularly close if they are near in age, when there was an emphasis on family unity, if they shared a bedroom or walked to school together. In later life closeness is maintained by shared reminiscences.[34]

There are common sources of friction between siblings. Jealousy and envy of a newly born sibling by young children is common, and particularly difficult in families where the mother has a close and harmonious relationship with a daughter before the newborn sibling arrives.[35] During childhood there is a lot of rivalry, and during later years it is hard to avoid comparing success against that of the others. In one study 71% of adult subjects had rivalrous feelings towards their siblings. The most common cause was parents preferring one sibling over another, treating them unfairly or making comparisons between them (57%), or another sibling vying for parental recognition and love (56%). Sibling rivalry is based on comparisons along particular dimensions, especially:[36]

achievement and success	27%
physical attractiveness	17%
intelligence	16%
interpersonal competence	11%
maturity	9%

There is always much interest in how well the others are doing. This is particularly so with brothers, and we have seen that they interact much less if they have different degrees of occupational success. Another source of friction, as we have seen, is grievance that other siblings are not doing their share of looking after elderly parents, and sometimes there is discord over the division of property in wills.

Siblings sometimes identify with and model themselves on each other, but more commonly they do not. Often they say that they feel 'different' rather than 'alike', and this has been interpreted as 'de-identification'. It is common in two-child families, and for the first two of three-child families, but not between the first and third of three-child families. It is based partly on identification with different parents – if the first identifies with mother, the second often identifies with father.[37]

Birth order is often important, not only in how the siblings relate to each other, but also how they relate to other people. There is some evidence that men and women with older brothers or sisters are more socially skilled than first borns. For example, they have more rewarding interactions with strangers of the opposite sex in experimental studies.[38]

Of the three possible sibling links, we have seen that the bond between sisters is by far the strongest, that between brothers usually the weakest. Sisters, when adult, still have a great deal in common, and play similar roles even if they belong to different social classes, whereas this is not true of brothers. Quite often one sibling is preferred by all the others. Often the nearest-age sibling of the same sex is liked best. If two siblings remain single, they may live together, and will see each other much more frequently than married siblings. Married siblings who have no children are also likely to see each other regularly.

Grandparents

Not all young people have grandparents, but when they do this is often the closest relationship outside the immediate family. About 68% of those over sixty-five have grandchildren. There is more contact with grandparents than with cousins, because the parents keep in closer touch with *their* parents while they are alive. The grandparents' home is the setting for family gatherings and rituals, and the grandparents are the head of the family. The grandmother is particularly important, especially in relation to her daughters and their families. She comes to the rescue in times of crisis, adult children in trouble can stay with her, or have children accommodated there, and grandma can mediate in disputes. The parents form a bridge between the children and the grandparents, and it is especially the mother who maintains this bridge. Grandparents are often quite close to their grandchildren, as if there was no generation gap. This is because grandparents have no disciplinary responsibility, and can simply enjoy the company of the young. They may take the children's side in conflict with the parents. As we have seen they may help grandchildren financially, by paying school fees, or via inheritance.

The concept of grandparenthood means a number of different things to grandparents.[39] It is often central to their lives, in the same way that the concept of parenthood is to parents. There is the satisfaction derived from passing on traditions and being respected in that role, and of 'clan immortality' or the feeling of biological continuity in grandchildren. There is often a reinvolvement with the past in reliving one's earlier life and identifying with one's own grandparents. There is also an attitude of indulgence and leniency towards grandchildren.

On the other hand, the position of 'valued grandparent' is an earned one, and is not given automatically. And there are wide variations in the nature of this relationship. While most grandparents find this a satisfying role, and take it in a 'fun-seeking' or 'formal and proper' manner, a quarter are 'distant figures', and a third find it difficult, mainly because of disagreements over upbringing. Grandmothers are more successful in establishing a good relationship with grand-daughters than grandfathers with grandsons – because of the greater continuity of female roles and interests. The main sources of satisfaction for grandparents are a feeling of biological continuity, and of emotional self-fulfilment.[40] On the other hand, there appears to be little or no connection between grandchildren and life satisfaction – friends are more important.[41] It is likely that there is such a link for a minority of grandparents, those who have succeeded in establishing a close relationship with the grandchildren; this may take the place of other attachments, and add to overall satisfaction with life.

Cousins, uncles, nephews, etc.

Frequency of contact with cousins and the others is much less than for primary kin – typically once a month if they live in the same neighbourhood or small town, yearly or less if they are further afield. There seems to be no obligation to keep in touch by phone or letter, as there is for parents and siblings. Social contacts are usually not deliberately sought, but occur through reunions of the parents, who are of course siblings, especially for working-class people, since they live nearer.

Often people have quite a number of cousins, of whom one or two are liked more than the rest. The best-liked cousin is very likely to be of the same sex, to be related through the mother, and especially through her sister – because of the close links between sisters. The preferred cousin is usually one who lived near during childhood and was a childhood companion.[42] People feel closer to cousins if they have no siblings themselves, and to cousins in the same social class and who share the same values. Again females have closer links with their cousins. Again, working-class people have closer contacts with cousins, and choose same-sex cousins more.

Contacts with cousins and the rest are more voluntary than contacts between closer kin; they are a matter of personal preference and shared values, for example with 'favourite cousins', as with friends. Whether or not they see one another is much more affected by distance than is the case with primary kin. Cousins can, however, substitute for other kin, for example siblings, and are more important for the unmarried.[43]

There is little evidence of 'selfish gene' processes having much effect. On the other hand the finding that being a childhood companion creates a closer relationship suggests that the early intimacy may be relevant for siblings too.

In-laws

In-laws come at the intersection of the two closest relationships, marriage and parent–child, which in turn are completely different. In-laws are sometimes regarded as part of the family, sometimes not. This can be a good relationship, but often it is found to be a difficult one. The most difficult kind is that between a husband and his mother-in-law; the reason is plain – the marital bond is liable to conflict with the strongest parent–child one, between mother and daughter. Mothers-in-law in myth and joke are portrayed as old and bitter, and surveys find that they are quite often seen like that. The mother is liable to be possessive and jealous of her daughter, but the most frequent source of irritation between mother and daughter-in-law centres around the children/grandchildren.[44] And sons or daughters-in-law find that they can tolerate short visits but not longer ones. There is often uncertainty about how to address parents-in-law, and they may end up as 'you' or 'granny'. There is often a feeling of ambivalence about accepting help from in-laws, especially between mother and daughter-in-law, which may be interpreted as interference or meddling. Fischer[45] found that mothers-in-law are more likely to *give* things, and mothers to *do* things for married daughters. This is evidently a relationship which is difficult, and which needs special rules or skills to deal with it. However, daughters-in-law sometimes look after their husband's elderly parents if they have no daughter.[46]

In some primitive societies there are such rules – usually about not looking at, or not interacting with, in-laws. We have found that the following rules are agreed as providing a guide to this relationship.

TABLE 10. Rules for In-Laws: Both Parents and Children

1. Respect the other's privacy.
2. Keep confidences.
3. Don't engage in sexual activity.
4. Invite each other to family celebrations.
5. Don't criticise the other person in public.
6. Remember birthdays.
7. Repay debts, favours or compliments.
8. Stand up for the other in their absence.
9. Share news of success.
10. Show emotional support.
11. Look the other person in the eye during conversation.

Additional Rules for Parents-In-Law

1. Address the other by first name.
2. Respect bond between son or daughter-in-law and spouse.
3. Offer help and advice when asked for.
4. Avoid proximity in living arrangements.
5. Establish good relations with the other in-laws.
6. Don't interfere in domestic issues.

Additional Rules for Son/Daughter-In-Law

1. Make the in-laws welcome.
2. Visit regularly.
3. Remember birthdays, anniversaries, etc.
4. Help and support parents-in-law in their old age.
5. 'Buy the parent-in-law the occasional present.

The nature of kinship relations

The great majority of people keep in touch with adult children (or with parents). Most keep up regular contact with one or more siblings, fewer with grandparents, cousins or more distant kin. Women are more active in kinship than men are, and the links between women are strongest – mother–daughter and between sisters. Working-class people keep up kinship links more than middle-class people do, because working-class wives often have to find confidants other than their husbands. Frequency of contact falls off with geographical distance, but it falls off least for the closest relationships, especially parent–child.

Are there rules for behaviour towards kin? The clearest examples are the rules of who should not be married. These are highly functional: for example, the rule of marrying outside the clan has the effect of binding different family groups together. The rule of recognising descent through one parent creates large and strong kinship groups. Within our own society we found that there are two important rules for closer kin – to provide help when needed, and to keep in touch. There are rules about in-laws in some cultures, i.e. avoiding them, but our own society has failed to develop an effective way of dealing with this relationship. We have found a number of further rules, which people think should be followed in different kin relations.

What is the basis of kinship bonds? Mutual compatibility and the exchange of rewards are certainly factors, and lead to a preference for one sibling or cousin over another. On the other hand relations with parents are kept up in nearly all cases, and relations with close kin apparently last for ever, and so do not depend on regular rewards as friendship does. The 'selfish gene' theory could give an explanation of kinship bonds, but the data do not fit very well. More is done for children than for siblings, both of whom share 50% of the genes. Perhaps this is because we have a concern for those blood relations for whom we have been responsible in the past. A close relationship is formed with cousins if they have been childhood companions. This supports the idea that the intimacy of the nuclear family creates permanent bonds by some kind of conditioning or imprinting.

We can underline the nature of kinship by comparing it with friendship. Both are important to people, but they are experienced as

very different, and friends and kin are usually kept apart.
1. People often live with kin, or very close to them.
2. Kin are less voluntary, though there is some choice in keeping up with siblings, and more choice in the case of cousins. There is a feeling of obligation to keep up close relationships.
3. Kin relationships last longer, indeed for ever, while friendships can be quite short, and often end when one person moves.
4. Kin are a source of major help, whereas friends are not.
5. Quite different activities are shared – leisure, eating and drinking (with friends), chat, keeping in touch, and tangible help (with kin).

On the other hand there is some evidence that friends may become substitutes for kin, for example in the case of the 20% of people over sixty-five who have no close kin living. Sometimes one kind of relationship takes on some of the properties of another, as when someone says 'She's more like a sister than a friend'.

Figure 1 provides one example of substitution – the widowed and divorced often live with one of their children, while single people often live with a sibling. Old people who have no sibling are more likely to have seen a child in the past week (81%) than those who saw a sibling during the same period (62%). The widowed and divorced are more likely to have seen a child in the last two days (66%) than the married (41%). Cousins are seen more often if there are no siblings. It looks as if children, sibling and spouse contact are to some extent inter-changeable, and can substitute for each other.

The history and cultural variations of kinship

The earliest human societies were the hunters and gatherers, who lived a simple nomadic existence. They also had a very simple kinship system: children traced their descent equally from both parents; there was an incest taboo and a certain amount of polygamy; married couples did not live near either parent; there was little property to inherit, so there were few rules about that.

When settled agriculture had developed, and families owned land, herds and other property, kinship rules became more complicated. Descent was traced from one parent, usually the father. Married couples lived near the home of the parent, and inherited his property. This led to the development of large groups of kin, sharing the same male ancestors (or sometimes female). Marriage had to be to one or more women from another clan, but within the same tribe; the constant exchange of women held the different clans together. Often brides had to be paid for, by money or property, since they were seen as an investment to produce children. A cross-cultural comparison of 549 primitive societies found that families were more extended when families owned property, and when all members of the family helped with the work.[47]

In modern industrial society kinship has changed again. The main attachments are now within the nuclear family. It has been shown that the nuclear family fits the demands of industrial society better than the more extended families and clans of previous times: workers and their families are free to move to where the work is, successful individuals can rise in the system without being encumbered by numerous kin who want a share; similarly those who are not very good at the work do not have to be given the best jobs because of their family connections. The nuclear family gives close social support which helps to deal with work stress.[48] Comparisons of Italian and American families show that Italians have much more frequent contact with their kin. The Italians have not moved as far as the Americans towards the nuclear family.[49]

The nuclear family itself is monogamous, has fewer children, and may not live near the parents (except for certain ethnic groups). Despite the closeness of these families, they exercise less control than before over the choice of mate by their children. The main kin who are recognised outside the nuclear family are siblings, grown-up children and parents. All other kin are much less important.

The way in which these kinship systems have emerged can be explained in terms of their functions. They are examples of group problem-solving, over long periods of time. The simplest is the rule of descent from one parent, found in agricultural societies. The direct result is the formation of large, strong kinship groups who can band together for mutual protection and support. However this is usually combined with the rule of exogamy – marrying into other family groups – which has the effect of creating bonds, mainly female ones, between the different clans. In modern society we do not need the protection of large kinship groups, since other kinds of social organisation have grown up to take their place. Another example of the emergence of rules comes from those societies where descent is through the mother, and where couples usually live near the wife's family, like the Ashanti in Ghana and the Trobriand Islanders. The men still rule and control property. Inheritance is not to their own children, but to sisters' sons; this is because there is no doubt over who the mother is, though there may be doubt who the father is, so they can be sure that their inheritance is going to a blood relative. This happens particularly where there is much extra-marital intercourse. For similar reasons there is little concern over pre-marital intercourse – no one cares who the father is.[50]

Sibling relations also take different forms in some other cultures. A common pattern is for the older brothers and sisters rather than the mother to look after the younger children, as in Polynesian and African societies. In India and other parts of Asia it is the duty of brothers to provide dowries for their sisters, and to arrange suitable marriages. In many parts of the world the sibling group is very important and influential in managing family affairs, and they often continue to live close together.[51]

FURTHER READING

Allan, G. (1979) *A Sociology of Friendship and Kinship* London: Allen & Unwin

Blood, R. (1972) *The Family* London: Collier-Macmillan

Troll, L., Miller, S. & Atchley, R. (1979) *Families in Later Life* Belmont, Ca: Wadsworth

10

Social Relationships at Work

Most men, and an increasing number of women, spend a great deal of their lives at work—7 to 8 hours a day, 5 to 5½ days a week, from the age of 18 to 65 or longer, nearly 100,000 hours in all. Most of those who are unemployed wish that they were at work. Most work involves collaboration with others, and a proportion of the time at work is spent in the company of others.

As we saw in Chapter 4, some friendships arise out of contacts at work. On the other hand most people at work do not become friends in the usual sense, although there may be a close relationship with them of a rather different kind. We saw that middle-aged men often have few close friends. One of the differences between friends and workmates is that the things they do together are quite different. Another difference is that workmates are brought together partly by the working organisation and the work-flow system – because they work next to each other, or on the same job, rather than because they necessarily choose to spend time together.

There is something of a puzzle about these relationships. On one hand there is a good deal of evidence that they make a big difference to job satisfaction, and can play an important part in buffering the effects of stresses at work. Job satisfaction is strongly related to life satisfaction, both affecting each other.[1] But there is also evidence that work relationships are seen as more superficial, less rewarding, and as generating more conflict than, for example, friends or family. We shall try to resolve this issue. It comes up again in connection with those who retire or lose their jobs: people who say that they do not like their jobs are often even less happy when they lose them.

Another problem concerns the nature of the attachments between people at work. On one hand work relationships are very important, not only for satisfaction and health, but also for keeping jobs and for careers. On the other hand many people do not appear to develop lasting bonds with their workmates, and may not bother to say good-bye when they leave.

The benefits from relationships

Do these work friendships convey benefits similar to those derived from friendships outside? Many studies have shown that satisfaction with co-workers, supervision and management are major components of overall job satisfaction. But work relationships differ from friendship, love, and other intimate relations in a number of ways. Cohen et al. found that friendship, work and love relationships between two people differed in the importance of goals and resources. In love and friendship the partner and the relationship are seen as more important than self, while in work relationships the opposite is true. Money and goods are seen as more important than esteem or affection. (Fig. 1)

Fig. 1   THE IMPORTANCE OF GOALS AND RESOURCES IN WORK, FRIENDSHIP
AND LOVE RELATIONSHIPS[2]

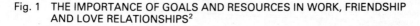
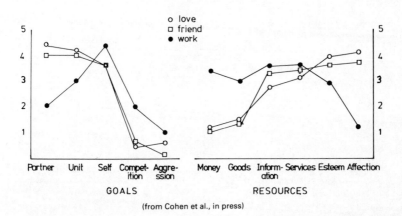

(from Cohen et al., in press)

Supportive relationships at work have often been found to be associated with lower levels of tension and illness. Other studies have found that when people at work have good relationships, especially with peers, they are less anxious, less depressed, and less ill in mind and body. Some of the research supports the 'buffering' hypothesis described earlier (p. 26f), i.e. social support operates only when it is needed, when the individual receiving the support is under stress. It is not known exactly how this works. Those who receive social support perceive events as less stressful, and supportive workmates can

Fig. 2   WORK RELATIONSHIPS PLOTTED ON DIMENSIONS 1 AND 2[6]

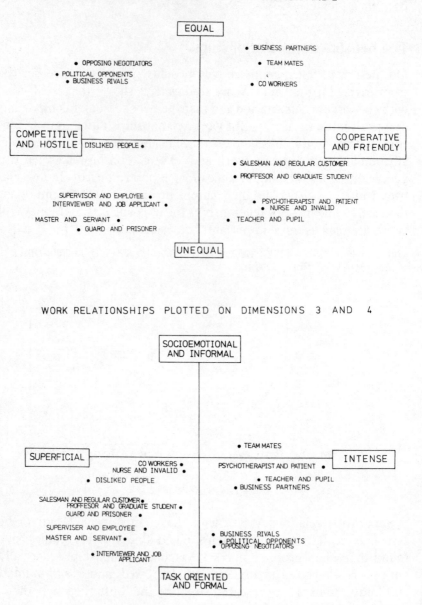

WORK RELATIONSHIPS PLOTTED ON DIMENSIONS 3 AND 4

actually help to deal with the problem.[3]

However, relationships with others can be a major *source* of stress at work. For shop-floor workers pressure to get things done, lack of consultation, others not pulling their weight, can be problems.[4] For managers, 'personality clashes' had troubled 20% of one small sample; loneliness, promotion to an awkward situation over someone's head, and a 'bad atmosphere', are other examples of this.[5]

Are work relationships important or not? In fact the results given below are really quite consistent. Many, perhaps most, work relationships provide rather little satisfaction and support – 45% of workers in one study[6] had no friends at work. On the other hand, under the right conditions, for example small and cohesive groups, work relationships are a very powerful source of satisfaction and support.

Clearly these close work relationships are very important, but what exactly are they like? A number of different work relationships were included in the dimensional study carried out by Wish and colleagues. (Figure 2).

Wish found that different types of work relationships were

Fig. 3   GROUP SOLIDARITY AND ABSENTEEISM IN WHITE COLLAR WORKERS[8]

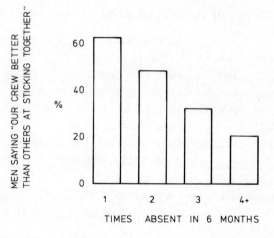

characterised by different positions along his dimensions. For example, the supervisor–employee relationship was seen as unequal, task oriented and formal, and more likely to be competitive and hostile than co-operative and friendly. However, co-workers were more equal, co-operative and friendly, and halfway between both task-oriented/formal and socio-emotional/informal. Others, such as teacher–pupil relations, were unequal but co-operative and quite intense. Thus both the benefits and conflicts are likely to differ according to the *type* of the work relationship.

In addition, the *nature* of the particular relationship is also important. Many studies have found that job satisfaction is high and absenteeism and labour turnover low in work teams that are small and cohesive. (See Figure 3.)

Satisfaction is greater for those under certain styles of supervision, for example those that allow more participation in decisions, and for people of higher status. On the other hand, many people at work are of low status, under the wrong kind of supervision, and do not belong to cohesive groups. This may explain the low levels of satisfaction with work relationships which we obtained in the study reported on p. 83.

In addition, the structure of the organisation itself is likely to affect interpersonal relationships. And the sorts of relationships people have at work will, in turn, affect their satisfaction with the job. We shall look more closely at the role of relationships and informal contact within the organisational structure in the next section.

Formal and informal contact at work

A large proportion of our time at work may be spent in interaction with others. For example, managers spend a lot of time talking to people. Rosemary Stewart[9] asked 160 managers in British firms to keep diaries, and she found that they spent between one-third and 90% of their time with other people (see Table 1). About 32% of the time appeared to be with others of similar status.

Other studies of managers have obtained similar results. Managers spend little time alone – 34% in this study, 22% and 20% in two others. They seem to spend most of their time talking, face to face or over the phone, and even when alone they may be reading or dictating letters. One manager read 97 items from the post and replied to 45 in three hours.[11]

The pattern of activity varies between different kinds of manager.

TABLE 1. How Managers Spend Their Time [10]

Alone	34%
With one other person	32%
With two or more people	34%
With immediate subordinate	26%
With boss	8%
With colleague	12%
With fellow specialists, elsewhere in the company	8%
With other internal contacts	5%
With customers	5%
With other external contacts	6%
Time spent on inspection	6%
Time spent on informal discussions	43%
Time spent on committees	7%
Time spent telephoning	6%
Time spent on social activities	4%

For example, the heads of large firms, compared with those of smaller ones, spend more time in formal meetings such as committees, while in smaller firms things are more informal, more time is spent in the works, and more time filling in for other people. Line managers spend more time with subordinates and on inspection, less time alone, while sales managers spend more time outside the company, in social activity and on entertainment, for example with customers.[12] But while the pattern of activity varies, a great deal of time is spent in interpersonal interactions, both of a formal and informal kind.

A great deal of social behaviour at work is not through choice of other people's company because we like them, but because they are part of the formal organisation. We receive orders from A, give orders to B, co-operate with C, help D, inspect E's work, negotiate with F, interview G, teach H, because it is part of the job. Relationships in working groups are different from those at home or with friends. They are based on co-operation in organised, hierarchical groups. This can be a great source of satisfaction, and prevents one form of loneliness (p. 77). Children enjoy team games, and students enjoy organising clubs and social events.

In addition there are social contacts which are not part of the job – for example at coffee breaks or lunch, and so on – usually known as the informal side of work. George Homans[13] proposed a theory about how the two kinds of social activity are related. He argued that people come to work in order to get the work done and to be paid for it; they have to co-operate with other people, discover that they like some of them, and start engaging in extra social activity with them. Working relationships are first brought about by the formal system of work, but are elaborated in several ways by informal contacts of different kinds, and the forming of work relationships. It is essential for such relationships to develop if co-operation at work is to succeed. This informal system then affects the pattern of work itself, through the formation of norms about how much work to do, division into sub-groups, and emergence of a status hierarchy not recognised by management, all of this affecting the way work is done.

There is a well-known study of a group of men in the Bank Wiring Observation Group, in a factory in Chicago. Their patterns of playing games and of friendship are shown in Figure 4.

Fig. 4   INFORMAL ACTIVITY AND FRIENDSHIP AT WORK

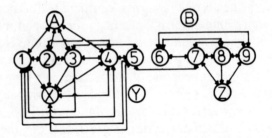

Men who played games

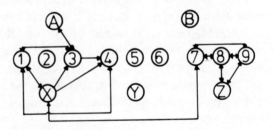

Men who were friends

Fig. 5   INFORMAL COOPERATION AT WORK

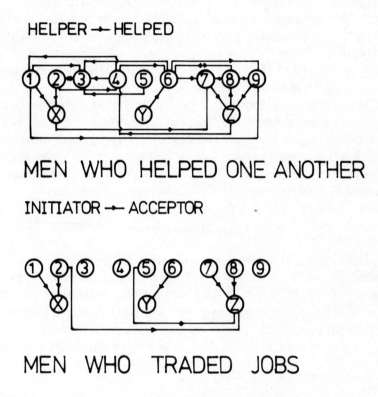

HELPER → HELPED

MEN WHO HELPED ONE ANOTHER

INITIATOR → ACCEPTOR

MEN WHO TRADED JOBS

Informal co-operation at work in the Bank Wiring Room is shown in Figure 5.

We can see from these figures how friendship patterns coincide with informal cooperation pathways. However, friendship is not necessary for co-operation or for informal social activities such as playing games together.

So far we have described relations between pairs of people, but there are also sub-groups, or cliques, which may think that they are superior to other subgroups, and may feel hostile towards them. Each of these groups will form norms, for example about how much work it is necessary to do. Again A may know C, who is in a quite different section, and this becomes a new channel of co-operation, or simply of gossip – part of the 'grapevine'. A may fail to co-operate with D, whom he does not like.

Within a working group, where all have the same rank on the organisation chart, some become regarded as unofficial leaders – because they are older and more experienced, or more highly skilled, or better at dealing with the authorities. This affects the way the pattern of work is controlled, for example in decisions about how hard to work.

The hierarchy has a big effect on relations between people, and the way in which they communicate with one another.

1. Equal status relations inside the working group. Here people may co-operate and engage in reciprocated help, but they can also be rivals for promotion. Equal status relations with members in other groups outside the formal organisation can be easier, can be useful in getting things done quickly, or simply as another channel in the grapevine. About 40% of messages between managers are to others at the same level, many of them outside official channels. And the larger and more complex the organisation is, the more lateral communication takes place.[16]

2. Relationships between people of different status are more difficult, especially where one is the direct supervisor of the other. If they are two levels apart, or not in the same line of command, things can be easier. The relationship of superior and subordinate, where one has power over the other, usually creates a certain distance between those involved. We shall discuss the skills for handling this relationship later.

Sex, age and status differences in work relationships

Sex Both sexes enjoy and need intimate relationships as well as involvement in structured groups. However males are more involved in groups, females in intimate relationships (p. 76f). Women are more concerned with the social side of work relationships than men, and this is one of the main sources of job satisfaction for them, partly because of the nature of female work. Many women work in one or two main types of job. Some are teachers, nurses, social workers, or personnel officers, all of whom look after other people. Some women are secretaries, clerical workers, or shop assistants, all of whom help other people, and work in small working groups. Perhaps for these reasons the job satisfaction of women is usually higher than that of men. Women who are at work have on average a greater sense of happiness and well-being than those who are not, especially if they lack other involvements (for example if they are single or have no children), if they are hard up, and if they enjoy their work.[17]

In a study of work relationships that we carried out with Rob McIlveen in a large production plant in northern England we found that women reported slightly more satisfaction with their jobs when first starting, and also slightly greater feelings of stress at the time of the survey. However, women also reported having more friends at work, more work colleagues, and also more people at work that they don't get on with. Women seem to work in jobs in which they have larger social networks than men do. And this includes both more friendly and more conflict relationships, which is perhaps why they find their jobs both more satisfying and more stressful than men do.

Women in managerial positions have some special problems however. More seems to be expected of them than of their male equivalents, and they have more domestic work to do, so it is not surprising that the main stresses they report are work overload (35%), and time pressures and deadlines (25%).[18] They have some problems dealing with the male managers too: they may have difficulty integrating with groups of males, miss the social support of other females, and would like to be more confident and assertive, and to be able to deal with men at work more successfully. Sexual harassment is surprisingly common: over half a sample of British female managers had experienced it, though women at work may play flirtatious games too, in order to gain some advantage. On the other hand many women are helped by a male superior who acts as 'mentor' and helps them in their career. In fact, on-the-job training and experience is positively related to job satisfaction for women managers but not for men.[19] As supervisors women are often credited with more 'consideration' (see p. 260), and often they are more considerate, though research suggests that the same styles of leadership are needed by both sexes. They rarely have any difficulty with male subordinates, but are more likely to have trouble with women, who sometimes dislike having a female boss.[20] Some research has shown that women employees have a fear of success and this stops them trying to gain advancement. However, more recent work has shown that fear of success is really fear of loss of femininity. Younger people and those at lower pay grades and with fewer years spent with the organisation show more fear of success.[21]

Age Young people at work have to be 'socialised' into the ways of work; they have to learn how to work as a member of a group, and under the direction of a supervisor. This 'socialisation for work' takes place first at school, but it is not successful in all cases. There are a proportion of people who are unable to work in the usual way – because they cannot cope with authority, think they are unable to do the work, or for some other reason.[22]

For young people at work the peer group is important; and for older workers, especially those who have not been very successful, or those whose main achievements are behind them, again the social contacts may be more important than the work itself.

Status   More senior people at work have a quite different pattern of social relationships from those lower down. Managers spend a great deal of time with their subordinates and secretaries, especially if they have a large staff under them, and in committee meetings. Senior people at work are less often members of a relaxed peer group; they are at the centre of a complex social network and have to deal with a lot of conflict. They have to sustain a number of interlocking relationships; other people are the main source of stress – unsatisfactory subordinates, demanding superiors, and rivalrous colleagues.[23] Higher status people are of course more influential, which may be one reason

Fig. 6   EFFECT OF MANAGEMENT LEVEL ON INFLUENCE AWAY FROM THE COMPANY

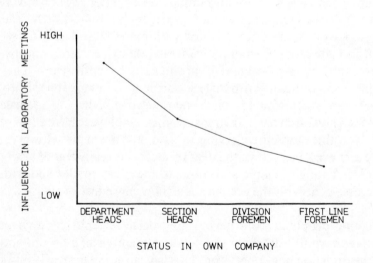

why their job satisfaction is much higher. They are also found to be more influential when at meetings away from their own company – probably because they simply adopt the same style of behaviour and establish the same relationships as in their home company (Figure 6).

Cultural variations in work relationships

The pattern of work relationships which we have described is not found in all parts of the world, and management theories of American or European origin do not necessarily work elsewhere. Here are some of the main ways in which relationships at work may vary.

Supervisory hierarchy   Wider changes in society, backed by social science research, have led to less authoritarian relationships, smaller differences of power and status between the levels in the hierarchy, and more consultative and persuasive leadership styles. However, attempts to replicate research on the optimal style of supervision elsewhere have found that authoritarian leadership is just as effective, or more effective, in countries such as India and Japan. This is the style they are used to, and it reflects the greater power differences in the hierarchy. In Japan managers are trained for obedient behaviour in hierarchies by management courses in which they are compelled to go on 25-mile route marches by night, on little food, ordered to shout or sing the company song, and to learn and recite meaningless texts.[25]

We found that superior–subordinate relations in Japan and Hong Kong are very rule-bound: work superiors should keep their distance, and not disclose feelings or problems to their subordinates; but there are also rules about the paternalistic care of subordinates.

Importance of small groups   In many parts of the world great importance is attached to loyalty to the clan or other group, including work-groups and company; 'individualism', in which individuals act independently, is disapproved of. Examples are the Israeli kibbutz, the Russian collective, Chinese collectivism, and Japanese firms, which look after members of the firm for life, as if they were members of the family. One consequence is a higher level of conformity. On the other hand these groups may form only among members of the same tribe or clan, and there may be distinct lack of co-operation between members of different tribes.[26]

In Indonesia, Japan and other parts of the East, great value is placed on harmonious relations between people, on avoiding conflict, and on saving face. It may be necessary for negotiators to make substantial concessions to avoid the other side losing face. The positive side is that these groups are very supportive, and in Japan company members know that they have a secure job for life.

Industrial democracy   This is an important development in industrial organisation, first seen in Yugoslavia, Norway and West Germany. It consists of joint consultative committees, on which several levels of personnel are represented, and which have the power to make important decisions. Another part of the scheme is the use of worker–directors. Our interest here is not in how well it works, but in its effect on relationships. One effect is to strengthen the position of those at the lowest level, and to weaken the position of their supervisors, since there is a readily available channel through which to challenge their authority.[27]

Informal working arrangements   In Western culture children are 'socialised' for work at school: this prepares them for working regular hours, under supervision, in a disciplined way. In Third-World countries there are often difficulties in getting people to work in such a regimented fashion. For some kinds of work it is possible to hand the job over to a group, under its own leadership, to finish the job in their own way, and their own time. Unfortunately this cannot be done with assembly-line work, or other work where men and machinery are closely interdependent.[28]

Rules   These differences in structure are reflected in different sorts of rules. As we have seen in Chapter 3, rules about privacy and keeping confidences are shared across our Eastern and Western cultures, but Eastern work relations, particularly in Japan, are characterised by less intimacy and less emotional expressiveness towards the other person. There are rules about not expressing affection or feelings at work.

WORKMATES AND COLLEAGUES

We have seen that people at work spend a great deal of time with others of similar status to themselves. We can distinguish between several levels of intimacy here:

1. Many people at work are seen simply through formal work contacts,

and not at any social occasions at work, such as coffee breaks. We have called these 'work colleagues'. These relatively superficial and task-oriented encounters can, however, be enjoyable, and often are. In addition, more serious collaboration over the work itself, over and above the formal requirements of the job, is enjoyable, since the other person is instrumental in providing help on the job.

2. Chatting, jokes and games at breaks, lunch and drinks in club or canteen, are often extremely euphoric and enjoyable occasions. This interaction is usually between members of the immediate working group, who are known for this reason, and who are regarded as members of a closely-knit 'in-group'.

3. When two people see each other a good deal at work, either through purely social activities, or through the work, or more commonly both, we can call them 'friends-at-work'. They are different from friends in the normal sense in that they are not invited home, and do not engage in joint leisure activities. In the Goldthorpe study (below), 55% of manual workers said they had one or more close friends at work, but only 27% met these friends outside, and most did not ask their friends home.

4. Then there are friends in the normal sense, who are known through work. We call them 'social friends'. We showed above that quite a lot of friends are made in this way – 25% in one survey. They are different from friends known through the neighbourhood or leisure activities, since they are seen regularly in at least two different settings, i.e. at work and at home or in the community. We saw that middle-class people make friends more readily at work, because their work contacts often encourage friendship, for example social events at which spouses are invited, and leisurely lunches. Manual workers also make friends at work.

There are two main kinds of activity shared with workmates, though the two are closely intertwined – co-operation over work, and primarily social activity. Both can be very satisfying, especially when shared with a social friend or friend-at-work, but also with work colleagues who are not friends. In our study of work relationships we asked over a hundred workers of a large processing plant in northern England to select four work colleagues: one who was also a friend outside work, one who was a friend-at-work, one who was just a work colleague and not associated with at break or meal times, and a fourth who was a disliked work colleague. We asked each to rate how much satisfaction they derived from certain activities for each of the four work peers. We can see in Table 2 that both work and social activities at work are more satisfying with social friends and friends-at-work, but even, for some people, with disliked work colleagues.

TABLE 2. Percentage of Workers Reporting a Fair Amount or Great Deal of Satisfaction from Interactions with Four Different Peer Relationships at Work

	Social friend	Friend at work	Work colleague	Disliked colleague
Working together on a joint task	75.3	53.2	34.6	15.2
Giving advice on work matters	64.5	43.6	37.9	34.4
Receiving advice on work matters	61.3	45.7	26.3	16.1
Joking or teasing	58.1	45.8	31.5	23.7
Chatting casually	67.7	56.0	28.3	17.3

As Figure 5 and Table 4 show, workers may help one another, usually on a reciprocal basis, over and above what is required by the formal arrangements. Help and co-operation take a variety of forms, in different settings, and are the basis for successful work-teams. Workmates may also provide each other with information, including information on technical and organisational matters. The primarily social interchanges take place at coffee breaks and over lunch, and also during social encounters on the job. Usually there is much overlap between those who help each other and those who engage in social activities together. Manual workers engaged in boring, repetitive jobs may invent all sorts of games and comic routines to relieve the monotony. A group of factory workers was studied who had devised regular events at certain times each day: one man would steal and eat another's banana, another would share out peaches at a certain hour, another would open a window, creating a row about the draught, and so on. 'If it weren't for the talking and fooling, you'd go nuts.'[29]

Studies of different organisations have found quite a variety of relationships between equals. In a large oil company, for example, these links had the quality of being gentlemanly, cool, and cordial.[30] However, this was a company where the managers were very ambitious, and cautious about establishing strong links with others who might not be their colleagues for very long, and indeed who might become their subordinates. Other organisations – many American ones, and marketing or advertising sections – are often marked by euphoric and jokey, but rather superficial, relationships. It depends on the 'culture' of the firm.

A study of industrial workers in Luton was carried out by Goldthorpe, and some of the findings are given in Table 3.

TABLE 3. Social Interaction Between Industrial Workers [31]

Frequency of talking to workmates

A good deal	Now and then	Hardly at all
47%	39%	12%

Feelings about being moved away from present workmates

Very upset	Fairly upset	Not much bothered	Not bothered at all
4%	23%	32%	36%

Number of workmates regarded as 'close friends'

None	1 or 2	More than 2
45%	25%	31%

Meetings with workmates regarded as close friends outside the plant

Visiting at home	Arranged meetings	Semi-casual meetings	Purely casual meetings or none at all	No workmates regarded as close friends
16%	11%	11%	17%	45%

It can be seen that there was quite a lot of conversation and that much of this took place on the job, for example between machine setters and assemblers. And much of this conversation was irrelevant to the job. On the other hand relationships were rather weak, as is shown by the lack of concern about being moved away from workmates. Comparison of different working groups confirmed what was said above – spatial factors had a big effect on forming relationships. On the other hand technology was only one factor: the men most favourably placed for social attachments to develop were the toolmakers, and they talked a great deal, but were not concerned about being moved away from their mates. While 55% of this sample of manual workers had one or more 'close friends' at work, only 27% of them met outside the plant by arrangement, and 16% visited each other at home. Most of their friends were *not* workmates.

But workmates can involve quite close relationships, and this will make a difference to the type of social interaction at work. In our study of work relations we found there was a great deal of informal social interaction at work even with the disliked colleague, as Table 4 shows.

TABLE 4. *Percentage of Workers Engaged in Work and Social Activities More than Several Times a Day at Work*

	With			
	Social friend	Friend at work	Work colleague	Disliked colleague
Helping other with work	52%	32%	18%	8%
Discussing work	49%	52%	32%	17%
Chatting casually	72%	63%	26%	15%
Joking with the other	72%	54%	24%	13%
Teasing the other person	46%	32%	18%	20%
Discussing personal life	30%	19%	13%	11%
Discussing personal feelings	26%	10%	5%	5%
Asking for or giving personal advice	33%	19%	8%	6%

In fact, we found that the frequency of engaging in certain activities at work correlated with reported work stress and satisfaction. But these associations depended upon the nature of relationships with the work peer with whom the interaction took place. For example, people were highly satisfied if they engaged in a lot of discussion about work, or teaching or showing the other person something about work, or asking or giving personal advice, and even teasing, and they were less satisfied with work if they did little of these things. But this relationship held only for friends-at-work, not for any other category of work colleague. Stressfulness was low if people engaged in a lot of these activities, and in social interaction like chatting casually at work, or discussing their personal life and feelings. Low frequency of all these activities was associated with high stress. Again, this relationship held for only one category of work colleagues, but this time it was social friends. Apparently, then, the more often we engage in talking about work or about ourselves with friends-at-work, the more *satisfied* we are with the job, but the more we interact with our social friends at work, the less *stressful* we find the job[31a].

We have seen that relationships at work are a powerful source of social support, and can help to reduce stresses at work. It seems likely that friends from work could be particularly important here – problems can be discussed quietly away from the work-place, and the other can be relied on as an ally at work.

We can add a little more about how to make the best of work relationships from our rules study. We found a number of rules for dealing with 'co-workers', which include these and also the rather less close work relationships described in the next section.

TABLE 5. Rules for Co-Workers

1. Accept one's fair share of the work load.
2. Respect other's privacy.
3. Be co-operative with regard to the shared physical working conditions (e.g. light, temperature, noise).
4. Be willing to help when requested.
5. Keep confidences.
6. Work co-operatively despite feelings of dislike.
7. Don't denigrate to superiors.
8. Address the co-worker by first name.
9. Ask for help and advice when necessary.
10. Look the co-worker in the eye during conversations.
11. Don't be over-inquisitive about each other's private lives.
12. Repay debts, favours and compliments no matter how small.
13. Don't engage in sexual activity with the co-worker.
14. Stand up for the co-worker in his/her absence.
15. Don't criticise the co-worker publicly.

We then asked 120 people how dissatisfied they would be if eleven of these rules were broken by their own work colleagues. The greatest dissatisfaction was reported for disclosing confidences, denigrating others to a work superior, not accepting a fair share of the work load, and criticising the other person publicly. And rule violations of keeping confidences, public criticism, failing to help when asked and failing to support the other person in his/her absence led to much higher dissatisfaction if committed by a 'friend-at-work' than by someone labelled as 'just a work colleague'. But all work peers – whether good friends, friends-at-work, work colleagues, or even 'people we don't get on with at work' – were expected to accept their fair share of the work load, respect privacy, not denigrate others to a work superior, repay debts and favours, and be co-operative about shared work conditions. Violations of these rules were equally frowned upon, regardless of friendship. Apparently, even friends are not excused from keeping task-related or informal work rules. And in the case of certain rules, they are even more strongly bound to a role of help and support.

SUPERIOR–SUBORDINATE RELATIONSHIPS

Even groups of two start to form a hierarchy – if there are two males at least. In larger groups a very definite informal hierarchy forms, and groups are more effective at tasks if they do have a settled hierarchy. The relationship between a supervisor and his or her subordinates at work is one of the most basic and important social relationships. In working organisations there is nearly always a formal hierarchy, where the leader is appointed from outside, rather than elected by the group. It is difficult for one person to supervise more than ten to fifteen others, so the larger the organisation the more levels there will be in the hierarchy. Very large organisations become very bureaucratic, with ten or more different ranks. In an informal group the person who emerges as the leader is usually the one who is more expert or who knows most about the task in hand; promotion in organisations depends on similar principles, in theory.

Formally appointed leaders have some power, to reward or punish. In prisons they can punish, in industry they can reward – by controlling promotion and extra payments. In voluntary associations, in universities and hospitals, supervisors can also appeal to the inner commitments of their followers, and they may also have power based on their expertise. A supervisor may have power derived from his personal ties with subordinates, so that he can call on their loyalty.

However, subordinates have power too. They can gang together, in trade unions or in smaller groups, which give them collective power, since the boss usually cannot sack all of them. They can make him dependent on receiving rewards from them, either in the form of hard work, or simply of interpersonal rewards, which can be withdrawn if the leader does not behave himself.

Is there an exchange of help or other rewards between superiors and subordinates? A supervisor is in a position to help subordinates by helping them earn good money, get promoted, and in other ways advance their welfare. He can also help them on the job, though this may be seen as promoting his own interests. People at work are rewarded by the working organisation in various ways; supervisors are able to manipulate these rewards so that they are contingent on efficient performance.

Subordinates help their boss by doing a good job of work. It has been suggested that supervisors work out a different exchange of rewards with each subordinate, so that some are more favoured, while more is expected of them. However there is a limit to this, in view of group norms that govern the fair division of rewards. It has also been suggested that deferring to the supervisor's higher status is another reward given by subordinates.[32]

The supervisor of a group of workers, or the manager of a group of lesser managers, usually works in the same area, sometimes in the same room. He keeps in touch with them and their work intermittently, by a combination of formal meetings, perhaps once a week, and more frequent informal ones, in the work-place and over tea-breaks. He may or may not be a member of the immediate informal group. For example, the actual work performed by first-line supervisors varies greatly, depending on details of technology, spatial arrangements, and whether or not they are responsible for such things as production planning, inspection, machinery maintenance, overtime arrangements, and so on.[33]

Much of the interaction between superiors and subordinates is initiated by the superior; it includes instruction about the work to be done, and how to do it, comments on the subordinate's performance and suggestions for different ways of doing things. The subordinate may initiate things too: it might be expected that he would seek help or advice, but often this is sought from the peer group, in order to avoid appearing incompetent; subordinates report progress with the work –often this is distorted or delayed until the boss is in a good mood, in the case of bad news; subordinates make suggestions and complaints, though these are often ignored. There may be straightforward discussion of work problems, in which the supervisors need not always take a dominant role.

Rosemary Stewart's managers spent on average 26% of their time with their subordinates, and 8% with *their* superiors. The number of people supervised – the 'span of control' – is fairly small for managers: five to seven plus a secretary; it is larger for first line supervisors, up to twenty or more but more typically about fifteen.

What do managers actually do? Mintzberg[34] maintains that they do ten jobs:

Interpersonal roles
   Figurehead – official duties, ceremonies.

Leader – initiates, pursues organisational goals, hiring and firing.

Liaison – with other organisations and the outside world.

Informational roles

Monitor – finds out what is happening inside the organisation and outside, reads reports.

Disseminator – passes on information to members of the organisation.

Spokesman – transmits information to people outside.

Decisional roles

Entrepreneur – takes action to improve some situation, by delegation or supervision.

Disturbance handler – deals with emergencies.

Resource allocator – authorises expenditure, etc., on different projects.

Negotiator – with unions, sales, or on other matters.

The amount of time spent on these different jobs varies between different management specialities. Line managers spend more time on the decisional roles, especially disturbance handling, while staff managers are more active in the informational roles, especially monitor and spokesman. Sometimes these roles are shared out between two or three managers. The activities of higher levels of management are rather different from those lower down. There is more figurehead, more liaison and spokesman to the outside world, and less disturbance handling and negotiating.

How does the supervisor–subordinate relationship compare with others that we have looked at? In the Wish study (Fig. 2) it appears to be seen as *superficial, very unequal,* and somewhat *hostile* and *competitive.* In our study of satisfaction and conflicts, supervisors were seen as a very weak source of satisfaction, little better than neighbours, but as a major source of conflict, second only to spouse. Again we have the problem that Wish's subjects, and some of ours, had either little work experience, or experience of a limited kind. Sofer,[35] in his study of middle management in large firms, found that supervisory relations were gentlemanly and informal; though the fact that superiors had to assess their subordinates created a problem. These men were greatly concerned with promotion; their immediate superiors were of course very important here, sometimes giving a lot of help to their protégés.

What is the source of conflict between supervisors and subordinates? Some people are hostile to authority, others are made anxious by superiors. Hostility can be brought about by unfair treatment, anxiety by the fear of punishment. The basic problem perhaps is that superiors have power, particularly power to punish, or to withhold rewards. There is also bound to be restriction on self-disclosure, on both sides.

On the other hand there is evidence to show that job satisfaction, absenteeism and labour turnover are greatly affected by relations with the supervisor. Here are two aspects of supervisory skills which have been found to affect the satisfaction of subordinates:

Fig. 7 GRIEVANCE RATE AS A FUNCTION OF CONSIDERATION AND INITIATING STRUCTURE

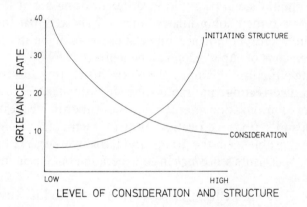

We shall explain what these dimensions of supervision mean shortly. Meanwhile the point we want to make is that although many people do not have very good relations with their supervisors, others do, and this depends heavily on supervisors handling them in the right way.

Supervisors also affect health. The studies on social support described earlier found that a supportive supervisor – one who scores high on 'consideration' – generates better bodily and mental health. The reason is partly that he is in a position to solve work-related problems and hence to remove the source of stress. In addition, he may be approached with all sorts of personal problems. In a survey of industrial foremen it was found that they spend an average of 2.5 hours each week discussing moderate or serious problems of their subordinates. The most common were work-related problems such as job dissatisfaction and difficulties with other employees, but there were also a large number of more personal problems such as marital and sexual difficulties, nervousness and depression, and problems with children, alcohol or drugs. Most foremen felt positively about being cast into the role of helper and considered this an important part of their job.[37] Conversely a bad supervisor is one of the very worst sources of stress. A study by Caplan *et al.*[38] suggests that while support from supervisors reduces anxiety and depression, support from colleagues has slightly more effect. Other studies show that support from supervisors has a 'buffering' effect. This means that supervisor support affects health when there is stress, but otherwise has no such effect (see p. 26f).

So what should supervisors do in order to bring about the right relationship with their subordinates? Figure 7 showed that Initiating Structure and Consideration are important sources of job satisfaction. These dimensions of supervision can be defined as follows:

1. 'Initiating structure': planning the work, instructing and training, checking and correcting, and motivating subordinates.

2. 'Consideration': looking after the needs of subordinates, establishing a warm and supportive relationship with them, and dealing with interpersonal problems in the group. Industrial workers are happiest when their supervisors score *high* in consideration but *low* in initiating structure.

But how about the effects of supervisors on productivity? *Both* consideration and some degree of initiating structure are needed – but not too much. Consideration delivers the rewards needed to support initiating structure. This is part of the key to successful supervision. The supervisor rewards behaviour which promotes organisational goals – he links rewards to the desired behaviour. However there is a snag: people dislike being given orders, even if rewards are attached. Another complication is that these supervisory skills have different effects in different kinds of work setting. Table 6 shows their effects in manufacturing and service departments. The asterisks refer to correlations which are significant, that is, they are high enough, given the size of the sample, to reflect real relationships rather than being chance associations. For example, a high level of consideration by supervisors is strongly associated with less proficiency and reduced absenteeism for manufacturing settings, but it is linked only with fewer accidents in service departments. A high level of initiating structure improves proficiency but increases grievances in manufacturing. In the service setting it is only related strongly to high turnover.

TABLE 6. Relations between Supervising Style and Effectiveness [39]

	Proficiency	Absenteeism	Accidents	Grievances	Turnover
Consideration					
Manufacturing	−0.31*	−0.49*	−0.06	−0.07	0.13
Service	0.28	−0.38	−0.42*	0.15	0.04
Initiating Structure					
Manufacturing	0.47*	0.27*	0.15	0.45*	0.06
Service	−0.19	0.06	0.18	0.23	0.51*

How do supervisors give orders without reducing job satisfaction? The answer lies in how the orders are given, and the best way is in the *democratic–persuasive* style. The democratic–persuasive style consists of motivating people by explanation and persuasion rather than by just giving orders, allowing subordinates to participate in decisions and using techniques of group discussion and group decision. There is a major difficulty about the use of participatory methods however: they only work under some conditions and not others. In the first place only

TABLE 7. Rules for Superiors

1. Plan and assign work efficiently.
2. Keep subordinates informed about decisions affecting him/her.
3. Respect the other's privacy.
4. Keep confidences.
5. Consult subordinates in matters that affect him/her.
6. Encourage the subordinate's advancement.
7. Advise and encourage subordinates.
8. Fight for subordinate's interests where necessary.
9. Don't be jealous of the subordinate's ability.
10. Don't give commands without explanation.
11. Be considerate regarding the subordinate's personal problems.
12. Look the subordinate in the eye during conversations.
13. Don't criticise the subordinate publicly.
14. Don't visit the subordinate socially, unannounced.
15. Don't supervise too closely.
16. Don't engage in sexual activity with the subordinate.
17. Repay debts, favours and compliments.
18. Don't discuss personal finances with the subordinate.

some kinds of subordinates want them and find them rewarding. Those of authoritarian personality do not, nor do those from most cultures outside Europe and North America. And participation is less successful if there are time pressures, or with an unpopular or not very powerful supervisor. It is very successful at higher levels of leadership, and in personnel and service departments.

We can add some more guidance for the successful handling of this relationship from our findings about the rules which should be followed, on both sides. In our English sample, the agreed rules for work superiors were as in Table 7.

We also found corresponding rules for subordinates (Table 8).

TABLE 8. Rules for Subordinates

1. Don't hesitate to question when orders are unclear.
2. Use initiative where possible.
3. Put forward and defend own ideas.
4. Complain first to superior before going to others.
5. Respect other's privacy.
6. Be willing and cheerful.
7. Don't be too submissive.
8. Be willing to accept criticism.
9. Keep confidences.
10. Be willing to take orders.
11. Don't say derogatory things about the superior.
12. Look the superior in the eye during conversation.
13. Obey the superior's instructions.
14. Don't visit the superior socially unannounced.
15. Don't criticise the superior publicly.

We have seen that the superior–subordinate relationship at work is seen by most people as full of conflict and as providing little satisfaction. On the other hand supervisors *can* have a considerable effect on health and satisfaction, if the right skills are used. Supervisors have power to reward or punish, and there is usually not a very close relationship here, and no permanent bonds are formed. However this is not always the case, and it is interesting that the teacher–pupil relationship came out much more positive than that between work supervisors and subordinates, in the study reported in Figure 2. In Japan there is sometimes a close relationship between supervisors and subordinates, the so-called *oyabum-kobun* relationship, in which the supervisor adopts a kind of godparent role.

It looks as if the barriers created by differences of power and status can be reduced by the use of certain supervisory skills, and reduced even more by an attitude of concern for the other.

RIVALS, COMPETITORS AND ENEMIES

Conflict between individuals and between groups is a normal part of working organisations as we know them. These can be seen as coalitions of interest groups, which are in a perpetual state of internal struggle and of partly resolved conflicts.[40] It has been argued that conflict has some positive effects: groups are energised to compete, the best solution wins, and issues are brought into the open.[41] Other conflicts are less valuable, for example, between those of different power and status; these too may be unavoidable, since they reflect conflicts in the wider society.

There are also a number of difficult relationships at work. Some of these are the result of friction between individuals because they have different jobs, or because of rivalries over status, or simply because of incompatible personalities. It may be necessary to sustain some kind of working relationship, perhaps for many years, with these people, whereas outside work one would simply avoid them.

Interpersonal conflicts

There may also be conflicting pressures and expectations about role behaviour. A person's clients want him to do one thing, his colleagues want him to do something else. Foremen and supervisors often find that their superiors and subordinates want them to do different things. As many as 48% of industrial employees experience role conflict of some kind. This makes them tense and unhappy and produces psychosomatic illness; they also become ineffective. One way in which they react is to reduce their social contacts with those who are exercising the contrary pressures. Or they may engage in 'role bargaining' to find something that will keep both parties happy. Curiously the individuals who have the most trouble with role conflict are the reasonable, easy-to-deal-with ones, since others think that they can be influenced; they soon give up with rigid and obstinate people. A lot of individuals at work have trouble over 'role ambiguity', where there is not enough general agreement on what the role consists of, what they should be doing.[42]

One of the commonest forms of role conflict at work is 'role overload', where there are pressures from all sides to do more than it is possible to do. The solution may be to work out a system of priorities, which is made clear to those making demands. A lot of conflict is due to status differences. Higher-status individuals at work are paid more, have pleasanter offices and working conditions, have greater power and influence over decisions. (It is not always realised that those at the top usually have to work longer hours, that the work can be very stressful, and that responsibility is a cause of heart disease and allied complaints.) This may be resented by those lower down, who may think they are just as good (and sometimes they are). There are often fierce rivalries for status and promotion. And there can be other problems: an older person who is less qualified is paid less than a younger person; someone thinks he has the authority to give orders, but others don't think so, and are unwilling to carry them out.

Sometimes two individuals at work simply do not get on, partly for organisational reasons, but more because they just don't like one another. They would never choose one another as friends, but the work requires that they work together, perhaps for years. In our study of work relationships we found certain common sources of conflict with disliked work colleagues. These are given in Table 9.

TABLE 9. Percentage of Workers Reporting Difficulty over Certain Sources of Conflict with Disliked Work Colleagues

	Percentage	
Conflict over	some difficulty	moderate or great difficulty
Different opinions and beliefs	23.8	52.2
Competition for promotion or jobs	22.8	23.9
Demands on time	35.2	27.3
Competing for attention from others	28.3	28.5
His/her work habits	28.4	38.7
His/her personal habits	22.7	42.0
Work issues	28.3	45.5

As we can see, a great deal of conflict occurs over purely work matters, but also over interpersonal aspects as well.

Can we make any suggestions about how to alleviate the difficulties of these relationships? In our rules study we found the rules for dealing with one type of difficult relationship.

TABLE 10. Rules for People We Can't Get On With

1. Respect each other's privacy.
2. Strive to be fair in relations with one another.
3. Don't discuss what is said in confidence.
4. Don't invite to dine at a family celebration.
5. Don't engage in sexual activity with the other.
6. Don't feel free to take up as much of the other's time as one desires.
7. Don't denigrate the other behind their back.
8. Don't ignore the other person.
9. Don't visit the other person socially, unannounced.
10. Repay debts, favours or compliments no matter how small.
11. Look the other person in the eye during conversation.
12. Don't display hypocritical liking.

Another approach to resolving interpersonal conflicts is increasing the amount of communication between those involved, so that each side comes to understand and to trust the other more. Suspicion and hostility are increased by ignorance of what the other is up to. Some success has been reported from experiences in group meetings of various kinds, in which frank self-disclosure is encouraged (see Chapter 12). Role-reversal also helps to understand the other's point of view. Sometimes a third party can mediate or act as a go-between, or suggest alternative ways of co-operating.

Intergroup conflict

Other conflicts at work are derived from those between different groups. Different departments may have different interests or points of view. Marketing wants a variety of products to meet varied demands, while production prefers to have a few products, changing as little as possible. Production and personnel, technical and non-technical, and of course management and unions, can easily come into conflict.

Intergroup conflict is different from interpersonal conflict: members of the other group are treated alike, as members of the other group rather than as individuals. The two kinds of conflict can be combined, and one may be mistaken for the other. Two people may think that they dislike one another as individuals, whereas it is really the intergroup situation that divides them; they could have been good friends under different circumstances.

Members of groups usually distinguish between members of the 'in-group' and members of other groups. There is a universal tendency to overvalue members of the in-group, and to undervalue out-group members. This is legitimatised by discovering features of the in-group that are different and can be claimed to make the group superior, and to exaggerate the differences between the two groups. So, for example, members of a production department may see themselves as doing the real work, or possessing important skills, while members of staff departments think that they are superior, because of their technical qualifications and better working conditions. Such beliefs enable members of each group to bolster their self-esteem, and justify hostile behaviour towards the other group.[43] One reason for this is that in order to bolster our own self-esteem, we want to think well of groups to which we belong, and we discover respects in which our group is different, and therefore superior to the others.

These strong feelings about the in-group, and particularly about the out-group, are accentuated under certain conditions. There may be genuine competition between groups, for facilities, better payment or other material benefits. Or there may be a struggle for recognition, for status; one group may have been given an advantage which is not thought legitimate by the other.

One effect of intergroup conflict is a biased evaluation of the value of the in-group. Another effect is hostility towards the other group, and refusal to co-operate with its members. Differences between the two groups are seized upon, exaggerated, and made the justification for in-group superiority, and bad behaviour towards the other group. Another effect of intergroup conflict is greater cohesion and loyalty within groups, a tendency to choose authoritarian leaders and to demand more conformity.

How can intergroup conflicts be handled? Overlapping membership is one solution, so that on different criteria for membership some individuals belong first to one group, then to the other. Emphasising shared goals and removing the basis for conflict are other ways.

An interesting case of intergroup conflict is negotiation, for example between management and unions. Here again rules have emerged to enable the situation to be handled more effectively: 'unambiguous lies must be avoided, explicit promises have to be kept, invective is never to be used, explicit threats must not be issued, agreements in principle must not be blatantly violated when it comes to the execution of details, and mutual understandings must not be deliberately misconstrued later on.'[44] In addition, special social skills are needed to deal with the situation. It is found that the most effective negotiators (N) act as follows:[45]

1. N should make a strong case, make strong demands and give small concessions.
2. N should not be too tough, however, or there may be no agreement, and he should not attack or irritate the other side.
3. N should be open to a wide range of alternatives, and not plan a particular outcome in advance.
4. N should adopt a rational, problem-solving approach, in which he explores all the options, finds out a lot about the other side and their problems as well as giving information himself, and communicates clearly and without ambiguity.
5. N should create a reputation for honesty and firmness, and enhance the image of his party.

PROFESSIONAL AND SERVICE RELATIONSHIPS

Professional and service relationships cover our dealings with other individuals in a very specific and task-oriented capacity. These are the relationships that evolve from some direct exchange of goods and services, but they can, over time and with repeated interactions, turn into very intense relationships. For example, teachers and pupils, doctors and patients, psychotherapists and clients.

However, professional relationships can, and do, vary greatly in the degree of intimacy and in the length and intensity of the relationship, in the sort of feelings each participant has about the other, and in the balance of power. For example, teachers and students may be very close, akin to the parent–child relationship, while other relationships, such as landlord and tenant, may involve more conflict and hostility than liking and intimacy. Others, such as therapist and client, may involve very high intimacy and disclosure, but this relationship differs from intimate relationships by its non-reciprocity. The therapist, unlike a friend, is not expected to show self-disclosure or mutual exchange of feelings and attitudes. In some forms of psychoanalysis, this imbalance is very pronounced, the patient being expected to disclose intimate topics, while the psychiatrist may be completely silent and non-evaluative throughout much of the therapy session.

As in intimate and work relationships, conflict can occur within professional and service relationships, and rules operate to avoid such conflicts by regulating behaviour of both partners within certain limits. Professional relationships sometimes have a formal body of 'rules of conduct' – for example, the professional ethics of doctors and therapists, of company rules for salesmen. But again, as in any relationship, the less formal and more implicit interpersonal rules of relationships also operate. And for a particular relationship, rules about effective management of the task in hand are important – for example, rules about teaching for teachers and about learning for pupils, rules about healing for doctors and rules about receiving treatment by patients.

Teachers and pupils

The literature on teaching skills and practice is voluminous. A lot of research has been done comparing the amount learnt, or the exam results obtained, with different teaching skills.[46] Those which have been found to be most effective are as follows:

1. Introducing (structuring) topics or activities clearly;
2. Explaining clearly, with examples and illustrative materials;
3. Systematic and businesslike organisation of lessons;
4. Variety of teaching materials and methods;
5. Use of questions, especially higher-order questions;
6. Use of praise and other reinforcement, verbal and non-verbal;
7. Encouraging pupil-participation;
8. Making use of pupil's ideas, clarifying and developing them further;
9. Warmth, rapport and enthusiasm, mainly shown non-verbally.

However it is also important to establish the right *relationship* with the pupils, and schoolchildren have very clear ideas about this. It has been found that they have 'rules for teachers'; they disapprove of teachers who are arrogant and distant, who do not know the names of pupils, who cannot keep order, who are unfair, or give unjust punishment. If teachers break these 'rules' they are liable to be 'punished' – by verbal insults, creating disorder, or even physical violence.[47]

The teacher–pupil relationship has two aspects:

1. A task-oriented one, aimed at teaching knowledge;
2. An interpersonal one, involving a relatively long-term relationship.

There must be rules that are both task-oriented and intimacy-regulating for both teacher and pupil.

We found that the most important rules for teachers were, in order of importance[47a]:

TABLE 11. Rules for Teachers

1. Be well informed about what he/she is teaching.
2. Criticise the pupil's work constructively.
3. Treat pupil fairly.
4. Take the pupil's work seriously.
5. Prepare lessons thoroughly.
6. Be able to clarify questions.
7. Discipline the pupil when necessary.
8. Keep confidences.
9. Respect the other's privacy.
10. Be available at regular times.
11. Admit ignorance when necessary.
12. Be considerate regarding the pupil's personal problems.
13. Look the pupil in the eye during conversation.
14. Don't use swearwords in the company of the pupil.
15. Don't engage in sexual activity with the pupil.
16. Don't give commands without explanation.
17. Don't ask the pupil for material help.
18. Address the pupil by first name.
19. Show emotional support.
20. Don't discuss personal finances with the pupil.
21. Strive to present oneself in the best light possible.

Many of these rules are specific to the pupil–teacher relationship, dealing with the actual task of teaching rather than the personal relationship between the teacher and pupil. Others are concerned with regulating the level of intimacy: teachers should be supportive to students, but not divulge personal information.

We asked twenty-nine teachers to specify which rules they believed were important in the teacher–pupil relationship. These were the same as those listed by our group as a whole, except that teachers believed that the following rules were also important:

1. Talk to the pupil about religion and politics.
2. Talk to the pupil about sex and death.
3. Stand up for the pupil in his/her absence.
4. Engage in joking and teasing with the pupil.

We also asked our teachers to report on their own behaviour in the classroom. We found that there was a high degree of consistency between how important an individual believed a certain rule to be, and how often he/she behaved according to the rule in practice. However, there were other rules with no strong association between the importance of a rule and how often it was applied by the teacher in practice. And this includes some of the rules teachers judged were very important: clarifying questions, admitting ignorance when necessary, taking the pupil's work seriously, criticising constructively, respecting privacy, and being considerate about a pupil's personal problems. Apparently it is not always possible for a teacher to apply the rules she believes to be important as strongly as she thinks should be done in practice. But again, these tend to be task-related rules. Teachers are fairly consistent in their behaviour and views on interpersonal rules. If a teacher believes that it is important to discuss intimate topics, give emotional support, joke or tease the pupil, etc., she is very likely to do this regularly in practice; if a teacher believes that it is not important or applicable to the teaching situation, she will rarely or never do so. Perhaps this is the difference between teachers who just teach their subject and those who provide their pupils with a wider preparation for adulthood – the emphasis on teaching as an interpersonal relationship.

Rules are not only important for teachers, they also apply to pupils. In our main rules study, we found that people judged the following rules to be the most important for a pupil to apply in the teacher–pupil relationship:

TABLE 12. Rules for Pupils

1. Put forward and defend ideas.
2. Use initiative where possible.
3. Accept constructive criticism.
4. Don't hesitate to question when unclear.
5. Prepare assigned work.
6. Hand in exercises on time.
7. Don't be impertinent to the teacher.
8. Respect the teacher's privacy.
9. Don't disclose confidences.
10. Obey the teacher's instructions.
11. Look the teacher in the eye during conversations.
12. Share news of success with the teacher.
13. Don't be submissive to the teacher.
14. Don't engage in sexual activity with the teacher.
15. Don't use swearwords in the company of the teacher.

When we asked our teachers what they believed were the rules for pupils, these were virtually identical to the rules endorsed by our whole group. But in addition teachers thought it was important for pupils to:

1. Disclose personal problems and feelings to the teacher.
2. Talk to the teacher about religion and politics.
3. Talk to the teacher about sex and death.
4. Show distress or anxiety in front of the teacher.
5. Ask personal advice.
6. Present oneself in the best light possible.

Again, both teachers and non-teachers believe that task-oriented rules are the most important ones to follow, even for pupils, although, like teacher rules, rules about privacy and not disclosing confidences are also very important. But teachers are more likely than non-teachers to endorse intimacy rules as being important, indicating that teachers are putting more emphasis on the interpersonal relationship.

We also examined rules of the university tutor–student relationship by asking thirty students to rate the importance of rules for both the tutor and themselves as students in the relationship. The important task-related rules for tutor and students were very similar to those endorsed for teachers and pupils respectively. However, the intimacy-regulating rules become less relevant. There are no strongly endorsed rules proscribing swearing, sexual activity or discussion of personal information for the tutor–student relationship, as there are for teacher–pupil relations.

It seems that there are consistent task-related rules for the teacher to follow, whether this is a teacher in the school classroom situation or a tutor in the university. These rules are similar whether rated by teachers, students or a wider sample of old and young men and women. However, intimacy-regulating rules differ according to the situation, intimacy often being prescribed for pupils and proscribed for teachers, but not generally rated as extremely important for either.

Doctors and patients

Another important professional 'relationship' is the one between doctor and patient. Most of our visits to the doctor are for the treatment of physical ailments, but we also tend to use our G.P. for help with emotional and social problems as well as physical ones.

Historically, the family doctor's role was oriented strongly towards dealing with such problems, and even today doctors are seen as therapists and supportive agencies rather than just physical healers. In our study of separated or divorced people, we found that 42% of the group had contacted a doctor or other medical professional for advice on matters relating to the divorce or separation or on personal matters. And in interviews with heart attack patients, many men cited their doctor as a confidant – someone he would go to if he had a personal problem of some sort.

So the doctor–patient relationship involves more than the simple diagnosis and treatment of physical ills. Even when we do visit for a purely physical complaint, the interpersonal relationship between doctor and patient is an important issue. It has been found that patients describing good and poor consultations they had experienced placed more emphasis on the emotional content of the consultation and on the doctor's behaviour than on the clinical process involved. Overall, 35% of comments made about good consultations related to the clinical process, while 62% were about the emotional content of the doctor's behaviour, compared to 21% of negative comments about unsatisfactory clinical procedures and 70% about the doctor's behaviour or the emotional content in poor consultations. Good consultations involved:

1. The doctor making the patient feel confident and reassured;
2. The doctor making the patient feel the consultation was not a waste of time;
3. The doctor making the patient feel relaxed;
4. The doctor's behaviour being understanding, friendly or intimate, interested or egalitarian.

In bad consultations:

1. The doctor made the patient fearful;
2. The doctor made the patient feel the consultation was a waste of the doctor's time;
3. The doctor's behaviour was not understanding, was unfriendly, uninterested, superior, or hesitant.[48]

As in the case of teachers, there is a particular task to be carried out in the interaction (diagnosis and treatment), but there is also an interpersonal relationship of some degree of intimacy, and again we expect rules of behaviour to be both task-oriented and intimacy-regulating.

We found that the most important rules for doctors were:

TABLE 13. Rules for Doctors

1. Listen carefully to the patient.
2. Always explain very clearly.
3. Counsel on preventative medicine.
4. Be frank and honest.
5. Hold information obtained from the patient in strictest confidence.
6. Keep confidences.
7. Respect patient's wishes.
8. Don't criticise the patient publicly.
9. Look the patient in the eye during conversation.
10. Respect the patient's privacy.
11. Show emotional support.
12. Don't engage in sexual activity with the patient.
13. Come to a clear diagnosis.
14. Appear neatly or smartly dressed when with the patient.
15. Don't use swearwords in the company of the patient.
16. Don't become personally involved with the patient.
17. Don't show distress or anxiety in front of the patient.
18. Strive to present yourself to the patient in the best light possible.
19. Don't ask the patient for material help.

Rules for the doctor include task-oriented ones (explanation, counselling) but there are rules both encouraging intimacy (be frank and honest, and eye contact) and protecting intimacy (respect privacy, keep confidences).

Rules for the patient were:

TABLE 14. Rules for Patients

1. Question doctor if unclear or uncertain.
2. Give doctor all relevant information.
3. Follow the doctor's instructions carefully.
4. Be completely honest.
5. Ensure cleanliness for the medical examination.
6. Don't waste the doctor's time.
7. Don't make unreasonable demands on the doctor's time.
8. Have confidence in the doctor.
9. Respect the doctor's privacy.
10. Present problems one at a time.
11. Look the doctor in the eye during conversations.

For the patient, too, there are task-oriented rules, and rules both promoting and regulating the intimacy of the exchange.

Householders and repairmen

While teacher–pupil and doctor–patient relationships may be fairly long-term and relatively intense, many service relationships may be quite casual and superficial, and restricted to only a single interaction or meeting. This includes such relationships as customer–salesman, interviewer–applicant, bus-driver–passenger, and so on. While some of these may progress to more long-term acquaintanceship – such as the customer at the village shop – most are more transitory. As a result, there are fewer rules governing the exchange, since the interaction is not seen as an ongoing one. Perhaps this is why we find the situation in which someone confides a great deal of intimate information to a stranger, for example a fellow train passenger, whom he/she never expects to meet again. Because there is no prospect of continued interaction, there are fewer repercussions of what is said or done, and therefore fewer restrictions on certain kinds of behaviour.

For most service relationships therefore there are fewer intimacy-regulating rules, but there are rules governing the actual task in hand.

TABLE 15

Rules for Repairman

1. Respond quickly in times of emergency.
2. Clear up any mess that is made.
3. Be prompt in keeping appointments.
4. Respect the householder's privacy.
5. Keep confidences.
6. Have a standard charge for service.
7. Obey the instructions of the householder.
8. Don't waste time by socialising on the job.
9. Look the householder in the eye during conversation.
10. Don't criticise the householder publicly.

Rules for Householder

1. Prepare space and facilities for the other.
2. Respect the other's professional skills and advice.
3. Offer refreshments.
4. Keep confidences.
5. Respect the repairman's privacy.

As an example of short-term service relationships we have selected the householder–repairman relation, since this is an interesting case, in the sense that it is potentially more intimate by its occurrence in the home or other physical territory of one of the participants. Therefore, we argue, it should be slightly more rule bound, especially regarding intimacy-regulating rules, than other short-term service relationships.

As we saw in Chapter 3, there are very few rules for this relationship, and they are rated as less important than in most other relationships. The important rules for the repairman and householder can be seen in Table 15.

While we still have the two general intimacy-regulating rules, these are endorsed less strongly than for other professional relationships, such as doctor–patient or teacher–pupil. And again, most of the rules are task-oriented – aimed at regulating the task in hand rather than the interpersonal relationship.

FURTHER READING

Argyle, M. (1972) *The Social Psychology of Work* Harmondsworth: Penguin
Homans, G. (1950) *The Human Group* London: Routledge & Kegan Paul
Bass, B. & Ryterband, E. (1979) *Organizational Psychology* New York: Allyn & Bacon

11

Neighbours

The relationship with neighbours is the weakest relationship which we shall consider, but it is nevertheless of considerable theoretical interest and practical importance. The *Shorter Oxford Dictionary* defines a neighbour as 'one who lives near or next to another; e.g. in an adjoining house, or in the same street or village.' However, we shall here be discussing relationships with those neighbours who are known and recognised. These overlap with friends, kin and workmates, and the neighbourhood is one of the main sources of friendship. In this chapter we shall deal with those neighbours, the great majority, who are not as intimate as friends, who, for example, are not entertained to meals, or are companions on joint outings. We shall find that there are class differences in the use of some of these labels – working-class people in Britain do not distinguish much between neighbours and friends. We shall also include some of those who live in the same neighbourhood, and who are seen regularly at pubs, church or other voluntary associations, in shops or in the street.

The largest survey of neighbours in Britain was carried out by Market Opinion and Research International who sampled 1,801 adults (see Table 1). Respondents were offered various definitions of 'neighbours', and the following were the most popular definitions:

36% 'live next door'
36% 'live in same street or block of flats'
22% 'live fairly near by or in same few streets'

According to town planners, 'neighbourhoods' are quite large units of 10–15,000 people, with their own schools and shopping centre, occupying about half a square mile, with boundaries such as main roads and railway lines. However, if people are asked to draw their own neighbourhood on a map, they mark out a much smaller area, of about 100 acres, containing 3,000–3,500 people, usually including their church, shops, pub and other meeting places.[2] It is a proportion of these people, who are known and seen regularly, but who are not really friends, that we shall regard as neighbours.

If people are asked to name the others with whom they have the strongest ties or the closest relationships, neighbours and workmates come at the bottom of the list, well below family, kin and friends. However, neighbours seem to be fairly numerous: in the MORI survey 22% could name over twenty neighbours, 47% could name eleven or more, and only 16% named three or fewer. And, like workmates, neighbours may be seen quite frequently, more than kin outside the home, for example. A number of studies have provided evidence about frequency of contact with neighbours. In the MORI survey the frequencies of several kinds of neighbour interaction were found (Table 1).

TABLE 1. Frequency of Contacts with Neighbours [1]

	Once a day or more	Once a week but less than once a day	Once a month, less than once a week	Less than once a month
You speak to a neighbour	61	30	6	3
You visit the home of a neighbour	12	29	15	43
A neighbour calls round for a chat	17	30	14	38
You have a neighbour in for a meal	0	2	4	92
You have a neighbour in for a drink	2	7	8	81
You meet for a drink in a pub or club	2	10	7	79

It can be seen that most people speak to their neighbours frequently, and 41% visit a neighbour's house once a week or more, but having a drink together is much less common, and a meal rather rare. Other studies show that 53% of people are active members of clubs, and 52% go to the pub at least once a month.[3] This does not count people talked to in the street or in shops.

We can distinguish between different types of neighbourly relations by the settings in which people meet.

1. Domestic proximity. Those who are literally next-door neighbours,

or who live very close, who may meet over the garden fence, on the doorstep, or in the hallway of an apartment block.

2. In public places. The most common meeting place in 'Yoredale' is in the street, followed by pubs, cafes, and grocery shops.[4] Towns are usually designed with a central square or other places where people can meet informally.

3. Voluntary associations. We have seen that most people belong to one or more voluntary associations; these are churches, social clubs, evening classes and sports clubs, many of them in the immediate neighbourhood.

Network analysis

It is useful to study the whole network of linkages in a group or community. Links between pairs of individuals can be seen as part of a larger pattern; 'network' is often a more useful concept than 'group', when only a few of the possible links are taken up actively. Networks can be traced by asking all the people in a neighbourhood to name those whom they feel closest to, or interact with most often. More details can be obtained about the nature of the link, whether it involves help and support or is purely sociable, whether it involves information and advice, influence e.g. in getting jobs, material or financial help, doing things together, and so on. Networks are important since they are the routes through which all this information, help, and support flows. The network in a neighbourhood will include others who are friends, kin, workmates, or just neighbours. A link can have more than one strand – another person may be a workmate as well as a neighbour.

Networks differ in several ways. One of the most important is *density*: the density of a network is the proportion of possible links that are active. A survey in Detroit found the proportions of people who were surrounded by more-or-less dense networks; in a dense network an individual's three closest friends also knew each other well, as in Figure 1a.

Networks are more dense or interconnected, under certain conditions: when people need greater help or protection, because these are not provided by the authorities, within ethnic minority or religious groups, among older married people, in traditional working-class areas like Bethnal Green in Britain, and where those involved are similar in class, age, or in other ways.

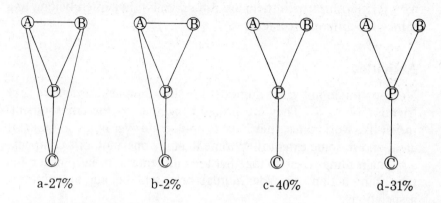

a-27%   b-2%   c-40%   d-31%

Fig. 1   NETWORKS OF DIFFERENT DENSITIES

In dense networks there is more social influence, and a pair of individuals, like husband and wife, who share the same links, are held together by the network. While such networks can be very supportive, we shall see that looser networks also have their advantages – there is less conformity pressure for example. Similarly there are advantages in networks based on a variety of different kinds of linkage, since they provide access to a wider variety of others who might be useful in some way. (cf p. 68f)[6]

Networks also vary in *homogeneity* – the degree of similarity between the members. Groups of neighbours are the *least* homogeneous in terms of education, wealth and occupational level, compared with kin, friends, etc. (see Table 2).

TABLE 2. *Similarity of Friends by Source of Friendship: Percentage With Same Status as Respondent* [7]

	Occupational level	Income	Education	Ethnicity	Age
Neighbours	39	42	43	32	53
Work	60	81	51	23	49
Childhood	40	50	49	42	56
Association	54	60	53	42	56
No known roles	36	49	46	31	60
Total	45	56	48	34	58

This may be a crucial finding about neighbours, and could explain why relationships with them are rather cool – they often belong to a somewhat different social class.

Activities

Neighbours do not share domestic life (like families), or leisure (like friends), or work. They are brought together by the environment, rather like workmates, they have to co-operate over living in the same area, and to some extent they come to enjoy one another's company. The main things they do together are talk, entertain, keep order and take joint action, provide mutual help and belong to voluntary associations.

Talk   Perhaps the main thing neighbours do is talk. Some of it is local news – who has moved, had a baby, what the council is planning. Some of it is 'gossip' – the careers and incomes of other families, illicit sexual liaisons, misbehaviour of teenagers, etc. Some is sheer chat, especially between wives, but not at a very high level of self-disclosure. This talk is most common among wives who are not working, especially among those who have young children, and the retired, who are also at home. For working-class people in Britain, this talk may be over the garden fence, on the doorstep, in the street or in shops; for middle-class women it is more often in the home. Some talk takes the form of more serious help and co-operation and will be considered later.

It is very common in the U.S.A. for wives at home to hold coffee parties, and some middle-class British wives who have no job, or who work part-time, do the same. However, neighbours, apart from those who become real friends, are not invited to meals. It is a case of 'garden party only', as it was once described in some social circles. Neighbours are kept at a distance by the non-intimate level of entertainment. It is also common in the U.S.A. to hold block parties, which all the families attend, with cookouts, and games for the young. This is very rare in Britain, apart from occasions like royal weddings.

Keeping order and taking action   Neighbours keep order in the street and near by. They bring pressure to bear on parents of noisy children or the owners of badly behaved pets. The other side of this is the need felt to keep up with the Joneses, by keeping front gardens equally tidy, or acquiring similar possessions. Neighbours sometimes have to deal

Fig. 2   MINOR HELP BY NEIGHBOURS OVER THE LAST YEAR
(PERCENTAGE OF SAMPLE)
MORI 1982

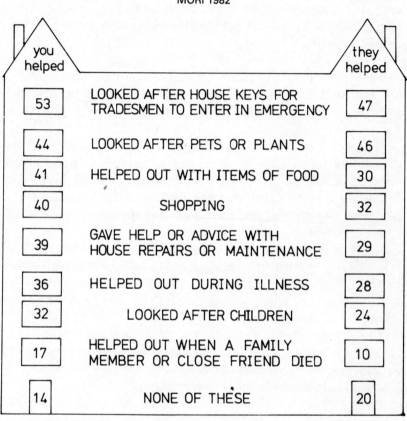

you helped		they helped
53	LOOKED AFTER HOUSE KEYS FOR TRADESMEN TO ENTER IN EMERGENCY	47
44	LOOKED AFTER PETS OR PLANTS	46
41	HELPED OUT WITH ITEMS OF FOOD	30
40	SHOPPING	32
39	GAVE HELP OR ADVICE WITH HOUSE REPAIRS OR MAINTENANCE	29
36	HELPED OUT DURING ILLNESS	28
32	LOOKED AFTER CHILDREN	24
17	HELPED OUT WHEN A FAMILY MEMBER OR CLOSE FRIEND DIED	10
14	NONE OF THESE	20

with outside threats. Then they join together to deal with the outside world. In Britain it is increasingly common for groups of neighbours to form protest groups – about a new by-pass, a proposed prison, a new housing estate, and so on. They may collect signatures, organise demonstrations, lobby councillors. In the U.S.A. it is increasingly common for householders in a block to organise their own policing, to deter criminals.

Mutual help   This is probably the most important thing neighbours do. The MORI survey found that neighbours had given each other a great deal of help in small matters over the previous year or so (Figure 2).

However, people did not approach their neighbours for more demanding forms of help. For financial problems only 3% would approach a neighbour, for help or advice with a death in the family 7%, about unemployment 3%, and about marriage break-up 4%. For problems like these people turned to their spouses (in the first three cases) and to other members of the family.

Help varies with the time of life, and with other variables. Young wives help each other with children and baby-sitting, older people are helped with shopping, gardeners lend each other tools and exchange seedlings, motorists help with cars that fail to start or are stuck in the snow.

There is more help among working-class people (p. 291). There is also a lot of mutual help in the country, between farmers, who co-operate over the use of heavy machinery, sheep-dipping, or providing labour to help with urgent jobs on the farm.[9]

Another kind of help consists of the provision of advice or information on medicine, law, gardening, fashion and many other matters. It has long been known that there are 'opinion leaders' – individuals who are known to be well informed on a certain topic. Often the first step in tackling a problem is to discuss it with one of these people, before seeing a doctor, psychiatrist, lawyer, or what-ever. One of the functions of social networks is to provide access to the right person and sometimes the local expert will actually provide the service needed. For example, there are some people who are good at listening to problems, who become in effect local psychotherapists, and it has been found that they are as successful as the properly trained ones.

Mutual help groups This is something of a new social movement, from the U.S.A. It consists of the organising of local groups of people who share a similar problem. To some extent it has been going on for a long time – groups of young mothers who help each other with child-minding, and who can give one another useful advice, for example. One of the first kinds of organised groups was Alcoholics Anonymous. Now there are groups of widows, the recently divorced, parents of handicapped children, families of prisoners, neurotics, gamblers, obese people, and others. These groups sometimes have an inspirational, almost religious, air about them. They often have the following characteristics:

1. The members share a common problem, which they can talk about, and feel understood.
2. The members meet regularly to provide mutual help and support.
3. Those who need help progress to providing help for others, which in turn helps them.
4. By associating with the others, members come to see themselves as normal, instead of deviant.
5. There is a shared group determination to work together on a problem, such as losing weight, gambling, etc.
6. Members receive information and education, through belonging to the group.
7. There is shared action and involvement, which reduces passivity and promotes the attainment of goals.[10]

To some extent such groups depend on natural informal leadership from those who are better educated or informed, and who know how to cope with the problem or how to deal with the authorities. The groups may also be helped by a social worker or other relevant professional. In practice there is often close collaboration between professional and lay leaders. Professionals may take the initiative in bringing groups together, and provide expert information or help where needed. They may also recruit lay para-professionals to help them. In a project in Philadelphia a number of informal helpers were identified in their local networks, and trained in various helping skills, especially in dealing with life crises. In another project hairdressers were trained in counselling techniques, since clients often discuss their problems with hairdressers.[11]

Voluntary associations Many people belong to clubs, classes, churches, and so on. These are mainly based on local neighbourhoods, and are more formally organised than the groups we have considered so far. The extent of this activity is shown in Table 3.

The Young and Willmott survey of Londoners found that 53% of married men working full time were active members of at least one club, and that 16% were officers of clubs. In addition, 52% of them went to a pub once a month or more, and 15% to church regularly. The MORI survey shows that for many people those they know best are found in pubs and clubs of various kinds. Bracey's study of young families in the suburbs of Bristol found that men were more often members of athletic and educational groups than women. There was a

TABLE 3. Membership of Voluntary Associations

Survey by Young and Willmott [12]

Active members of one or more clubs	53%
Officers or committee members	16%
Church (at least once a month)	15%

Survey by Bracey [13]	*men*	*women*
Members of social clubs	17	14
Members of athletic clubs	9	1
Members of parent–teacher associations	—	3
Attend evening classes, or other educational and cultural groups	6	1

'Social Trends' survey [14]		
Dancing (in last 4 weeks)	14	16
Watch football	7	1
Bingo	2	6
Darts	15	4
Social and voluntary work	8	9
Amateur music/drama	4	3

	People known best	
MORI survey [15]	*men*	*women*
People at local pub or club	23	10
Members of church	7	12
Members of sporting club	11	5
Members of club associated with hobby or interest	10	7
Members of a voluntary association	2	3

famous study of 'Yankee City' by Lloyd Warner[16] which found very extensive club membership. He found that many of these associations and branches were quite small – 28% had under ten members, 54% had twenty or fewer. He also found that members of these groups often spanned three or four of his six social classes, though some groups were exclusively drawn from one or two adjacent classes, and women favoured these more exclusive groups.

The rewards and costs of neighbours

Compared with other relationships, neighbours afford a rather low source of satisfaction and conflict, a little below workmates, as our results in Figure 5 (p. 83) show. Nevertheless 36% of people say that they are 'very satisfied' with their neighbours.

We have just shown that neighbours do provide a certain amount of help, especially at crises, and especially for old people. In addition people engage in quite a lot of sheer sociable activity, around the home and at clubs. Does frequent contact with neighbours lead to better health or happiness? Many studies have looked into this, and the answer seems to be that good or frequent contacts with neighbours, and membership of churches or other local groups, *is* clearly associated with greater happiness, well-being, health and mental health, and that this is independent of the effects of marriage or other forms of social support. There is some evidence, not very conclusive, that this is because contact with neighbours is an aid to good health etc., rather than vice versa. On the other hand the effects of neighbours are definitely weaker than the effects of being married, or of friends or relations.

A study of a Chinese–American community in Washington found that a measure of neighbourhood social support predicted freedom from psychiatric symptoms. It is interesting to see the items that made up the index of neighbourhood support (shown in Table 4.)

The effects of neighbours and neighbourhood groups are greater for the elderly, for those of lower social class, and for those in poor health. In Britain 29% of 65–74-year-olds, and 47% of those 75 or over, live alone, and many of them feel lonely. In addition a lot of them have no children, or no kin living near, and many of their earlier friends have died. For them neighbours and neighbourhood groups are very important.[18]

Neighbours are also a source of annoyance of various kinds, though

TABLE 4. *Some items from the Neighbourhood Social Support Scale* [17]

Feelings about the neighbourhood
Feelings about people nearby
Frequency of talking with neighbours
Close friends in D.C. area
Get together with friends from old country
Involved in Chinese activities
Involved in Chinese association
Officer in Chinese association
Satisfied with job

the typical level of this is low. Seventy-eight per cent in the MORI survey had no problems with neighbours over a two-year period. The most common problems reported were noise (7%), pets (4%), and behaviour of children (4%). Other studies show that there is a concern with privacy – neighbours are usually not really friends yet they live so close they know a great deal about us – hence the need for fences, trees, and net curtains. Sometimes there is anxiety about gossip – people know that the neighbours discuss them and pass on the latest news. There is the problem that many of the neighbours are of slightly different social class – their houses, gardens, children and pets are a little dirtier and more disreputable, or the reverse. Respectable working-class people do not want to be involved with the 'rough' families down the road. And while people want to feel that they can call on neighbours to help them in time of need, they do not want either to feel indebted to them, or to be called on too much themselves.

Are people worried about 'keeping up with the Joneses'? The MORI survey asked about ways in which respondents felt that their neighbours were better off. About half felt that the neighbours *were* better off in some way. Some were thought to be happier (14%), or to have better cars, or jobs (both 13%), children or social life (both 12%). However very few admitted that they envied these things – only 11% in all, the most envied items being cars (3%).

Effects of the physical environment

This is what neighbours are all about – they are people who know each other mainly or partly because they live near each other. Many studies have shown that physical proximity is important in whether people know or like each other. Sometimes the effect is very strong: Festinger and his colleagues[19] found that in halls of residence for students no fewer than 41% of next-door neighbours were chosen as friends; for married students living in houses 27% of next-door neighbours were chosen. However, proximity and frequency of interaction can have the opposite effect and lead to disliking, though this is less common. In older and less homogeneous groups, who have well-established networks outside the neighbourhood already, the effects of proximity are much less marked. In an older working–class area of Oxford, only 40% accepted their neighbours, though 60% had no friends at all.[20] In a large apartment building in New York, although the residents were similar in income, age, and religion, few said more than hello to each other.[21] People will like their neighbours more if they see them more often – if they are not away at work, if they are in a small group of houses, or in a cul-de-sac.

Contacts between neighbours are greatly affected by the details of the architecture. Baum and Valins[22] compared students living in groups of thirty-four off a long corridor with a lounge, and others in groups of three, sharing a lounge but with no corridor. Students in the corridor buildings felt crowded, lacked privacy, wanted to avoid others, and did not form good relations with one another.

Another example is the tower block, and some other kinds of large apartment building, in which people often do not get to know each other. It is a help if there are areas for social contact and leisure activities. A problem with these buildings is that there are dark corners which no one controls, and which become arenas for delinquency. The solution is to have areas that are visible to, and can be controlled by, small groups of residents – 'defensible space'.[23] However, most people get on better with their neighbours if they live in single-family houses. The percentages of families who had contact with neighbours in the previous month, in a study in New Zealand, were:[24]

single-family houses	61%
two-family housing	47%
multiple housing	19%

However, in an Australian study it was found that people living in high-rise buildings were not particularly isolated. They only knew people who lived in the same building, and they saw them less frequently than those in other forms of housing, but they talked for longer when they did meet, and they knew a larger number of people.[25]

In the traditional English village, where virtually everyone worked on farms, there was a very close-knit community of neighbours and kin, in which people depended on each other a great deal for help, because they had to. 'Whether gossip, bickering and family feuds were or were not a more prevalent feature than a wholesome sense of togetherness could vary from village to village'.[26] However, all this has changed with the decline in the number of agricultural workers and the big influx of commuters, whose work and main social life is outside the village. They are often resented by the original villagers, who look back to a partly mythical golden age of social unity.

Some sociologists forecast that the growth of city life would lead to increasing social isolation, and the decline of family, kin, neighbourhood, and other face-to-face groups. It has been found that in general the larger the community the less people know their neighbours. In an American survey respondents were asked 'About how many people in this neighbourhood do you know by name?' The answers were:[27]

	under 3	over 20
In large cities	22%	27%
Outside cities	3%	70%

So it is really true that people know their neighbours better in villages. However within cities there are areas of quite different kinds. Run-down, inner-city areas, near factories and docks, do have the features feared by the early sociologists – people living alone, in isolation from each other, high rates of crime and mental disorder. On the other hand well-established working-class areas, often now demolished as 'slums', like the East End of London, have been found to be as cohesive and as full of neighbourly activity as villages. In the U.S.A. there has been an extensive move out towards the suburbs, especially by younger and more prosperous families. Sociologists made gloomy predictions about suburbs too – they would develop a tribal-like conformity, with limited social involvements and attachments. In fact American suburbs have more active social life and involvement in the neighbourhood than other parts of American cities, more localised friendships, but less contact with the kin left behind.[28] British suburbs and housing estates are not all so neighbourly, partly because of lack of clubs and social facilities (see below p. 292).

I DON'T MIND GENERAL GORNFORTH RELIVING HIS MEMORIES OF LIFE OUT EAST — IT'S THESE DAMN SANDSTORMS I OBJECT TO !

K.Lamb 81

Private Eye

When do people get to know their neighbours? We can now gather together some of the main points made in this chapter by listing the conditions under which two people will establish a neighbourly relation.

Which people are most involved with neighbours? They are those who are at home during the day – wives and the retired, also people with children, and long-term residents. Women see neighbours from the street more frequently, while men spend more time in clubs.

Which neighbours are chosen? The main factors in choosing them are: living near, living within the same enclave, being similar in age, social class and ethnicity, and having other things in common – religion, politics, occupation, or having the same problems.

Which neighbourhoods are the most neighbourly? They are small units, such as villages, streets in the slums, some new housing estates, provided that there are good meeting places and social clubs. Tower blocks and the like are less neighbourly than streets of single houses. Areas that are homogeneous, especially in age and social class, are more neighbourly, especially working-class areas.

Age, sex, class and national differences

Age   Contact with neighbours varies with the stages in the life cycle, and corresponding family composition. Married people with children see a lot of their neighbours, and depend on them a lot for help with the children, shopping, etc. Forty-five per cent of them visit the home of a neighbour weekly, compared with 35% for single adults or pairs of adults without children. Old people also see their neighbours, and call on them a good deal, though they do not know very many. It is partly a matter of being at home during the day: young wives with children and retired folk of both sexes are at home most, and see most of their neighbours. The older people are, the more their friends are drawn from the same neighbourhood. Young people are not usually much concerned with the next-door neighbours, though they do attend the neighbourhood social facilities, and make friends with those in adjoining rooms at college.

Sex   We have seen that women who are at home spend a lot of time with other similar women, and that what they mainly do is talk, both gossip and passing on useful information. Women are less active in clubs than men, especially athletic clubs.

Class   Neighbours are defined rather differently in different social classes. For traditional working class people in Britain, neighbours are those who live next door or quite near in the same street, and they are the main source of friendship and help. 'I suppose people who come from outside think it's an awful place, but us established ones like it. Here you can just open the door and say hello to everybody.'[29] Exactly the same was found in a slum in New York: neighbours were very important. People met in local bars and settlement houses, and people felt 'at home' in their own street, where they often sat and talked when the weather was warm.[30] Working-class people live close to their neighbours, and do not really distinguish them very clearly from friends, while kin are also included in the network. Working-class people help each other a lot on a day-to-day basis, lending items like cups of sugar, loaves of bread, towels.

For the middle classes, friends are drawn from further afield, though often in the same neighbourhood; those who live near, but belong to a different class, are not really seen as neighbours at all.[31] Middle-class people invite their neighbours into the house, though not for meals, while working-class folk talk to their neighbours in the street or in the pub. Middle-class people are quite self-sufficient, though they may borrow garden tools. The middle classes are more likely to belong to voluntary associations, and are much more likely to be officers or committee members (see Figure 3).

The MORI survey used the 'Acorn' method of classifying neighbourhoods, into eleven basic types. There was most social contact in modern family housing for manual workers, and in rural areas, least in overcrowded and low-income areas with immigrants, though a lot of neighbours could be named in overcrowded areas. There was most help in modern family housing for those with higher incomes, in student and high-status non-family areas, and in traditional high status suburbia. There was least help in low-income areas with immigrants, and urban local-authority housing.

National differences Similar studies have been carried out on neighbours in the U.S.A., and a number of interesting differences have appeared. Bracey[33] compared somewhat similar housing estates in the

Fig. 2 MEMBERS AND OFFICERS OF CLUBS (MARRIED WORKING MEN)

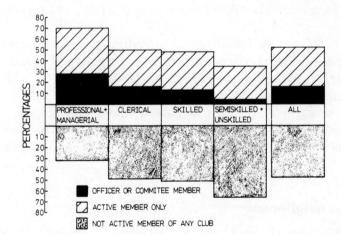

two countries, and found that there was greater neighbourliness in the U.S.A., while many of the English wives interviewed were quite lonely, though in both countries people kept the neighbours at a distance. The American wives had more coffee parties and there were neighbourhood picnics and barbecues. There were also more social organisations in the American neighbourhoods, while the English families complained that community facilities, especially for children, were inadequate. Other studies have shown that 85% or more of Americans belong to clubs and other associations, compared with about 50% for the British. American churches, for example, offer a wide range of social facilities in addition to the church services. A comparison of two small towns[34] found that people met in different physical settings. In the British small town they met in the street; the next most frequent meetings were in pubs and shops. The Americans met most frequently in schools; the next most frequent meetings being in the street and shops. The Americans met on many occasions organised for, or by, adolescents or children.

What is the explanation for these national differences? Part of the explanation probably lies in the greater mobility of Americans. They are used to moving house and to welcoming and assimilating others who have just moved in, including immigrants from abroad. The churches and other institutions are geared towards helping new arrivals to the community. In addition, the hot summer weather and open-air life makes for easy contacts between families. However the amount of neighbourliness varies with the physical setting, and we described above another American setting where almost no contact with neighbours developed.

The MORI survey found some interesting regional differences inside Britain. The Scots could name by far the largest number of neighbours – 39% could name twenty or more. People in the North called round for a chat most often, those in the Midlands went out to the pub for a drink with their neighbours most, and people in the South went to the pub, and also asked neighbours in for a meal rather more than others – 28% sometimes did this, compared to 16% in the North.

Rules for neighbours

Neighbours were included in our rules study, and twelve rules were strongly endorsed as applying to neighbours (see Table 5).

TABLE 5. Rules for Neighbours

1. Be willing to help in an emergency.
2. Respect the neighbours' privacy.
3. Be considerate about noise, pets, children, activities.
4. Watch each other's houses when the others are away.
5. Keep confidences.
6. Always greet one another in public.
7. Attempt to maintain neighbourhood standard of property.
8. Make an effort to get to know one another.
9. Don't encroach over shared boundary.
10. Seek to repay debts, favours or compliments no matter how small.
11. Look the other person in the eye during conversation.
12. Don't feel free to take up as much of the other's time as one desires.

We found that older subjects endorsed a number of these rules more strongly, possibly reflecting their greater experience of relations with neighbours.

These rules are exactly as we predicted from knowledge of the problems facing neighbours. Residents need to be helped in emergencies (rule 1), but are worried about privacy (2), and gossip (5), and want to avoid annoyances such as noise (3), and over boundaries (9) and property standards (7). They do not want help to be one-sided (4 and 10), or to have to spend too much time (12), but an effort should be made to set up some sort of relationship (6 and 8). We think that this is a very useful set of rules, and that those who follow them will be better neighbours.

The nature of the neighbour relationship

We can now point to the key features of this curious relationship. It is unlike any of the others we have considered, in that neighbours live nearer, but are less similar, and the relationship is less intimate. There is frequent interaction, but this does not usually lead to a close relationship, rather to one that is 'cordial but distant'. Privacy is a problem because neighbours are not usually similar enough or intimate enough to know as much about each other as they are likely to do. The most important activity of neighbours is helping one another when needed – everyday help between mothers and children, and between working-class wives who borrow things, regular co-operation between farmers, help in domestic crises, and the formation of mutual help groups. There is also a lot of sheer sociability, in the street, over the garden fence, and at pubs and clubs. There are special and familiar difficulties with neighbours, over noise, dogs, children and fences.

Neighbours living under the same roof

Many people, particularly the young and students, share accommodation. This involves a relationship that is very close in one respect since the participants are living in close physical proximity and often sharing costs and facilities, but is not an intimate interpersonal relationship. While room-mates or people sharing flats and houses are often friends before living together, there are many who do not know each other beforehand, as in the case of most student accommodation. We have already noted that proximity and contact encourage liking and friendship (p. 70), but may also, under certain circumstances, lead to dislike and conflict.

The sorts of concerns we have noted for neighbours are also likely to occur, in even more extreme forms, for those sharing accommodation. Privacy becomes a critical issue, since there are usually no physical boundaries to hide behind within shared housing. And co-operation over annoyances is also important.

TABLE 6. Rules for Sharing Accommodation

1. Respect the other's possessions.
2. Share the housework.
3. Be considerate about noise, visitors, hot water, etc.
4. Share expenses or establish rules for doing so.
5. Address the other person by first name.
6. Keep confidences.
7. Respect his/her privacy.
8. Be tolerant of each other's friends.
9. Show mutual trust.
10. Be willing to listen to each other's problems.
11. Look him/her in the eye during conversation.
12. Look after the other person when he/she is ill.
13. Be loyal to one another.
14. Repay debts, favours or compliments no matter how small.
15. Show interest in each other's daily activities.
16. Don't nag the other person.
17. Stand up for the other person in his/her absence.
18. Share news of success with him/her.
19. Don't criticise him/her in public.

We found the following rules for people of the same sex sharing accommodation. (See Table 6) Again, in the same way as for neighbours, we have rules about the problems and conflicts that can occur between people living in close proximity. But in addition, we have rules about intimacy and support, which overlap to some extent with the rules of friendship, cohabitation and marriage.

FURTHER READING

Bracey, C. (1977) *Neighbours* London: Routledge & Kegan Paul
Fischer, C. (1977) *Networks and Places* New York: Free Press

12

Training and Therapy for Relationships

Now that we have all this knowledge about relationships, what can be done with it? We shall start by describing existing methods of training and therapy for relationships, and then show how these could be improved on the basis of the new knowledge. We shall also describe how people can help themselves to handle their relationships better – by following the rules which we have found, by learning interaction skills, and by a deeper understanding of each relationship.

Intervention methods have traditionally focused on improving distressed relationships, for example, unhappy marriages, or the 'problem' child in the family. These methods have tended to be clinically based, and run by professionally trained personnel, such as psychiatrists, clinical psychologists, social workers, or trained counsellors, as in individual marital or family therapy. More recently, intervention methods have aimed at prevention: attempting to provide the individual, couple, or family with skills that will prevent or minimise the problem. As such, they focus on non-distressed relationships – those functioning at adequate or high levels of satisfaction and competence. They also operate to prepare individuals for dealing with potentially difficult life changes such as marriage.

There are also methods dealing with relationship enhancement for its own sake. These aim to attain the maximum potential from the relationship for the benefit of the individual, couple, or family. These include family and marital enrichment programmes, as well as sensitivity training methods.

In addition there are self-help techniques and organisations that may teach relationship skills or provide help with distressed relationships. Many teach-yourself manuals are available. Other help agencies include counselling offered by religious bodies, help or advice from general practitioners, informal advice from friends, family, neigh-

296

bours, and the like. Though these individuals may not be professionally trained therapists or counsellors, research has shown that they may be helpful in alleviating distress by informal 'psychotherapy'.

While most of these methods deal with our more intimate relationships, there are also methods of teaching professional and work relationships skills. These include the wide variety of teaching programmes used in management and supervisory training, in teacher-training, and the like.

EXAMPLES OF TRAINING AND TREATMENT FOR RELATIONSHIPS

Psychotherapy

The case for the use of psychotherapy in relationship problems is that a person may have internal problems – anxieties, conflicts, hostilities, lack of self-esteem, or mistaken beliefs – which prevent him or her from entering, or making a success of, certain relationships. These problems are usually attributed to difficult interpersonal relationships in childhood, especially with the opposite sex parent. Psychotherapy takes a variety of forms, Freudian and otherwise, and focuses on a distressed individual. The following techniques are common to all varieties of psychotherapy, used by therapists (T) for patients (P)[1].

1. T expresses a warm, accepting and often uncritical attitude of interested concern towards P, and creates a strong interpersonal relationship; it is a kind of ideal friendship, in which T participates emotionally, though it is restricted to the therapeutic hour.

2. P is encouraged to talk about his anxieties, conflicts and other bottled-up emotions; the cathartic expression of these feelings, and sharing them with another person who does not react critically, helps to relieve them, and enables P to think about painful problems.

3. T tries to explore P's subjective world of feeling and thinking, to understand P's point of view and to open up communication with him.

4. T tries to give P insight into why he reacts as he does, and thus to change him or her. This is done by the verbal labelling of P's behaviour; psychoanalysts and others will offer a theoretical interpretation as well, for example obsessional hand-washing may be explained as the symbolic cleansing of guilt.

5. T helps P to make plans and positive decisions – to try out new ways of dealing with people and situations and to make positive efforts, thus

becoming committed, rather than remaining indifferent and passive.

Psychoanalysts emphasise interpretation, (4) above; non-directive therapists emphasise uncritical acceptance (1); and existential therapists the taking of decisions (5). Cognitive and 'rational-emotive' therapists concentrate on removing unreasonable beliefs, such as the belief that one should be loved and admired by all; here the therapist acts as a kind of teacher. We shall offer an extension of this approach below, as applied to relationships.

In fact for many patients who receive psychotherapy the problems derive mainly from their relationships. Adolescents and older people may be in conflict with their parents – for example feeling both hostile and dependent, or being unable to break free and establish a relationship between equals. Indeed the classical psychoanalytic cases involved problems of this kind. Psychotherapeutic methods such as encounter groups or cognitive therapy have also been used to deal with the problems of loneliness, with apparent success.[2]

There is evidence that psychotherapy in general is moderately successful: it results *on average* in less anxiety, greater self-esteem, better adjustment and better work achievement, than for untreated controls.[3] However, there is a great deal of variation, with some psychotherapists showing consistently good results, and others consistently failing to make their patients better. It is also found that briefly trained housewives and students may be just as successful as professional therapists.

Social skills training

Social skills training (SST) is a structured learning method for teaching interaction skills. It aims to change specific interpersonal *behaviours* that affect our relationships with others, such as the level of assertiveness, listening and conversation skills, appropriate non-verbal skills, and other behaviours associated with social competence. The underlying ethos of SST is that social behaviour, like any motor skill (for example, driving a car, swimming) can be broken down into its component parts, and taught. Poor social habits can be unlearnt and replaced by more socially skilled behaviour, by means of techniques such as direct instruction, video-taped feedback, role-played performance, modelling (see below), and practice.

The basic technique is role-playing, in a three-stage sequence:

1. There is a lecture, discussion, demonstration, tape-recording or film about a particular aspect of the skill. This is particularly important when an unfamiliar skill is being taught or when rather subtle social techniques are involved. The demonstration is especially valuable: it is known as 'modelling'.

2. A problem situation is defined, and 'stooges' are produced, with whom trainees role-play for seven to fifteen minutes each. In group SST other trainees may take the part of 'stooge'. The background to the situation may be filled in with written materials, such as the application forms of candidates for interview, or background information about persona problems. The 'stooges' may be carefully trained beforehand to provide various problems, such as talking too much or having elaborate and plausible excuses.

3. There is a feedback session, consisting of verbal comments by the trainer, discussion with the other trainees and playback of audio- or video-tapes. Verbal feedback is used to draw attention constructively and tactfully to what the trainee was doing wrong, and to suggest alternative styles of behaviour. The tape-recordings provide clear evidence for the accuracy of what is being said.

There is often a fourth phase, in which the role-playing, phase 2, is repeated, giving practice in the new learnt behaviour. In micro-teaching this is known as 're-teaching'.

This basic method has now been extended to include a number of techniques in addition to straight role-playing, such as:

non-verbal communication
the perception of non-verbal signals
taking the role of the other
rewardingness
analysis of difficult social situations
conversational and sequence analysis
self-presentation[4]

Since specific skills are taught, it is necessary to modify these to fit the social class, or other aspects of the sub-culture of trainees. The skills which are most suitable for diplomats and senior managers would not be suitable for unemployed youth. Those going to work in another culture can be trained in the social skills used in that culture.

SST programmes have been applied to a number of different areas:

1. Initiation of new relationships, such as friendship acquisition, or making heterosexual contacts.

2. Being assertive, expressing positive and negative feelings and making or refusing requests of others, both in intimate relationships and with more impersonal contacts such as shopkeepers or waiters.
3. Training specific task skills such as interviewing, selling, teaching, or public speaking.

Extension of SST to marital therapy will be described below. In addition, it has been used to teach parenting skills[5] and to teach listening and conversational skills to lonely people, and to reduce both shyness and loneliness problems.[6]

SST has also been applied in training for work relationships. For example, the average manager deals with a wide range of different situations during the course of a working week, which may range from chairing a meeting, interviewing job applicants, dealing with clients, giving and taking orders, carrying out negotiations, disseminating information to peers, resolving conflicts, training juniors, and so on. All require different approaches, and somewhat different styles.

Similar methods have been applied to teaching a variety of professional–client work relationships, for example, the doctor – patient consultation and medical interviewing,[7] and teacher–pupil relationships. Most teaching programmes use SST methods, to improve teaching skills.[8] There are also programmes for training police officers in dealing with the public or in hostage negotiation.[9]

SST has been found to be as good or better than alternative methods, both for the professional training of teachers, interviewers, salesmen, doctors, etc., and for a wide range of mental patients.

Marriage guidance

Marital distress is one of the three most common reasons that people seek therapy.[10] Every year in Britain about 100,000 people approach some kind of marital agency or social worker for help with their marital problems. The main sources of help, in something like this order, are:[11]

doctors
National Marriage Guidance Council
social workers
family and friends
clergy
psychiatrists
Samaritans

We shall discuss briefly some of the main approaches to the problem. Most of them involve both partners being dealt with together, though some individuals also seek marriage guidance.

"I think we may have left it a little late, Mrs Plowright."

(Punch)

Marriage guidance counsellors are unpaid, and are not professional social workers or psychologists. They are, however, trained and experienced in dealing with marital problems, and act as lay therapists with couples. They listen, they try to help the couple solve their problems as a neutral third party, they usually offer guidance or advice, and they do their best to preserve the marriage.[12]

Behavioural marital therapy

There are two main approaches to marital therapy:

Communication skills training teaches people to state their feelings about problems in a clear, direct and open way without making accusations or laying blame. They make statements in a supportive

way by responding empathically. In this way, communication becomes clear, ambiguous and confused statements are avoided, and
problems can be negotiated.

Behavioural therapy is based on ideas from behaviour therapy and
from social psychology, and is administered by psychologists. There
are several main themes, which reflect some of the findings about
disturbed marriages we described earlier. Its aim is to increase the
mutual exchange of positive and rewarding behaviour. Like communication skills training, it often teaches communication skills and
problem-solving techniques. It also uses methods of negotiating and
contracting.

The process starts by couples facing up to their problems. Each is
taught to present his or her side of the case tactfully, so as not to annoy
the other, with quite specific complaints, not derogating the other,
admitting to his or her part in the problem, and trying to solve the
immediate problem. Couples and their therapists then try to work out
a solution focusing on one problem at a time, often involving more
rewarding behaviour on the part of each and the making of contracts.
1. Increasing rewards. Each partner discovers the things the other
finds most rewarding, and tries to provide more of them. Sometimes
one day a week is defined as a 'love day' and special efforts are made to
increase the rewards. In one version each partner lists three kinds of
behaviour he or she wishes the other would perform more frequently,
and they then give each other points for the number of times they do it.
2. Improved communication. Partners are trained to be better senders
and receivers, for example of non-verbal cues for emotions and
intentions, sometimes using video techniques and modelling; listening skills are improved and empathy increased. They may need some
social skills training to learn how to put their case to their spouse
tactfully, and constructively. Some behavioural marital therapists are
now using the process of 'relabelling', which recognises the importance of people's causal attributions about behaviour.[13] Distressed
couples may be inferring the wrong reasons for their partner's
negative behaviour, and clarifying or changing such attributes can
improve the relationship.
3. Contracting. Changes are negotiated: if he does this, she will do
that. For example he agrees to take her out once a week, she agrees to
sex games of his choice once a week. A common exchange is for the
wife to agree to more sex in exchange for the husband engaging in

more conversation.[14] Part of the contract is that partners will not specify changes in behaviour that are unreasonable or aversive for the other spouse. Formal contracts may be written out.[15] There are two main types of formal contracting.[16] The 'quid pro quo' (tit for tat) contract means each person's behaviour change is contingent on a particular change in the partner's behaviour. For example, he agrees to take her dancing once a week on condition that she goes with him to watch football on Saturday afternoons. Usually the two events involve things done together, so that the contract results in more joint activities. Another kind is the 'Good Faith' contract, where each agrees to receive certain rewards only if they have kept their side of the bargain, and this doesn't always depend on what the other does. For example, he agrees to be able to watch TV only if he has engaged in conversation with her first.

Many follow-up studies have been carried out of this kind of therapy, with generally positive results.[17] Behavioural marital therapy tends to show more long-term change, although both methods generally show short-term improvement.[18] Marital therapy has positive benefits on about 65% of clients.[19]

Pre-marital counselling

This tends to emphasise the rule-governed nature of relationships. Its aim is to increase self-awareness and improve communication and interaction skills with the long-term goal of providing couples with the competencies that are related to marital satisfaction (see Chapter 6). Some programmes are structured to teach specific skills such as listening and speaking skills, discovering which behaviours are pleasing or displeasing to the partner, assertiveness and making requests, contracting and behaviour monitoring and 'pleasuring.'[20] Others emphasise interpersonal skills of self-disclosure, empathy and problem-solving.

Relationship enrichment

Enrichment programmes are aimed at well-functioning, non-distressed, committed relationships. They aim to help healthy couples or families to achieve their full potential for relationship growth by maximising the quality of the interactions and awareness of own and partner's or family's feelings and needs. The aim is to increase the love and intimacy component of relationships by enhancing skills of marital communication, sexuality, conflict negotiation, and problem solving, with generally more emphasis on the expression of feelings and empathic listening skills than on conflict and problem-solving techniques.

Methods used in these programmes are diverse, and can include structured discussion, lectures, experimental exercises, role-played simulations, feedback, set reading, and 'homework'. There are many such enrichment programmes operating in the United States,[21] and their popularity is increasing.

Family therapy

This is another kind of group psychotherapy, typically with two parents and a disturbed teenage child. The goal is to improve understanding, communication and problem-solving. In addition attempts are made to modify the family unit, as a system in equilibrium. The primary aim of family therapy is to encourage change in the individual by altering the social environment in the family system. Eighty-five per cent of family therapists regard improved communication as important for all families, compared to only 23% for improvement in an individual's symptoms.[22] Family therapy emphasises:

1. Clear and effective communication between members;
2. Making implicit rules explicit so that these may be examined and dealt with directly;
3. Teaching negotiation skills to deal with conflict situations.

Self-help

In addition to the professional services providing intervention or clinical treatment facilities, there are also a number of self-help and non-professional agencies which operate as sources of aid for distressed relationships, or as organisations that provide opportunities for establishing new relationships. English examples include Network and Gingerbread, and many other local or national organisations established by individuals to aid others in similar circumstances, such as post-divorce or single parenting.

Divorce support groups are proliferating in the United States, and there is some evidence that the social support of peers in these groups helps to improve self-confidence and emotional autonomy and aids in successful adjustment after separation.[23] There are support programmes for the lonely, such as volunteer visitors to provide companionship for the elderly.[24]

There are also commercial agencies such as computer-dating services which help the establishment of new relationships. And we have already noted the effects of neighbourhood and community organisation in facilitating meetings and continuing interactions between people (see Chapter 11), nor should we underestimate the importance of family and friends in providing help and support with distressed relationships (see Chapter 3).

Another kind of self-help is obtained by reading books written for the purpose, and containing exercises. Some success has been found with such materials on weight reduction, study behaviour and exercise.[25] In the social skills sphere there are books on inter-cultural skills and assertiveness. We discuss below the value of giving people a better understanding of relationships and how they work.

NEW METHODS OF TRAINING AND TREATMENT

We have a number of ideas for increasing the effectiveness of training for relationships, which arise out of the research that has been described in the course of this book.

Rules of relationships

We have presented rules for each of the relationships discussed, and in some cases we have produced evidence that breaking the rules results in damaging the relationships. Teaching people the rules could quite easily be incorporated in a didactic kind of therapy or in self-help schemes.

These rules can be divided into two broad areas. There are rules of rewardingness – rules about exchange and intimacy – and rules about conflict, both avoiding and confronting it. In addition, we shall discuss two other types of rules: task-related rules which deal with the practical side of task relationships such as work or professional service relations; and self-presentation rules: the more formal rules of etiquette and appearance.

Rules of rewardingness Later in this chapter we shall discuss two important ways of being rewarding – through intimacy and support – but what sorts of rules are applied in relationships that reflect these skills? How do we express and reflect intimacy? The following rules are ways of doing this.

1. Addressing the other person by their first name.
2. Showing an interest in the other person's activities.
3. Sharing news of success.
4. Trusting and confiding in the other person.
5. Showing the other person positive unconditional regard.
6. Acknowledging birthdays and special occasions.
7. Striving to make the other person happy while in each other's company.
8. Inviting the person to family celebrations or other intimate affairs.
9. Making the other person welcome.
10. Showing affection.
11. Discussing intimate topics such as sex or death, religion or politics.

As we have seen in previous chapters, these are among the most important rules that people endorse for close relationships such as marriage, family, friends and heterosexual relations. They are, however, rarely applied to more distant relationships – those with work colleagues, neighbours, or professional and service relations. These are therefore rules which are specific to our intimate relationships, and the relevance of applying these sorts of rules will change as the closeness of a relationship changes.

If we do not apply intimacy behaviours as a way of making our less intimate relationships rewarding, how do we do this? Rules of support and exchange are important for both intimate and non-intimate long-term relations, but the type of exchange and support will differ according to the nature of the relationship. The following are examples of such rules:

1. Volunteer help in time of need or when requested or in an emergency.
2. Look after the other person when he/she is ill, or look after the children when the other is unwell.
3. Stand up for the other person in his/her absence.
4. Be emotionally supportive.
5. Offer advice, encouragement or guidance and be willing to listen to advice.

6. Repay debts, compliments and favours, however small.
7. Fight for the other's interests where necessary.
8. Be considerate about the other's personal problems.

These sorts of rule were endorsed for both intimate and less intimate relationships such as those with neighbours, work colleagues and superiors. Of course, the kinds of support and help that are offered will differ between the two. Friends are expected to give emotional support, but work relations and neighbours generally are not. Work colleagues are expected to help in practical ways related to the work situation. And the idea of equitable exchange varies across relationships. Neighbours and both parent-in-law and son/daughter-in-law are expected to repay debts, compliments and favours however small, while for friends, spouses and family, such 'tit-for-tat' exchanges are not endorsed. In our most intimate relations, we do not have to repay such exchanges directly.

Rules of conflict The notion of rules as proscriptions designed to avoid problems is more familiar than rules prescribing rewarding behaviour. For example, we have rules of the road to avoid accidents and allow smooth flow of traffic, and we have rules for playing sports to ensure an orderly game. Similarly, we have rules designed to allow relationships to operate smoothly by avoiding common sources of conflict which may disrupt that relationship.

The specific rules will depend to a large extent on the type of relationship. For example, rules about faithfulness may be very important in certain relationships such as husband–wife or dating relations, but will hardly be relevant to work colleagues or kin relationships, since in these latter cases issues of faithfulness or infidelity are not likely to be sources of conflict. However, we have already seen, in Chapter 3, that there are some general rules which are applied across relationships and cultures. These deal with issues that may lead to conflict in any relationship – privacy, keeping of confidences, and public criticism.

What are these conflict-regulating rules? We list some of the most important ones below, together with the relationship to which they apply.
1. Should respect the other's privacy (all relationships).
2. Should not disclose confidences (all relationships).
3. Should not criticise the other person in public (most relationships).
4. Should be faithful (dating, cohabiting, and husband–wife).

5. Should be punctual/prompt in keeping appointments (dating, repairman, student).
6. Should not be overprotective/overpossessive (sibling, parent).
7. Should not encroach shared boundaries (neighbour).
8. Should accept fair share of the work load (work colleague).

We can see that all these rules are designed to avoid conflict by regulating behaviour so that the conflict situation does not occur. And in many instances the conflict would occur only in certain relationships so that the rule is relationship-specific. Again we can see the functional role that such rules play in regulating relations between people.

Task-oriented rules   Many of our rules are prescribed so that a particular discrete task is carried out. This is particularly true of task-focused relationships, such as doctor–patient, teacher–pupil, householder–repairman, and other work relationships. For these relationships we have rules about the most effective way of dealing with the job at hand – for example, rules about preparing lessons thoroughly for teachers, planning and assigning work efficiently for work superiors, counselling on preventive medicine for doctors, following doctor's instructions for patients. These rules are aimed not at avoiding conflict, but at completing the task at hand more effectively.

Rules of self-presentation   In addition we have rules about self-presentation – the more formal rules of social appearance and public behaviour. Although we asked about the importance of smart or neat appearance, and about 'striving to present oneself in the best possible light', such rules were rarely endorsed as important in our culture, and ranked well below our other classes of rules for all relationships.

Rules in a changing relationship   We have already seen that different sorts of rules apply to different relationships. But do rules also differentiate between stages of relationships? We know from our own experience that relationships change in both type and quality over time: close friendships may fade, work colleagues may become friends, heterosexual relations can change to marital, and spouses become divorcees. Do rules also change under these circumstances?

We have seen in Chapters 4 and 5, that in order to establish a relationship, we must be seen as 'attractive' to the other person – not only physically, but also in our social competence and the like. It is at this stage that rules of self-presentation are probably the most important ones to apply, since our appearance and superficial behaviour are the only aspects by which the other person can judge us as a desirable or undesirable potential relationship.

But as we develop the relationship, such rules become less important, and attractiveness of appearance plays a secondary role to the less accessible areas of personality and behaviour. Rules about rewardingness become important in maintaining a relationship. As people get to know each other better, there is increased self-disclosure, but this should be gradual and reciprocated, so that rules about both regulating and enhancing intimacy come into play (for example, respect other's privacy, but also share news of success). Exchange and support rules are also relevant here. Offers of help, favours and debts should be reciprocated.

Conflict-avoidance rules are also important, especially the keeping of confidences, since the exchange of intimacy that has occurred so far in the relationship makes this a vulnerable area for potential conflict. Mutual trust becomes increasingly important.

As a relationship continues to become a very close one, intimacy rules are the most important ones, in order to sustain this high level of intimacy. Support rules are important and help and support are expected; rules of reciprocating by direct exchange become less relevant. Conflict avoidance rules may become less important and conflict-negotiation rules may become more important.

Relationships may also lapse. As relations disengage, intimacy-enhancing rules will give way to intimacy-regulating ones (for example, proscription rather than prescription of emotional expression, discussion of intimate topics, and self-disclosure).

How are we to apply this information to improve our relationships? By looking at the rules and skills at each stage, we can provide some guidelines. For example, in establishing a relationship, first impressions are important. How we appear and behave in this initial period is often crucial, whether the relationship is a potential friendship or date, or even a more formal meeting with work superior or interviewer. Self-presentation rules and skills are important. Social skills training, for example, often focuses on these initial meetings between people by teaching appropriate conversation topics, skilful non-verbal behaviours, listening skills, and even grooming and appearance.

Rules and skills for maintaining relationships are also applied in, for example, marital or family therapy or counselling. Exchange rules may be explicitly applied in the form of behavioural contracting as we have already described. Regulating rules may be explicitly stated, especially where these may have been infringed – for example respecting the partner's privacy. And to enhance rather than maintain a relationship, communication skills are taught, and this usually involves invoking some of our intimacy rules. Couples are taught to communicate and to engage in self-disclosure, and to be more rewarding to each other. We have already seen in Chapter 6 that unhappily married couples are more likely to produce and to reciprocate displeasing verbal remarks and nonverbal acts. They also produce less self-disclosure, and husbands in particular are not as good at expressing their emotions or interpreting their wives' feelings as those who have happy marriages. Rules about communicating feelings, expressing emotions and being emotionally supportive are obviously important ones to apply.

These sorts of rules and skills are important not only for marriage, but for other close relationships such as friendship. Just as in marriage, rewardingness is critical for friendship. Applying intimacy and exchange rules is important in maintaining a close friendship, and as we have seen in Chapter 4, failing to keep to some of these rules is implicated in causing the breakdown of actual friendship. Exchange rules are especially important here, since we look upon our friends as important sources of support.

Teaching relationship skills

The rules contain a great deal of information about conducting and maintaining relationships. But they do not always tell us how to do it. As we said earlier, there is the *performance* aspect to consider. Exactly how can one be emotionally supportive, for example? A handbook of motoring or springboard diving in one sense tells you how to do it, but it is also necessary to receive instruction and to have a lot of practice in order to do it successfully.

Let us start with *rewardingness*. The rules listed above on page 306f list the main ways in which people should be rewarding in most relationships. But a great deal of rewardingness is embodied in details of non-verbal and verbal styles of behaviour. Popular people, for example, are more rewarding, and it is found that the most important difference in behaviour between popular and unpopular people is that the popular ones are more rewarding – they are cheerful and friendly, take an interest in others, are helpful and kind, interesting and amusing. Unpopular people are gloomy and hostile, boastful and mainly interested in themselves, and try to get other people to do things for *them*.[26] Individuals may also be popular because they are in a position to provide tangible help of one kind or another. Those whose job consists of giving out rewards are more popular than those who administer punishments. Physically attractive individuals, of either sex, are more popular.

A lot of rewardingness is non-verbal – smiling, looking, touching, using a friendly tone of voice. But words are important too, saying things in a kind and sympathetic way, rather than being critical, sarcastic, hostile or superior.

Rewardingness in relationships can also be divided into two interrelated areas – intimacy and support. Our closest relationships are highly intimate ones. We derive enjoyment from shared intimacies, both physical and social–emotional. The physical intimacy of sex is one important (though as we have seen not *the* most important) ingredient in heterosexual relationships. Non-sexual touching is also highly rewarding, as in cuddling between parent and child, or a hug between same-sex close friends. It serves to strengthen the bond and emphasises closeness of the relationship. Verbal intimacy is also highly rewarding. We share good news with our friends and family, and re-experience the pleasure of its happening in relating the event. We also disclose intimate thoughts and feelings in our close relationships, and this reinforces our sense of self-worth and personal identity and of being accepted. One of the skills of rewardingness in relationships is therefore the ability to be intimate – to share experiences by self-disclosure, and to allow *mutual* self-disclosure.

Relationships are also rewarding because they are supportive. When we have difficulties, we tend to turn to our friends and kin as sources of social support. This help may be practical (in the form of financial or material help, for example), or it may be psychological or emotional support. One of the skills of relationships is therefore how to be helpful. For example, the skill of empathic listening to give someone emotional support, or the ability to give non-critical advice.

A second general area of social skill is *influencing other people*. A person who is rewarding simply by giving way to others all the time would not be able to achieve either personal or professional goals. What are the social skills of influencing people?

1. The central core is the verbal request. This must be polite, and

persuasive, i.e. offer good reasons or advantages for the other, in doing what you want.

2. The verbal request should have the right non-verbal accompaniments, including such elements of assertiveness as a loud voice (but not too loud), a serious facial expression, an erect posture, direct gaze.

3. At the same time there must be sufficient warmth and rewardingness, both verbal and non-verbal, to sustain the relationship.

4. Influence can be achieved simply by rewarding or punishing aspects of the other's behaviour by verbal agreement or disagreement, or by non-verbal rewards and punishments, such as smiling, head-nodding, looking, or the reverse.

5. Influence is easier if one has recently done things for the other, which should be reciprocated, or if one has power to give or withhold favours.[27]

Then there is *dealing with conflict*. We have seen that most relationships involve a certain amount of conflict, particularly in the cases of marriage, superior–subordinate and other work relations, and parent–child relations. In all these it may be necessary to sustain the relationship, perhaps over a long period, even though both sides find it difficult.

The best way of handling all these difficult relationships is shown by our rules, and by other studies: avoid being aggressive, use a reasonable degree of assertiveness instead, listen to the other's point of view and try to understand it, try to find a solution which is acceptable to both, and be prepared to give way to some extent. The details vary between relationships. In marriage we have seen that conflict is common, and that there are advantages in facing up to it and working it through. *Behavioural marital therapy* offers a very formal way of doing so, but this sounds rather like management–union bargaining. Marriage has the advantage that these discussions may well occur in the context of a good meal, a comfortable sofa, or even in bed. In other words domestic intimacy and rewardingness can play a role in bringing about a solution. In supervisor–subordinate conflict there is no corresponding advantage in working through all forms of conflict, and it may be better simply to avoid them. These conflicts are sometimes exposed in encounter-group training, not always with favourable results.

Some special areas of social skill should be mentioned. We mentioned *non-verbal communication* (NVC) in connection with rewardingness. NVC is also very important as a means of communicating emotional states, for example happy–sad and attitudes to others, like friendly–hostile. This is done mainly via facial expression and tone of voice.[28] Some people are not very good at expressing the state they are in, some are not very good at interpreting the signals sent by others. It has been found that in disturbed marriages there is rather poor sending and receiving of non-verbal signals for emotions, on the part of husbands.[29] As a result neither can tell very clearly what the other is feeling. This suggests that some training in non-verbal communication for husbands could well be incorporated into marital therapy.

Another area of social skill is the *management of sequences of interaction*, such as conversation. We showed earlier that in disturbed marriages there are often cycles of behaviour that lead to rows. These may consist simply of one negative message, for example criticism, leading to a negative reply, or of more complex cycles, with negative outcomes.[30] In the case of loneliness, and people who have difficulty making friends, a common problem is an inability to conduct a conversation. In all such cases it is possible to give training in the skills of handling sequences of behaviour.[31]

This kind of problem can be tackled by an extension of SST in which the focus is on the couple rather than on either individual. A couple is asked to 'role-play' some situation which has often caused them difficulty, the encounter is video-taped, followed by feedback and discussion of the sequence of moves made.

We will now look in more detail at the *skills needed for friendship*:

1. Friendship goes through a series of stages, and certain skills are needed at each: (*i*) We select possible friends by observing which people we like the look of, in terms of their appearance and behaviour; (*ii*) we invite one of those chosen to a drink, meal or other social event, where a certain amount of self-disclosure takes place; (*iii*) if the second stage is passed, regular meetings of some kind are instituted.

2. Rewarding the other is important, especially by showing that we like them, both by what we say, and by the facial expression, tone of voice, etc., with which we say it. This is often the focus of social skills training.

3. Physical attractiveness is important for friendship as well as for heterosexual affairs; it may be easier to change appearance than behaviour.

4. Self-disclosure indicates trust, and is essential if a relationship is to deepen; however it should be gradual and reciprocated.

Let us look at the *skills needed by supervisors of working groups*. The *rules* were given earlier, but how about the *skills*?

1. It is essential to carry out the supervisor's job of planning and scheduling the work to be done, making sure that supplies are available and the equipment working, instructing and training subordinates, checking and correcting their work, telling them how well they are doing, and motivating them to work effectively. However, all this has to be done with a very light hand and in a very tactful way – people do not like being ordered about.

2. It is also essential to look after the members of the working group, helping them to attain rewards and to avoid punishments, establishing a friendly relationship with them, taking a personal interest in individuals, being understanding about mistakes, and dealing with interpersonal problems in the group. This is again partly a matter of non-verbal communication.

3. The secret of keeping control of the group and staying on good terms with its members lies in the way orders are given. There are advantages in the 'democratic–persuasive' style, in which subordinates are motivated by explanation and persuasion, rather than just the giving of orders. This allows them to participate as far as possible in decisions that affect them. It also involves the use of the rather difficult techniques of group discussion and group decision.[32]

Learning the facts of life: what one needs to know about relationships

We mentioned 'cognitive therapy' above, that is treating people by the removal of incorrect beliefs. Some forms of social skills training also contain an educational component. For example, training people to work in other cultures usually includes teaching them the different ways of the new culture, including aspects of social behaviour and relationships. We would like to suggest that both in preparatory training and in therapy it may be useful to remove incorrect beliefs and to teach those concerned some of the relevant facts of life about relationships. Indeed this book is partly written for this very purpose, and we hope it will be found useful.

We do not want to repeat or to summarise the whole book, but we shall select a few key facts of life, which are both very important and not as widely known as they should be.

Marriage 1. There is sharing of many aspects of life, including property, money, and the production of children; this involves much joint, co-operative work.

2. The relationship is intense, and is usually deeply satisfying; this is due to sexual rewards, close companionship, and the provision of social support. It has a positive effect on health, mental health and happiness. There is great distress when it is ended by divorce or bereavement.

3. There is also a great deal of argument and conflict, which is nevertheless compatible with a happy marriage; it is necessary and valuable to work these conflicts through.

4. Marriage is changing in that women now earn more money and have more power, men do more of the housework. However the full dual-career family has additional sources of conflict.

5. The divorce rate is increasing, partly because of higher expectations and unwillingness or inability to deal with conflict. However, divorce leads to a period of great distress, and second marriages are less likely to work than first. The alternative is to follow the rules and learn the skills needed to make the first marriage succeed.

Parent–adolescent relations 1. This is the worst period in the parent–child relationship. Marital happiness is at its lowest, and teenagers are often lonely and depressed.

2. However the parent–child relationship survives adolescence in nearly all cases; this is a temporary difficulty in a relationship which may last fifty years. The attachments formed during early childhood seem to be permanent; frequency of contact when the children become adults does not fall off with time.

3. The conflict is due to the child's desire to be adult and independent, and to acquire an identity that is his own, not a reflection of the family. Parents are concerned about behaviour which seems to be both deviate and sometimes dangerous and unwise.

4. As in all kinship relations, major help is provided in either direction, when it is sought.

Friends 1. Friends are people with whom we enjoy talking and doing things. To keep a friend it is necessary to be rewarding, but a commitment and concern for the other also develops. Only minor forms of help are expected from friends.

2. The activities shared with friends are distinctive – joint leisure,

talking, eating and drinking.

3. Friendship is particularly important from adolescence to marriage, and in old age; it is less important in between. It takes rather different forms for men and women, and in different social classes.

4. Friends exist not in isolated pairs, but as part of a social network. It is important to bear the others in mind, to avoid problems of jealousy, to keep confidences, etc.

Work relationships   1. People are brought together by the working environment and organisation. Co-operation, help and information are needed both by individuals and to produce an effective enterprise.

2. Individuals need social support at work; relationships there can be a source of support, satisfaction and health, or the reverse – depending on the relationship established.

3. A variety of relationships are formed at work, from close friendship to hostility. A common form is friendship that is confined to the work-place, based on gossip, jokes and games in tea-breaks and lunch intervals.

Practical arrangements for handling relationships

Some of the findings about the conduct of relationships lead to advice of a rather different kind. There are clear implications for how to choose a partner for each relationship, what to do with him or her, where to do it, and how to relate to others.

First, whom to choose. Sometimes we have no choice, or very little choice – family, workmates, and neighbours for example. With friends we have complete freedom of choice. Someone who wants to have more friends should seek others of similar background and interests, of similar values and outlook, who are seen or can be seen frequently. Such people are found at work, in leisure activities, and in the neighbourhood. The easiest thing is to join a club, church, or other group of like-minded people, in the neighbourhood. Choice of a potential spouse is also quite voluntary, in our culture at least. He or she does not need to live near – they will soon do that anyway. And, possibly for biological reasons, we are attracted to people other than the girl next door, who are strangers. However, if we marry someone who is too different, the chances of a successful marriage are reduced. He or she should be of similar background, interests and values, as in the case of friends. Marriage between couples from different countries, ethnic groups, or religions, is less likely to work.

Then there is choice of activities. Any relationship consists basically of doing things together, and for each relationship there is a characteristic range of activities. Friends, for example, engage mainly in eating, drinking, talking and joint leisure. Married couples spend a great deal of time together, especially in bed, watching TV, at meals, and in co-operating over running the home and family. It may be particularly important to do rewarding things together and to talk to each other in order to sustain a shared view of the world. With kin it is important to keep in touch, simply to see them, and to provide help when needed. With friends at work there are gossip and jokes in the intervals from work, and help with the work. With neighbours there is chat over the garden fence and provision of minor help.

The physical environment is important and partly under our control. We saw, for example, that it is dangerous for marriages if the couple live apart, for example when changing jobs, or even for one partner to have a bolt-hole in college or club to retreat to after rows. Friends are more likely to stay friends the nearer they live, and the more often they are encountered. The architectural arrangements of colleges and flats affect whether or not neighbours will become friends. The physical environment at work, and the arrangements for tea-breaks and lunch, have similar effects. Just as the physical environment can help to sustain relationships, so can the social network. A pair of friends or a pair of spouses are more likely to stay together if they have a shared social network.

Conclusion

We began this book by showing the great benefits to health, mental health, happiness and length of life which are obtained from satisfactory relationships. A great deal of unhappiness and ill-health results for those who fail to manage their relationships successfully. Marital partners, friends, kin and workmates are all extremely important in different ways.

We have tried to analyse the main features of each of these relationships, including the sources of satisfaction and conflict, the basis of bonding, the activities involved, and how these relationships vary with age, sex, social class, culture and history. And we have tried to give some understanding of them, and to correct common misunderstandings. Finally we have presented the main rules which should be followed, and the skills which should be used to handle each relationship successfully.

FURTHER READING

Brannen, J. & Collard, J. (1982) *Marriages in Trouble* London: Tavistock

Duck, S. & Gilmour, R. (1984) *Personal Relationships vol. 5: Repairing Personal Relationships* London: Academic Press

Jacobson, N. & Margolin, G. (1979) *Marital Therapy* New York: Brunner/ Mazel

References

Chapter 1

1. B. Wellman (1979) 'The community question: the intimate networks of East Yorkers' *American Journal of Sociology*, *84*, 1201–31.
2. M. Wish, M. Deutsch & S. J. Kaplan (1976) 'Perceived dimensions of interpersonal relations' *Sociometry*, *40*, 234–46.
3. D. T. Campbell (1975) 'On the conflicts between biological and social evolution and between psychology and moral tradition' *American Psychologist*, *30*, (12), 1103–26.
4. G. A. Allan (1979) *A Sociology of Friendship and Kinship* London: Allen & Unwin.

Chapter 2

1. A. Campbell (1981) *The Sense of Well Being in America: Patterns and Trends* New York: McGraw–Hill.
2. J. L. Freedman (1978) *Happy People* New York & London: Harcourt Brace Jovanovich.
3. J. W. Reich & A. Zautra (1981) 'Life events and personal causation: some relationships with satisfaction and distress' *Journal of Personality and Social Psychology*, *41*, 1002–12.
4. M. Morgan (1980) 'Marital status, health, illness and service use' *Social Science and Medicine*, *14A*, 633–43.
5. M. Young, B. Benjamin & C. Wallis (1963) 'Mortality of widowers' *Lancet*, *2*, 454–6.
6. M. S. Stroebe & W. Stroebe (1983) 'Who suffers more? Sex differences in health risks of the bereaved' *Psychological Bulletin*, *93*, 279–301.
7. B. L. Bloom, S. R. Asher & S. W. White (1978) 'Marital disruption as a stressor' *Psychological Bulletin*, *85*, 867–94.
8. J. J. Lynch (1977) *The Broken Heart* New York: Basic Books.
9. W. R. Gove (1979) 'The relationship between sex roles, marital status, and mental illness' *Social Forces*, *51*, 34–44.
10. Lynch, *The Broken Heart*.
11. A. Campbell, P. E. Converse & W. L. Rodgers (1976) *The Quality of American Life* New York: Sage.

12. L. F. Berkman & S. L. Syme (1979) 'Social networks, host resistance, and mortality: a nine-year follow-up study of Almeda county residents *American Journal of Epidemiology*, *109*, 186–204.

13. F. Kobrin & G. Hendershot (1977) 'Do family ties reduce mortality: Evidence from the United States 1966–68' *Journal of Marriage and the Family*, 39, 737–45.

14. L. M. Verbrugge (1983) 'Multiple roles and physical health of women and men' *Journal of Health and Social Behavior*, *24*, 16–30.

15. Lynch, *The Broken Heart*.

16. J. H. Medalie & U. Goldbourt (1976) 'Angina pectoris among 10,000 men' *American Journal of Medicine*, *60*, 910–21.

17. M. R. DiMatteo & R. Hays (1981) 'Social support and serious illness' in B. H. Gottlieb (ed.) *Social Networks and Social Support* Beverly Hills: Sage.

18. P. Warr & G. Parry (1982) 'Paid employment and women's psychological well-being' *Psychological Bulletin*, *91*, 478–516.

19. H. T. Reis (1984) 'Social interaction and well-being' in S. Duck (ed.) *Personal Relationships. 5. Repairing Personal Relationships* London: Academic Press.

20. Gove, 'The relationship between sex roles. . .'

21. M. Hughes & W. R. Gove (1981) 'Living alone, social integration and mental health' *American Journal of Sociology*, 87, 48–74.

22. W. W. Eaton (1978) 'Life events, social support, and psychiatric symptoms: a re-analysis of the New Haven data' *Journal of Health and Social Behavior*, *19*, 230–4.

23. R. J. Turner (1981) 'Social support as a contingency in psychological well-being' *Journal of Health and Social Behavior*, 22, 357–67.

24. R. L. Leavy (1983) 'Social support and psychological disorder: a review' *Journal of Community Psychology*, *11*, 3–21.

25. G. W. Brown & T. Harris (1978) *Social Origins of Depression* London: Tavistock. C. S. Aneshensel, R. R. Frerichs & V. A. Clark (1981) 'Family roles and sex differences in depression' *Journal of Health and Social Behavior*, 22, 379–93.

26. A. Tyerman & M. Humphrey (1983) 'Life stress, family support and adolescent disturbances' *Journal of Adolescence*, 6, 1–12.

27. F. Andrews & S. Withey (1976) *Social Indicators of Well Being* New York: Plenum.

28. Campbell, Converse and Rodgers *The Quality of American Life*.

29. A. Peplau & D. Perlman (1982) *Loneliness* New York: Wiley.

30. E. S. Paykel, B. McGuiness & J. Gomez (1976) 'An Anglo-American comparison of the scaling of life-events' *British Journal of Medical Psychology*, *49*, 237–47.

31. A. D. Kanner, J. C. Coyne, and C. Schaefer (1984) 'Comparison of two modes of stress measurement: daily hassles and uplifts versus major life events' *Journal of Behavioral Medicine 4*, 1–39.

32. R. Cochrane (1980) 'Life stresses and psychological consequences' in P.

Feldman & J. Orford (eds) *Psychological Problems* Chichester: Wiley.

33. J. M. Innes (1981) 'Social psychological approaches to the study of the induction and alleviation of stress: influences upon health and illness' in G. M. Stephenson & J. H. Davies (eds) *Progress in Applied Social Psychology*, *1*, Chichester: Wiley.

34. Bloom, Asher & White, 'Marital disruption . . .'

35. S. Henderson & P. Duncan-Jones (1981) *Neurosis and the Social Environment* Sydney: Academic Press.

36. S. C. Kobasa (1982) 'The hardy personality: towards a social psychology of stress and health' in G. S. Sanders & J. Suls (eds) *Social Psychology of Health and Illness* Hillsdale, NJ: Erlbaum.

37. H. M. Lefcourt, R. S. Miller, E. E. Ware & D. Sherk (1981) 'Locus of control as a modifier of the relationship between stressors and moods' *Journal of Personality and Social Psychology*, *41*, 357–69.

38. K. Parkes (1984) 'Locus of control, cognitive appraisal and coping in stressful episodes' *Journal of Personality and Social Psychology 46*, 655–680.

39. C. S. Carver & C. Humphries (1982) 'Social psychology of the type A coronary prone behavior pattern' in Sanders & Suls *Social Psychology of Health and Illness*.

40. J. C. Coyne, C. Aldwin & R. S. Lazarus (1981) 'Depression and coping in stressful episodes' *Journal of Abnormal Pyschology*, *90*, 439–47.

41. S. Cohen & G. McKay (1984) 'Social support, stress and the buffering hypothesis: a theoretical analysis' in A. Baum, J. E. Singer & S. E. Taylor (eds) *Social Psychological Aspects of Health*, vol. IV, Hillsdale, NJ: Erlbaum.

42. K. B. Nuckolls, J. Cassell & B. H. Kaplan (1972) 'Psychosocial assets, life crisis and the prognosis of pregnancy' *American Journal of Epidemiology*, *95*, 431–41.

43. S. Cobb (1976) 'Social support as a moderator of life-stress' *Psychosomatic Medicine*, *38*, 300–14. S. Gore (1978) 'The effect of social support in moderating the health consequence of unemployment' *Journal of Health and Social Behavior*, *19*, 157–65.

44. Brown & Harris, *Social Origins of Depression*.

45. Henderson & Duncan-Jones, *Neurosis and the Social Environment*.

46. I. G. Sarason & B. R. Sarason (1982) 'Concomitants of social support: attitudes, personality characteristics, and life experiences' *Journal of Personality*, *50*, 331–44.

47. J. Suls (1982) 'Social support, interpersonal relations, and health: benefits and liabilities' in Sanders & Suls, *Social Psychology of Health and Illness*.

48. A. H. McFarlane, G. R. Norman, D. L. Streiner & R. G. Roy (1983) 'The process of social stress: stable, reciprocal and mediating relationships' *Journal of Health and Social Behavior*, *24*, 160–73.

49. W. R. Gove, M. Hughes & C. B. Style (1983) 'Does marriage have positive effects on the psychological well-being of the individual?' *Journal of Health and Social Behavior*, *24*, 122–31.

50. Brown & Harris, *Social Origins of Depression*.

51. Leavy, 'Social support and psychological disorder. . .'
52. H. T. Reis 'Social interaction and well being' . . .
53. Leavy, 'Social support and psychological disorder. . .'
54. J. D. Fisher *et al.* (1982) 'Recipient reactions to aid' *Psychological Bulletin, 91*, 27–54.
55. P. Warr (1983) 'Work, jobs and employment' *Bulletin of the British Psychological Society, 36*, 305–11.
56. C. A. Nathanson (1980) 'Social roles and health status among women: the significance of employment' *Social Science and Medicine, 14A*, 463–71. P. Warr & G. Parry (1982) 'Paid employment and women's psychological well-being' *Psychological Bulletin, 91*, 478–516.
57. J. S. House (1980) *Occupational Stress and the Mental and Physical Health of Factory Workers* Ann Arbor: University of Michigan Survey of Research Center.
58. R. Larson (1978) 'Thirty years of research on the subjective well-being of older Americans' *Journal of Gerontology, 33*, 109–25.
59. N. Lin *et al.* (1979) 'Social support, stressful life-events, and illness: a model and an empirical test' *Journal of Health and Social Behavior, 20*, 108–19.
60. McFarlane *et al.*, 'The process of social stress. . .'
61. R. C. Kessler & M. Essex (1982) 'Marital status and depression: the importance of coping resources' *Social Forces, 61*, 484–507.
62. Reis, 'Social interaction and well-being'. S. S. Brehm (1982) 'Social support processes: a theoretical model'; unpublished, University of Kansas.
63. S. Cohen & H. M. Hoberman (1982), 'Positive events and social supports as buffers on life change stress: maximising the prediction of health outcome'; unpublished, University of Oregon.
64. House, *Occupational Stress.* . .
65. S. M. Plant & S. B. Friedman (1981) 'Psychosocial factors in infectious disease' in R. Ader (ed.) *Psychoneuroimmunology* New York: Academic Press.
66. W. E. Broadhead *et al.* (1983) 'The epidemiologic evidence for a relationship between social support and health' *American Journal of Epidemiology, 117*, 521–37.
67. Broadhead *et al.*, 'The epidemiologic evidence . . .'
68. B. E. Vanfossen (1981) 'Sex differences in the mental health effects of spouse support' *Journal of Health and Social Behavior, 22*, 130–43.
69. Leavy, 'Social support and psychological disorder. . .'
70. D. Schmidt *et al.* (1982) 'Social alienation and social support' *Personality and Social Behavior Bulletin, 8*, 515–21.
71. M. S. Stroebe & W. Stroebe (1983) 'Who suffers more? . . .'
72. D. P. McAdams & G. E. Valliant (1982) 'Intimacy, motivation and psychological adjustment: a longitudinal study' *Journal of Personality Adjustment, 46*, 586–93.
73. R. Liem & J. Liem (1978) 'Social class and mental illness reconsidered:

the role of economic stress and social support' *Journal of Health and Social Behavior*, *19*, 139–56.

74. C. S. Fischer & S. L. Phillips (1982) 'Who is alone? Social characteristics of people with small networks' in L. A. Peplau & D. Perlman (eds) *Loneliness* New York: Wiley.
75. M. Hammer (1983) ' "Core" and "extended" social networks in relation to health and illness' *Social Science and Medicine*, *17*, 405–11.
76. Turner, 'Social support as a contingency. . .'
77. Broadhead *et al.*, 'The epidemiologic evidence. . .'

Chapter 3

1. M. Argyle, A. Furnham & J. A. Graham (1981) *Social Situations* Cambridge: Cambridge University Press.
2. Argyle *et al.*, *Social Situations*.
3. L. Mann (1969) 'Queue culture: the waiting line as a social system' *American Journal of Sociology*, *75*, 34–54.
4. M. Harris (1968) *The Rise of Anthropological Theory* London: Routledge & Kegan Paul, 590.
5. W. Twining & D. Miers (1976) *How to do Things with Rules* London: Weidenfeld & Nicolson, p. 57.
6. T. Parsons (1951) *The Social System* Glencoe, Ill: Free Press.
7. L. Sharp (1952) 'Steel axes for stone-age Australians' *Human Organization*, *11*, no. 2, 17–22.
8. M. Argyle (1983) *The Psychology of Interpersonal Behaviour* (4th edn) Harmondsworth: Penguin Books.
9. M. Argyle (ed.) (1981) *Social Skills and Work* London: Methuen.
10. R. H. Price & D. L. Bouffard (1974) 'Behavioral appropriateness and situational constraint as dimensions of social behavior' *Journal of Personality and Social Psychology*, *30*, 579–86.
11. P. Marsh, E. Rosser & R. Harré (1978) *The Rules of Disorder* London: Routledge & Kegan Paul.
12. A. Campbell (1980) *Female Delinquency in Social Context* Oxford: Blackwell.
13. M. Argyle, J. A. Graham, A. Campbell & P. White (1979) 'The rules of different situations' *New Zealand Psychologist*, *8*, 13–22.
14. Argyle, *The Psychology of Interpersonal Behaviour*.
15. E. Goffman (1963) *Behaviour in Public Places* London: Collier – Macmillan.
16. E. Donald (1981) *Debrett's Etiquette and Modern Manners* London: Debrett's Peerage Ltd.
17. Donald, *Debrett's Etiquette. . .* , 311.
18. Donald, *Debrett's Etiquette. . .* , 311.
19. Donald, *Debrett's Etiquette. . .* , 251.
20. Argyle *et al.*, *Social Situations*.
20a. M. Argyle, M. Henderson and A. Furnham (in press) 'The rules of relationships.' *British Journal of Social Psychology*.
21. R. Brislin & P. Pederson (1976) *Cross-Cultural Orientation Programs* New York: Gardner Press, p. 10.

22. E. Hall & W. Whyte (1960) 'Intercultural communication: a guide to men of action' *Human Organization*, *19*, 5–12.
23. H. Morsbach (1977) 'The psychological importance of ritualized gift exchange in modern Japan' *Annals of the New York Academy of Science*, *293*, 98–113. H. Morsbach (1977) 'Some characteristics of Japanese interpersonal relations – a Westerner's view'; paper presented at the Conference of the British Psychological Society, London, December.
24. K. Shimoda, M. Argyle & P. Ricci Bitti (1978) 'The intercultural recognition of emotional expressions by three national racial groups: English, Italian and Japanese' *European Journal of Social Psychology*, *8*, 169–79.
25. T. Lebra (1976) *Japanese Patterns of Behaviour* Honolulu: University of Hawaii Press.
26. T. Doi (1971) *'Amae no kozo'* (The Anatomy of Dependence) Tokyo: Kodansha International.

Chapter 4

1. C. S. Fischer *et al.* (1977) *Networks and Places* New York: Free Press.
2. S. R. Parker (1964) 'Type of work, friendship patterns, and leisure' *Human Relations*, *17*, 215–19.
3. Fischer *et al.*, *Networks and Places*.
4. M. Young & P. Willmott (1973) *The Symmetrical Family* London: Routledge & Kegan Paul.
5. T. Brennan (1982) 'Loneliness at Adolescence' in L. Peplau and D. Perlman *Loneliness: A Sourcebook of Current Theory, Research and Therapy* New York: John Wiley.
6. D. D. Clarke & C. M. B. Allen (unpublished) 'The effects of different types of residential accommodation on individuals' numbers and types of friendships: an exploratory study' Department of Experimental Psychology, Oxford University.
7. A. Szalai (ed.) (1972) *The Use of Time* The Hague: Mouton.
8. N. Shulman (1975) 'Life-cycle variations in patterns of close relationships' *Journal of Marriage and the Family*, *37*, 813–21.
9. S. L. Feld & R. Elmore (1982) 'Patterns of sociometric choices: transitivity reconsidered' *Social Psychology Quarterly*, *45*, 77–85.
10. M. Hallinan (1979) 'Structural effects on children's friendships and cliques' *Social Psychology Quarterly*, *42*, 43–54.
11. R. C. Roistacher (1974) 'A microeconomic model of sociometric choice' *Sociometry*, *37*, 219–38.
12. J. Boissevain (1974) *Friends of Friends* Oxford: Blackwell.
13. Fischer *et al.*, *Networks and Places*.
14. B. H. Gottlieb (ed.) (1981) *Social Networks and Social Support* Beverly Hills: Sage.
15. S. W. Duck (1973) *Personal Relationships and Personal Constructs* Chichester: Wiley.
16. M. Lea & S. Duck (1982) 'A model for the role of similarity of values in friendship development' *British Journal of Social Psychology*, *21*, 301–10.

References

325

17. M. Henderson & A. Furnham (1982) 'Similarity and attraction: the relationship between personality, beliefs, skills, needs and friendship choice' *Journal of Adolescence*, 5, 111–23.
18. M. Snyder, S. Gangestad & J. A. Simpson (1983) 'Choosing friends as activity partners: the role of self-monitoring' *Journal of Personality and Social Psychology*, 45, 1061–72.
19. R. C. Bailey, P. Finney & B. Helm (1975) 'Self-concept support and friendship duration' *Journal of Social Psychology*, 96, 237–43.
20. L. Jacobs, E. Berscheid & E. Walster (1971) 'Self-esteem and attraction' *Journal of Personality and Social Psychology*, 17, 84–91.
21. M. S. Clark & J. Mills (1979) 'Interpersonal attraction and communal relationships' *Journal of Personality and Social Psychology*, 37, 12–24.
22. S. M. Jourard (1971) *Self-Disclosure* New York: Wiley.
23. Fischer *et al.*, *Networks and Places*.
24. J. M. Riesman (1981) 'Adult friendships' in Duck & Gilmour, *Personal Relationships* Vol. 2. *Developing Personal Relationships*.
25. A. J. Reiss (1959) 'Rural–urban and status differences in interpersonal contacts' *American Journal of Sociology*, 65, 182–95.
26. J. Tognoli (1980) 'Male friendship and intimacy across the life span' *Family Relations*, 29, 233–9.
26a. L. Wheeler, H. Reis and J. Nezlek (1983) Loneliness, social interaction and social roles. *Journal of Personality and Social Psychology*, 45, 943–53.
27. P. Shaver & D. Buhrmester (1983) 'Loneliness, sex-role orientation and group life: a social needs perspective' in P. B. Paulus (ed.) *Basic Group Processes* New York: Springer-Verlag.
28. R. L. Selman & D. Jacquette (1977) 'Stability and oscillation in interpersonal awareness: a clinical-development analysis' *Nebraska Symposium on Motivation*, Vol. 25, Lincoln, Neb: University of Nebraska Press.
29. G. A. Fine (1981) 'Friends, impression management and pre-adolescent behaviour' in S. R. Asher & J. Gottman (eds) *The Development of Friendship* Cambridge: Cambridge University Press.
30. Shaver & Buhrmester, 'Loneliness, sex-role orientation. . .'
31. C. Gilligan (1982) *In a Different Voice* Cambridge, Mass: Harvard University Press.
32. I. S. Kon (1981) 'Adolescent friendship: some unanswered questions for future research' in Duck & Gilmour, *Personal Relationships* Vol. 2.
33. D. Matteson (1979) 'From identity to intimacy: It's not a one way street' in *Symposium on Identity Development* Groningen, Rijksuniversitat.
34. J. C. Coleman (1974) *Relationships in Adolescence* London: Routledge & Kegan Paul.
35. Coleman, *Relationships in Adolescence*.
36. S. Chown (1981) 'Friendship in old age' in S. Duck & R. Gilmour (eds) *Personal Relationships* Vol. 2.
37. Young & Willmott, *The Symmetrical Family*.

38. G. Allan (1979) *A Sociology of Friendship and Kinship* London: Allen & Unwin.

39. L. M. Verbrugge (1977) 'The structure of adult friendship choices' *Social Forces*, 56, 576–97.

40. R. Brain (1976) *Friends and Lovers* New York: Basic Books.

41. M. Argyle & A. Furnham (1983) 'Sources of satisfaction and conflict in long-term relationships' *Journal of Marriage and the Family*, 45, 481–93.

42. H. Kelley & J. Thibaut (1978) *Interpersonal Relations: A Theory of Interdependence* New York: John Wiley.

43. E. H. Walster, G. W. Walster & E. Berscheid (1978) *Equity: Theory and Research* Boston: Allyn & Bacon.

44. H. Luyanski & G. Mikula (1983) 'Does equity theory explain the quality and stability of romantic attachments?' *British Journal of Social Psychology*, 22, 101–12

45. R. Lamb & P. Collett (1984) 'Can equity theory do justice to change?' Unpublished manuscript. Oxford University, Department of Experimental Psychology.

46. Lamb & Collett (1984). . .

47. C. E. Rusbult (1983). A longitudinal test of the investment model: the development (and deterioration) of satisfaction and commitment in heterosexual investments. *Journal of Personality and Social Psychology*, 45, 101–17.

48. A. Campbell, P. E. Converse & W. L. Rodgers (1976) *The Quality of American Life* New York: Sage.

49. Campbell *et al.*, *The Quality of American Life*.

50. L. F. Berkman & S. L. Syme (1979) 'Social networks, host resistance, and mortality: a nine-year follow-up study of Alameda county residents' *American Journal of Epidemiology*, 109, 186–204.

51. B. Bochner, B. M. McLeod & A. Lin (1977) 'Friendship patterns of overseas students: a functional model' *International Journal of Psychology*, 12, 277–94.

52. G. Arling, 'The elderly widow and her family, neighbours and friends' *Journal of Marriage and the Family*, 38, 1976, 757–68.

53. E. Cumming & D. M. Schneider (1961) 'Sibling solidarity: a property of American kinship' *American Anthropologist*, 63, 498–507.

54. S. Schneider (1972) 'Patterns of social interaction' in Szalai, *The Use of Time*, 317–33.

55. S. Henderson, D. G. Byrne & P. Duncan-Jones (1982) *Neurosis and the Social Environment* Sydney: Academic Press.

56. S. Chown (1981), 'Friendship in old age' in Duck and Gilmore, *Personal Relationships* Vol. 2.

57. MORI (1982) *Neighbours and Loneliness* London: Market Opinion and Research International.

58. J. G. Williams & C. H. Solano (1983) 'The social reality of feeling lonely' *Personality and Social Behavior Bulletin*, 9, 237–42.

59. J. M. Atkinson (1970) *Social Isolation and Communication in Old Age*, unpublished MS.

60. L. A. Peplau & D. Perlman (eds) (1982) *Loneliness* New York: Wiley.
61. C. Solano, P. Batten & E. Parish (1982) 'Loneliness and patterns of self-disclosure' *Journal of Social and Personality Psychology, 43,* 524–31.
62. W. H. Jones, S. A. Hobbs & D. Hockenbury (1982) 'Loneliness and social skill defects' *Journal of Personality and Social Psychology, 42,* 682–9.
63. C. Anderson, L. Horowitz & F. deSales (1983) 'Attributional style of lonely and depressed people' *Journal of Personality and Social Psychology, 45,* 127–36.
64. W. Jones, C. Sansone & B. Helm (1983) 'Loneliness and interpersonal judgements' *Personality and Social Psychology Bulletin, 9,* 437–41.
65. J. J. La Gaipa & H. D. Wood (1981) 'Friendship in disturbed adolescents' in S. Duck and R. Gilmour (eds) *Personal Relationships 3. Personal Relationships in Disorder* London: Academic Press.
66. M. Argyle and M. Henderson (1984) 'The rules of friendship'. *Journal of Social and Personal Relationships 1,* 211–37.
67. Argyle and Henderson 'The rules of friendship'.

Chapter 5

1. J. L. Freedman (1978) *Happy People* New York & London: Harcourt Brace Jovanovich.
2. Z. Rubin (1970) 'Measurement of romantic love' *Journal of Personality and Social Psychology, 16,* 265–73.
3. K. E. Davis & M. Todd (1982) 'Friendship and love relations' *Advances in Descriptive Psychology, 2,* 79–122.
4. L. Steck, D. Levitan, D. McLane & H. Kelley (1982) 'Care, need and conceptions of love' *Journal of Social and Personality Psychology, 43,* 481–91.
5. K. S. Pope *et al.* (1980) *On Love and Loving* San Francisco: Jossey-Bass, p. 4.
6. E. Walster & G. W. Walster (1978) *A New Look at Love* Reading, Mass: Addison–Wesley.
7. Walster & Walster, *A New Look at Love.*
8. J. Traupmann & E. Hatfield (1981) 'Love and its effects on mental and physical health in R. Fogel, E. Hatfield, S. Kiesler & E. Shanas (eds.) *Aging: Stability and Change in the Family* New York: Academic Press.
9. W. M. Kephart (1967) 'Some correlates of romantic love' *Journal of Marriage and the Family, 29,* 470–4.
10. E. J. Kanin, K. D. Davidson & S. R. Scheck (1970) 'A research note on male–female differentials in the experience of heterosexual love' *Journal of Sex Research, 6,* 64–72.
11. MORI (1983) Survey. London: Market Opinion Research International.
12. J. P. Forgas & B. Dubosz (1980) 'Dimensions of romantic involvement: towards a taxonomy of heterosexual relationships' *Social Psychology Quarterly, 43,* 290–300.
13. T. L. Huston *et al.* (1981) 'From courtship to marriage: mate selection as

an interpersonal process' in S. Duck & R. Gilmour (eds) *Personal Relationships 2. Developing Personal Relationships* (London): Academic Press.

14. Huston *et al.*, 'From courtship to marriage. . .'
15. Huston *et al.*, 'From courtship to marriage. . .'
16. C. H. Swenson (1972) 'The behavior of love' in H. A. Otto (ed.) *Love Today: A New Exploration* New York: Association Press.
17. I. Reid (1978) *Social Class Differences in Britain* (2nd edn) London: McIntyre.
18. MORI (1979) Survey. London: Market Opinion Research International.
19. R. Jessor, F. Costa, L. Jessor & J. Donovan (1983) 'Time of first intercourse: a prospective study' *Journal of Personality and Social Psychology*, *44*, 608–26.
20. L. A. Peplau, Z. Rubin & C. T. Hill (1977) 'Sexual intimacy in dating relationships' *Journal of Social Issues*, *33*, 86–109.
21. H. B. Braiker & H. H. Kelley (1979) 'Conflict in the development of close relationships' in R. L. Burgess & T. L. Huston (eds) *Social Exchange in Developing Relationships* New York & London: Academic Press.
22. Braiker & Kelley, 'Conflict in the development. . .'
23. Huston *et al.*, 'From courtship to marriage. . .'
24. H. H. Kelley *et al.* (1983) *Close Relationships* New York: Freeman.
25. R. A. Hinde (1979) *Towards Understanding Relationships* London: Academic Press.
26. B. I. Murstein (1970) 'Stimulus-Value-Role: a theory of marital choice' *Journal of Marriage and the Family*, *32*, 465–81.
27. E. H. Walster *et al.* (1966) 'Importance of physical attractiveness in dating behavior' *Journal of Personality and Social Psychology*, *4*, 508–16.
28. E. Berscheid *et al.* (1971) 'Physical attractiveness and dating choice: a test of the matching hypothesis' *Journal of Experimental Social Psychology*, *7*, 173–89.
29. G. Wilson & D. Nias (1976) *Love's Mysteries: The Psychology of Sexual Attraction* London: Open Books.
30. J. C. Touhey (1974) 'Effects of dominance and competence on heterosexual attraction' *British Journal of Social and Clinical Psychology*, *13*, 22–6.
31. R. Centers (1972) 'The completion hypothesis and the compensatory dynamic in intersexual attraction and love' *Journal of Psychology*, *82*, 111–26.
32. MORI (1983) Survey. London: Market Opinion Research International.
33. Huston *et al.*, 'From courtship to marriage. . .'
34. P. Bateson (1983) *Mate Choice* Cambridge: Cambridge University Press.
35. Bateson, *Mate Choice*.
36. R. Fox (1967) *Kinship and Marriage* Harmondsworth: Penguin.
37. M. R. Parks, C. M. Stan & L. L. Eggert (1982) 'Romantic involvement and social network involvement' *Social Psychology Quarterly*, *43*, 116–31.

38. J. Coleman (1963) *The Adolescent Society* Glencoe, Ill: Free Press.
39. E. E. Jones & C. Wortman (1973) *Ingratiation: An Attributional Approach* Morristown, NJ: General Learning Press.
40. H. Arkowitz *et al.* (1975) 'The behavioral assessment of social competence in males' *Behavior Therapy*, 6, 3–13.
41. M. Cook & R. McHenry (1978) *Sexual Attraction* Oxford: Pergamon.
42. H. T. Reis *et al.* (1982) 'Physical attractiveness in social interaction. II Why does appearance affect social experience?' *Journal of Personality and Social Psychology*, 43, 979–96.
43. M. D. Newcomb (1981) 'Heterosexual cohabitation relationships' in S. Duck & R. Gilmour (eds) *Personal Relationships 1. Studying Personal Relationships* London: Academic Press, p. 163.
44 and 45. D. Ramprakash & J. Morris (1984) *Social Trends no. 14* London: H.M.S.O.
46. Newcomb, 'Heterosexual cohabitation relationships'.
47. P. C. Rosenblatt & L. G. Budd (1975) 'Territoriality and privacy in married and unmarried cohabiting couples' *Journal of Social Psychology*, 97, 67–76.
48. C. T. Hill, Z. Rubin & L. A. Peplau (1976) 'Breakups before marriage: the end of 103 affairs' *Journal of social Issues*, 32, 147–68.
49. C. E. Rusbult (1980) 'Commitment and satisfaction in romantic associations: a test of the investment model' *Journal of Experimental Social Psychology*, 16, 172–86.
50. J. D. Cunningham & J. K. Antill (1981) 'Love in developing romantic relationship' in Duck & Gilmour, *Personal Relationships* Vol. 2.
51. Freedman, *Happy People*.
52. Walster & Walster, *A New Look at Love*, p 73.
53. A. Brown & K. Kiernan (1981) 'Cohabitation in Great Britain: Evidence from the General Household Survey' *Population Trends*, 25, 4–10.
54. Newcomb, 'Heterosexual cohabitation relationships'.
55. B. Thornes & J. Collard (1979) *Who Divorces?* London: Routledge & Kegan Paul.
56. P. Collett & R. Lamb (1984) personal communication.
57. C. Kirkpatrick & T. Caplow (1945) 'Courtship in a group of Minnesota students' *American Journal of Sociology*, 51, 114–25.
58. C. E. Rusbult, I. M. Zembrodt & L. K. Gunn (1982) 'Exit, voice, loyalty and neglect: reponses to dissatisfaction in romantic involvements' *Journal of Personality and Social Psychology*, 43, 1230–42.
59. L. A. Baxter (in press) 'Strategies for ending relationships: two studies' *Western Journal of Speech Communication*.
60. D. Tennov (1973) 'Sex differences in romantic love and depression among college students' *Proceedings of the American Psychological Association*, 8, 419–20.
61. Kirkpatrick & Caplow, 'Courtship in a group. . .'
62. Kephart, 'Some correlates of romantic love'.
63. Cunningham & Antill, 'Love in developing. . .'

64. Cunningham & Antill, 'Love in developing. . .'
65. Hill *et al.*, 'Breakups before marriage. . .'
66. Cunningham & Antill, 'Love in developing. . .'
67. Wilson & Nias, *Love's Mysteries*.
68. M. Schofield (1965) *The Sexual Behaviour of Young People* London: Longman.
69. K. K. Dion & K. L. Dion (1975) 'Self-esteem and romantic love' *Journal of Personality*, *43*, 39–57.
70. J. Goody (1976) *Production and Reproduction* Cambridge: Cambridge University Press.
71. W. J. Goode (1959) 'The theoretical importance of love' *American Sociological Review*, *24*, 38–47.
72. M. Guttentag & P. F. Secord (1983) *Too Many Women?* New York: Sage.
73. P. C. Rosenblatt & P. C. Cozby (1972) 'Courtship patterns associated with freedom of choice of spouse' *Journal of Marriage and the Family*, *34*, 689–95.
74. E. O. Wilson (1978) *On Human Nature* Cambridge, Mass: Harvard University Press.
75. Wilson & Nias, *Love's Mysteries*, p 128.
76. E. Berscheid & E. Walster (1974) 'A little bit of love' in T. L. Huston (ed.) *Foundations of Interpersonal Attraction* New York: Academic Press.
77. D. G. Dutton & A. P. Aron (1974) 'Some evidence for heightened sexual attraction under conditions of high anxiety' *Journal of Personality and Social Psychology*, *30*, 510–17.
78. Cook & McHenry, *Sexual Attraction*.
79. M. Hewstone, M. Argyle & A. Furnham (1982) 'Favouritism, fairness and joint profit in long-term relationships' *European Journal of Social Psychology*, *12*, 283–95.
80. C. Seligman, R. H. Fazio & M. P. Zanna (1980) 'Effects of salience of extrinsic rewards on liking and loving' *Journal of Personality and Social Psychology*, *38*, 453–60.
81. M. S. Davis (1973) *Intimate Relations* New York: Free Press.
82. Cunningham & Antill, 'Love in developing. . .'

Chapter 6

1. *Social Trends* (1984) no. 14, London: H.M.S.O.
2. MORI (1982) *A Woman's Place* London: Market Opinion Research International.
3. *Social Trends*.
4. G. H. Elder (1974) *Children of the Great Depression* University of Chicago Press.
5. J. P. Robinson (1977) *How Americans Use Time* New York: Praeger.
6. A. Oakley (1974) *The Sociology of Housework* London: Routledge & Kegan Paul.
7. S. Edgell (1980) *Middle-Class Couples* London: Allen & Unwin.
8. J. Miller & H. H. Garrison (1982) 'Sex roles: the division of labor at

home and in the work-place' *Annual Review of Sociology, 8,* 237–62.

9. R. Centers, B. H. Raven & A. Rodrigues (1971) 'Conjugal power structure: a re-examination' *American Sociological Review, 36,* 264–78.
10. Edgell, *Middle-Class Couples.*
11. J. Scanzoni (1979) 'Social processes and power in families' in W. R. Burr *et al.* (eds) *Contemporary Theories about the Family,* vol. 1, London: Collier-Macmillan.
12. H. H. Kelley *et al.* (1983) *Close Relationships* New York: Freeman.
13. B. Gray-Little & N. Burks (1983) 'Power and satisfaction in marriage: a review and critique' *Psychological Bulletin, 93,* 513–38.
14. E. J. Nettles & J. Loevinger (1983) 'Sex role expectation and ego level in relation to problem marriages' *Journal of Personality and Social Psychology, 45,* 676–87.
15. R. M. Sabatelli, R. Buck & A. Dreyer (1982) 'Non-verbal communication accuracy in married couples: relationship with marital complaints' *Journal of Personality and Social Psychology, 43,* 1008–97.
16. P. Noller (1984) *Nonverbal Communication and Marital Interaction* Oxford: Pergamon.
17. B. E. Vanfossen (1981) 'Sex differences in the mental health effects of spouse support' *Journal of Health and Social Behavior, 22,* 130–43.
18. L. Wheeler, H. Reis and J. Nezlek (1983) 'Loneliness, social interaction, and social roles.' *Journal of Personality and Social Psychology, 45,* 943–53.
19. M. P. Johnson & L. Laird (1982) 'Couple involvement and network structure: a test of the dyadic withdrawal hypothesis' *Social Psychology Quarterly, 45,* 34–43.
20. C. Walker (1977) 'Some variations in marital satisfaction' in R. Chester & J. Peel (eds) *Equalities and Inequalities in Family Life* London: Academic Press.
21. T. Lake (1967) *Relationships* London: Joseph.
22. K. A. Polonko, J. Scanzoni & J. D. Teachman (1982) 'Childlessness and marital satisfaction' *Journal of Family Issues, 3,* 545–73.
23. Kelley *et al., Close Relationships.*
24. R. Gilford & V. Bengtson (1979) 'Measuring marital satisfaction in three generations: positive and negative dimensions' *Journal of Marriage and the Family, 41,* 387–98.
25. *Social Trends no. 14.*
26. C. Gibson (1974) 'The association between divorce and social class in England and Wales' *British Journal of Sociology, 25,* 79–93.
27. I. Reid (1981) *Social Class Differences in Britain* (2nd edn) London: McIntyre.
27a J. Haskey (1983) 'Social class patterns of marriage'. *Population Studies,* no. 34, 12–19.
28. H. Locksley (1982) 'Social class and marital attitudes and behavior' *Journal of Marriage and the Family, 44,* 427–40.
29. J. L. Hawkins, C. Weisberg & D. C. Ray (1977) 'Marital communication style and social class' *Journal of Marriage and the Family, 39,* 479–90.
30. Oakley, *The Sociology of Housework.*

31. A. Heath (1981) *Social Mobility* London: Fontana. Reid, *Social Class Differences in Britain*.
32. J. Roth & R. F. Peck (1951) 'Social class mobility and factors related to marital adjustment' *American Sociological Review*, *16*, 478–87.
33. J. E. O'Brien (1971) 'Violence in divorce-prone families' *Journal of Marriage and the Family*, *33*, 692–8.
34. B. Blood & M. Blood (1978) *Marriage* (3rd edn) London: Collier Macmillan.
35. O. D. Duncan, H. Schumann & B. Duncan (1973) *Social Change in Metropolitan Detroit: the 1950s to 1971* New York: Sage.
35a. M. Argyle and A. Furnham (1982) 'The ecology of relationships: choice of situation as a function of relationship'. *British Journal of Personality and Social Psychology*, *21*, 259–62.
36. Reid, *Social Class Differences in Britain*.
37. Blood & Blood, *Marriage*.
38. L. K. White (1983) 'Determinants of spousal interaction: marital structure or marital happiness' *Journal of Marriage and the Family*, *45*, 511–19.
39. H. J. Locke (1951) *Predicting Adjustment in Marriage* New York: Holt, Rinehart & Winston.
40. B. Fletcher (1983) 'Marital relationships as a cause of death: an analysis of occupational mortality and the hidden consequences of marriage – some U.K. data' *Human Relations*, *36*, 123–34.
41. W. A. James (1983) 'Decline in coital rates with spouses' ages and duration of marriage' *Journal of Biosocial Science*, *15*, 83–7.
42. J. L. Freedman (1978) *Happy People* New York & London: Harcourt Brace Jovanovich.
43. J. Udry, F. Deven & S. Coleman (1982) 'A cross-national comparison of the relative influences of male and female age on the frequency of marital intercourse' *Journal of Biosocial Science*, *14*, 1–6.
44. H. J. Eysenck (1983) *'I do': Your Guide to a Happy Marriage* London: Century Publishing & Multimedia Publication.
45. D. P. J. Przybla & D. Byrne (1981) 'Sexual relationships' in S. Duck & R. Gilmour (eds) *Personal Relationships 1. Studying Personal Relationships* London: Academic Press.
46. N. Glenn & C. Weaver (1981) 'The contribution of marital happiness to global happiness' *Journal of Marriage and the Family*, *43*, 161–8.
47. M. Abrams (1973) 'Subjective social indicators' *Social Trends* no. 4, 35–50.
48. D. K. Snyder & J. M. Regts (1982) 'Factor scales for assessing marital harmony and disaffection' *Journal of Consulting and Clinical Psychology*, *50*, 736–43.
49. J. W. Howard & R. M. Dawes (1976) 'Linear prediction of marital happiness' *Personality and Social Psychology Bulletin*, *2*, 478–80.
50. J. Gottman *Marital Interaction* New York: Academic Press. D. K. Snyder (1979) 'Multi-dimensional assessment of marital satisfaction' *Journal of Marriage and the Family*, *41*, 813–23.

51. Abrams, 'Subjective social indicators'.
52. R. L. Burgess (1981) 'Relationships in marriage and the family' in Duck & Gilmour *Personal Relationships 1. Studying Personal Relationships*.
53. Blood & Blood, *Marriage*.
54. M. Straus, R. Gelles & S. Steinmetz (1980) *Behind Closed Doors: Violence in the American Family* New York: Doubleday.
55. R. Bluglass (1979) 'The psychiatric assessment of homicide' *British Journal of Hospital Medicine, 19*, 366–77. D. Mulvihill, M. Tumin & L. Curtis (1969) 'Crimes of violence: a staff report submitted to the National Commission on the causes and prevention of violence'; U.S. Govt Printing Office, Washington.
56. J. Wiggins (1983) 'Family violence as a case of interpersonal aggression: a situational analysis' *Social Forces, 62*, 102–23.
57. M. Henderson (1984) 'Personality and social skills in violent offenders'; D. Phil thesis, Oxford University.
58. Wiggins, 'Family violence. . .'
59. M. Argyle & A. Furnham (1983) 'Sources of satisfaction and conflict in long-term relationships' *Journal of Marriage and the Family, 45*, 481–93.
60. From Opinion Research Centre Survey for *Woman* Magazine, 1978, published in Eysenck, '*I do*'. . .
61. Gottman *Marital Interaction*.
62. Gilford & Bengtson, 'Measuring marital satisfaction. . .'
63. B. Braiker & H. H. Kelley (1979) 'Conflict in the development of close relationships' in R. L. Burgess & T. L. Huston (eds) *Social Exchange in Developing Relationships* New York: Academic Press.
64. R. M. Knudson, A. A. Sommers & S. L. Golding (1980) 'Interpersonal perception and mode of resolution in marital conflict' *Journal of Personality and Social Psychology, 38*, 751–63.
65. F. D. Fincham & K. D. O'Leary (in press) 'Causal inferences for spouse behavior in distressed and nondistressed couples' *Journal of Consulting and Clinical Psychology*.
66. Blood & Blood, *Marriage*.
67. A. M. Honoré (1978) *Sex Law* London: Duckworth.
68. MORI, *A Woman's Place*.
69. C. B. Ford & F. A. Beach (1952) *Patterns of Social Behaviour* London: Methuen.
70. M. Hunt (1974) *Sexual Behavior in the 1970s* New York: Dell.
71. N. D. Glenn & C. N. Weaver (1979) 'Attitudes towards premarital, extramarital, and homosexual relations in the U.S. in the 1970s'. *The Journal of Sex Research, 15*, 108–118.
72. Glenn & Weaver (1979))
73. MORI (1980) Survey. London: Market Opinion Research International.
74. I. Reiss, R. Anderson & G. Spinangle (1980) 'A multivariate model of the determinants of extramarital sexual permissiveness' *Journal of Marriage and the Family, 42*, 395–411.
75. Reiss et al. (1980)
76. Reiss et al. (1980)

77. R. Bell, S. Turner & L. Rosen (1975) 'A multivariate analysis of female extramarital coitus' *Journal of Marriage and the Family*, *37*, 375–84.
78. G. Gorer (1971) *Sex and Marriage in England Today* London: Nelson.
79. J. H. Gagnon (1977) *Human Sexualities* Glencoe, Ill.: Scott, Foresman & Co.
80. R. O. Blood (1967) *Love Match and Arranged Marriage* New York: Free Press.
81. W. J. Goode (1963) *World Revolution and Family Patterns* New York: Free Press.
82. G. D. Bartell (1971) *Group Sex: A Scientist's Eyewitness Report on the American Way of Swinging* New York: Wyden.
83. Blood & Blood, *Marriage*.
84. M. D. Newcomb & P. M. Bentler (1981) 'Marital breakdown' in S. Duck & R. Gilmour (eds) *Personal Relationships 3. Personal Relationships in Disorder* London: Academic Press.
85. R. Rapoport & R. N. Rapoport (1971) *Dual-Career Families* Harmondsworth: Penguin Books.
86. R. C. Kessler & J. A. McRae (1982) 'The effect of wives' employment on the mental health of married men and women' *American Sociological Review*, *47*, 216–27.
87. S. Lewis & C. L. Cooper (1983) 'The stress of combining occupational and parental roles: a review of the literature' *Bulletin of the British Psychological Society*, *36*, 341–5.
88. R. D'Amico (1983) 'Status maintenance or status competition? Wife's relative wages as a determinant of labor supply and marital instability' *Social Forces*, *61*, 1186–1205.
89. F. Pepitone-Rockwell (ed.) (1980) *Dual-Career Couples* Beverly Hills: Sage.
90. J. Scanzoni (1980) 'Contemporary marriage types' *Journal of Family Issues*, *1*, 125–80.
91. M. S. Davis (1973) *Intimate Relations* New York: Free Press.
92. R. H. Turner (1970) *Family Interaction* New York: Wiley.

Chapter 7

1. J. Haskey (1983) 'Remarriage of the divorced in England and Wales – a contemporary phenomenon' *Journal of Biosocial Science*, *15*, 253–71.
2. Adapted from *Social Trends* (1981) and *Social Trends* (1982) London: H.M.S.O. and *The Economist* 'Who pays for no-fault divorce?' April, 1982.
3. R. Chester (ed.) (1977) *Divorce in Europe* Leiden: Nijhoff.
4. Chester, *Divorce in Europe*.
5. Office of Population, Census and Surveys, *Monitor*.
6. MORI (1982) Survey. London: Market Opinion Research International.
7. G. Levinger (1966) 'Sources of marital dissatisfaction among applicants for divorce' *American Journal of Othopsychiatry*, *36*, 803–7.
8. G. Birchler (1979) 'Communication skills in married couples' in A.

Bellack & M. Hersen (eds) *Research and Practice in Social Skills Training* Plenum.

9. R. Blood (1969) *Marriage* New York: Free Press, 6–7.
10. J. Freedman (1978) *Happy People* New York: Harcourt Brace Jovanovich.
11. C. Gibson (1974) 'The association between divorce and social class in England and Wales' *British Journal of Sociology*, 25, 79–93.
12. R. F. Winch (1971) *The Modern Family* New York: Holt, Rinehart & Winston.
13. B. Thornes & J. Collard (1979) *Who Divorces?* London: Routledge & Kegan Paul.
14. G. C. Kitson & M. B. Sussman (1982) 'Marital complaints, demographic characteristics, and symptoms of mental distress in divorce' *Journal of Marriage and the Family*, 44, 87–101.
15. MORI (1982) Survey. London: Market Opinion Research International.
16. Kitson & Sussman, 'Marital complaints. . .'
17. G. Hagestad & M. Smyer (1982) 'Dissolving long-term relationships: patterns of divorcing in middle age' in S. Duck (ed.) *Personal Relationships 4. Dissolving Personal Relationships*.
18. K. A. Moore & L. J. Waite (1981) 'Marital dissolution, early motherhood and early marriage' *Social Forces*, 60, 20–40.
19. J. Haskey (1983) 'Marital status before marriage and age at marriage: their influence on the chance of divorce' *Population Trends*, 32, 4–14.
20. *Social Trends* no. 14.
21. Chester, *Divorce in Europe*.
22. Thornes & Collard, *Who Divorces?*
23. Kitson & Sussman, 'Marital complaints. . .'
24. J. Dominian (1981) 'Major factors which contribute to marital breakdown'; paper presented at Long-Term Relationships Conference, Oxford.
25. Thornes & Collard, *Who Divorces?*
26. Thornes & Collard, *Who Divorces?*
27. Thornes & Collard, *Who Divorces?*
28. Chester, *Divorce in Europe*.
29. M. Argyle & B. Beit-Hallahmi (1975) *The Social Psychology of Religion* London: Routledge & Kegan Paul.
30. Kitson & Sussman, 'Marital complaints. . .'
31. M. D. Newcomb & P. M. Bentler (1981) 'Marital breakdown' in S. Duck & R. Gilmour (eds) *Personal Relationship 3. Personal Relationships in Disorder*. J. Dominian (1968) *Marital Breakdown* Harmondsworth: Penguin Books.
32. J. R. Udry (1981) 'Marital alternatives and marital disruption' *Journal of Marriage and the Family*, 43, 889–97.
33. N. Hart (1976) *When Marriage Ends* London: Tavistock.
34. Hart, *When Marriage Ends*.
35. M. Rands (1980) 'Social Networks before and after marital separation: a study of recently divorced persons'; Ph.D thesis, University of Massachusetts.

36. G. C. Kitson (1982) 'Attachment to the spouse in divorce' *Journal of Marriage and the Family*, *44*, 379–91.
37. Newcomb & Bentler, 'Marital breakdown', p. 81.
38. R. R. Rindfuss & L. L. Bumpass (1977) 'Fertility during marital disruption' *Journal of Marriage and the Family*, *39*, 517–28.
39. J. H. Harvey *et al.* (1982) 'An attributional approach to relationship breakdown' in Duck, *Personal Relationships 4. Dissolving Personal Relationships*.
40. Hart, *When Marriage Ends*.
41. G. B. Spannier & F. F. Furstenberg (1982) 'Remarriage after divorce: a longitudinal analysis of well-being' *Journal of Marriage and the Family*, *44*, 709–20.
42. J. Haskey (1983) 'Children of divorcing couples' *Population Trends*, *31*, 20–6.
43. F. Furstenberg, J. Peterson, C. Windquist-Nord & N. Zill (1983) 'The lifecourse of children of divorce: Marital disruption and parental contact' *American Sociological Review*, *48*, 656–68.
44. F. Nye (1957) 'Child adjustment in broken and unhappy unbroken homes' *Marriage and Family Living*, *19*, 356–61.
45. R. E. Emery (1982) 'Interparental conflict and the children of discord and divorce' *Psychological Bulletin*, *92*, 310–30.
46. E. M. Hetherington, M. Cox & R. Cox (1977) 'The aftermath of divorce' in J. H. Stevens & M. Mathew (eds) *Mother–Child, Father–Child Relations* Washington: National Association for the Education of Young Children.
47. M. Rutter (1972) *Maternal Deprivation* Harmondsworth: Penguin.
48. J. Pardeck & E. Izikoff (1983) 'A comparative study of the self concepts of adolescents from intact and unintact families' *Personality and Individual Differences*, *4*, 551–3.
49. Newcomb & Bentler, 'Marital breakdown'.
50. N. D. Colletta (1979) 'Support systems after divorce: incidence and impact' *Journal of Marriage and the Family*, *41*, 837–46. B. Wilcox (1981) 'Social support in adjusting to marital disruption: A network analysis' in B. Gottlieb (ed.) *Social Networks and Social Support* Beverly Hills: Sage.
51. H. J. Rashke (1977) 'The role of social participation in postseparation and postdivorce adjustment' *Journal of Divorce*, *1*, 129–40.
52. Wilcox, 'Social support in adjusting. . .'
52a. M. Henderson and M. Argyle (in press) 'Source and nature of Social Support given to women at divorce/separation. *British Journal of Social Work*.
53. Hagestad & Smyer, 'Dissolving long-term relationships. . .'
54. Hagestad & Smyer, 'Dissolving long-term relationships. . .'
55. J. C. Meyers (1976) 'The adjustment of women to marital separation: the effects of sex-role identification and stage in family life'; unpublished MS, University of Colorado, cited by B. L. Bloom, S. R. Asher & S. W. White (1978) 'Marital disruption as a stressor' *Psychological Bulletin*, *85*, 867–94.

56. S. W. White & S. R. Asher (1976) 'Separation and divorce: a study of the male perspective'; unpublished MS, University of Colorado, cited by Bloom *et al.*, 'Marital disruption. . .'
57. Hetherington *et al.*, 'The aftermath of divorce'.
58. Spannier & Furstenberg, 'Remarriage after divorce. . .'
59. Adapted from *The Economist*, 'Who pays for no-fault divorce?', April 1982.
60. Haskey, 'Remarriage of the divorced. . .'
61. R. Blood & M. Blood (1978) *Marriage* (3rd edn) New York: Free Press.
62. Haskey, 'Remarriage of the divorced. . .'
63. Blood & Blood, *Marriage*.
64. N. Glenn & C. Weaver (1977) 'The marital happiness of remarried divorced persons' *Journal of Marriage and the Family*, 39, 331–7.
65. Blood, *Marriage*.
66. Blood & Blood, *Marriage*.
67. Haskey, 'Marital status before marriage. . .'
68. K. S. Renne (1970) 'Correlates of dissatisfaction with marriage' *Journal of Marriage and the Family*, 32, 54–67.
69. R. Chester (1983) 'Relationships with step-children'; seminar at Oxford.
70. D. E. Anspach (1976) 'Kinship and divorce' *Journal of Marriage and the Family*, 38, 323–30.
71. Winch, *The Modern Family*.
72. Chester, *Divorce in Europe 2*, p 314.

Chapter 8

1. J. W. M. Whiting & I. L. Child (1953) *Child Training and Personality* New Haven: Yale University Press.
2. I. Reid (1981) *Social Class Difference in Britain* (2nd edn) London: McIntyre.
3. D. Ramprakash & J. Morris (1984) *Social Trends* no. 14 London: H.M.S.O.
4. J. Newson & E. Newson (1963) *Infant Care in an Urban Community* J. Newson & E. Newson (1968) *Four Years Old in an Urban Community* J. Newson & E. Newson (1976) *Seven Years Old in the Home Environment* London: Allen & Unwin.
5. L. W. Hoffman & J. D. Manis (1982) 'The value of children in the United States' in F. I. Nye (ed.) *Family Relationships* Beverly Hills: Sage.
6. F. E. Kobrin & G. E. Hendershot (1977) 'Do family ties reduce mortality?' Evidence from the United States 1966–1968. *Journal of Marriage and the Family*, 39, 737–45.
7. J. Orford (1980) 'The domestic context' in P. Feldman & J. Orford (eds) *Psychological Problems* Chichester: Wiley.
8. G. W. Brown & T. Harris (1978) *Social Origins of Depression* London: Tavistock.

9. Newson & Newson, *Infant Care*. Newson & Newson, *Four Years Old*. Newson & Newson, *Seven Years Old*.

10. F. I. Nye (1982) 'A theoretical perspective on running away' in F. I. Nye (ed.) *Family Relationships* Beverly Hills: Sage.

11. J. Freedman (1978) *Happy People*. New York: Harcourt Brace Jovanovich.

12. H. R. Schaffer & P. E. Emerson (1964) 'The development of social attachments in infancy' *Monographs in Social Research and Child Development*, 29, no. 3.

13. M. D. S. Ainsworth (1982) 'Attachment, retrospect and prospect' in C. M. Parkes & J. Stevenson-Hinde (eds) *The Place of Attachment in Human Behaviour* London: Tavistock.

14. R. Parke & S. Asher (1983) 'Social and personality development' *Annual Review of Psychology*, 34, 465–509.

15. M. E. Lamb *et al.* (1981) *The Role of the Father in Child Development* New York: Wiley.

16. M. Main & D. Weston (1981) 'The quality of the toddler's relationship to mother and to father: related to conflict behavior and the readiness to establish new relationships' *Child Development*, 52, 932–40.

17. Freedman, *Happy People*.

18. J. Block, J. Block & A. Morrison (1981) 'Parental agreement – disagreement on child-rearing orientations and gender-related personality correlates in children' *Child Development*, 52, 965–74.

19. J. Money, J. G. Hampson & J. L. Hampson (1957) 'Imprinting and the establishment of gender role' *Archives of Neurology and Psychiatry*, 77, 333–6.

20. H. A. Moss (1967) 'Sex, age and state as determinants of mother–infant interaction' *Merrill-Palmer Quarterly*, 13, 19–36.

21. H. Barry, M. K. Bacon & I. L. Child (1957) 'A cross-cultural survey of some sex differences in socialization' *Journal of Abnormal and Social Psychology*, 55, 327–32.

22. R. Brown (1965) *Social Psychology* New York: Free Press, p. 161.

23. Newson & Newson, *Seven Years Old*.

24. E. C. Devereux (1970) 'Socialization in cross-cultural perspective: comparative study of England, Germany and the United States' in R. Hill & R. König (eds) *Families in East and West* Paris & The Hague: Mouton.

25. J. W. M. Whiting, R. Kluckhohn & A. Anthony (1958) 'The function of male initiation ceremonies at puberty' in E. E. Maccoby, T. M. Newcomb & E. L. Hartley (eds) *Reading in Social Psychology* (3rd edn) New York: Holt, Rinehart & Winston.

26. E. M. Hetherington (1965) 'A developmental study of the effects of sex of the dominant parent on sex-role preference, identification, and imitation in children' *Journal of Personality and Social Psychology*, 2, 188–94.

27. F. F. Schachter (1982) 'Sibling deidentification and split-parent identification' in M. E. Lamb & B. Sutton-Smith (eds) *Sibling Relationships* Hillsdale, NJ: Erlbaum.

28. N. Beail (1983) 'The psychology of fatherhood' *Bulletin of the British Psychological Society*, *36*, 312–14.
29. Schaffer & Emerson, 'The development of social attachments. . .'
30. MORI (1982) Survey. London: Market Opinion Research International.
31. Lamb *et al.*, *The Role of the Father*.
32. Newson & Newson, *Seven Years Old*.
33. J. J. Conger (1973) *Adolescence and Youth* New York: Harper & Row.
34. S. Crockenberger (1982) 'Infant irritability, mother responsiveness, and social support influences on the security of infant–mother attachment' *Child Development*, *52*, 857–65.
35. S. Salzinger, S. Kaplan & C. Artemyeff (1983) 'Mother's personal social networks and child maltreatment' *Journal of Abnormal Psychology*, *92*, 68–76.
36. D. Pilling & M. K. Pringle (1978) *Controversial Issues in Child Development* London: Elek.
37. L. W. Hoffman (1974) 'Effects of maternal employment on the child – a review of research' *Development Psychology*, *10*, 204–28.
38. Conger, *Adolescence and Youth*.
39. J. C. Coleman (1974) *Relationships in Adolescence* London: Routledge & Kegan Paul.
40. Coleman, *Relationships in Adolescence*.
41. D. B. Kandel (1983) 'On processes of peer influences in adolescence' in R. K. Silbereisen (ed.) *Perspectives on Youth Development*. Berlin: Springer.
42. U. Bronfenbrenner (1974) 'Children, families and social policy: an American perspective' in *The Family in Society, Dimensions of Parenthood* London: H.M.S.O., 161–2.
43. G. H. Elder (1968) *Adolescent Socialization and Personality Development* Chicago: Rand McNally.
44. Newson & Newson, *Four Years Old*. Newson & Newson, *Seven Years Old*.
45. J. H. Plumb (1975) 'The new world of children in eighteenth century England' *Past and Present*, *67*, 64–95.
46. M. E. Wood (1977) 'Changing social attitudes to childhood' in R. Chester & J. Peel (eds) *Equalities and Inequalities in Family Life* London: Academic Press.
47. R. Rapoport, R. N. Rapoport, Z. Strelitz & S. Kew (1977) *Fathers, Mothers and Others* London: Routledge & Kegan Paul.
48. Devereux, 'Socialization in cross-cultural. . .'
49. E. Zigler & I. L. Child (1968) 'Socialization' in G. Lindzey & E. Aronson (eds) *The Handbook of Social Psychology* (2nd edn) vol. 3 Reading, Mass: Addison-Wesley.
50. D. C. McClelland (1961) *The Achieving Society* Princeton: Van Nostrand.
51. Barry *et al.*, 'A cross-cultural survey. . .' H. Barry, I. L. Child & M. K. Bacon (1959) 'Relation of child training to subsistence economy' *American Anthropologist*, *61*, 51–63.

52. J. Levin (1982) *Grant and Levin: Family Law* London: Sweet & Maxwell.
53. S. Glueck & E. T. Glueck (1950) *Unraveling Juvenile Delinquency* Cambridge, MA: Harvard University Press.
54. R. Loeber & T. Dishion (1983) 'Early predictors of male delinquency: a review' *Psychological Bulletin, 94*.
55. M. L. Hoffman (1970) 'Moral development' in P. H. Mussen (ed.) *Carmichael's Handbook of Child Psychology*, (3rd edn) vol 2, New York: Wiley.
56. T. Smith (1983) 'Adolescent reactions to attempted parental control and influence techniques' *Journal of Marriage and the Family, 45,* 533–42.
57. G. H. Elder (1962) 'Structural variations in the child rearing relationship' *Sociometry, 25,* 241–62. G. H. Elder (1963) 'Parental power legitimation and its effects on the adolescent' *Sociometry, 26,* 50–65.
58. Elder, 'Structural variations. . .' Elder, 'Parental power. . .'
59. J. Riskin & E. E. Faunce (1976) (1970) 'III Discussion of methodology and substantive findings' *Archives of General Psychiatry, 22,* 527–37.

Chapter 9

1. R. Firth, J. Hubert & A. Forge (1969) *Families and Their Relatives* London: Routledge & Kegan Paul, p. 108.
2. E. Shanas, P. Townsend *et al.* (1968) *Old People in Three Industrial Societies* New York: Atherton.
3. B. Wellman (1979) 'The community question: the intimate networks of East Yorkers' *American Journal of Sociology, 84,* 1201–31.
4. Shanas *et al., Old People.*
5. Firth *et al., Families and Their Relatives.*
6. B. N. Adams (1968) *Kinship in an Urban Setting* Chicago: Markham.
7. R. Hill *et al.* (1970) *Family Development in Three Generations* Cambridge, Mass: Schenkman.
8. Firth *et al., Families and Their Relatives.*
9. B. Soldo (1980) 'The dependency squeeze on middleaged women'; paper presented at meeting of the Secretary to Advisory Committee on Rights and Responsibilities of Women; US Dept Health and Human Services.
10. Hill *et al., Family Development.*
11. G. K. Leigh (1982) 'Kinship interaction over the family life span' *Journal of Marriage and the Family, 44,* 197–208.
12. Adams, *Kinship in an Urban Setting.*
13. Adams, *Kinship in an Urban Setting.*
14. L. Fischer (1983) 'Mothers and mothers-in-law' *Journal of Marriage and the Family, 45,* 187–92.
15. Adams, *Kinship in an Urban Setting.*
16. Firth *et al., Families and Their Relatives.*
17. A. Lang & E. Brody (1983) 'Characteristics of middleaged daughters and help to their elderly mothers' *Journal of Marriage and the Family, 45,* 193–202.

18. Lang & Brody, 'Characteristics of middleaged daughters . . .'
19. Hill *et al.*, *Family Development*.
20. T. Caplow (1981) 'Christmas gifts and kin networks' *American Sociological Review*, *47*, 383–92.
21. Firth *et al.*, *Families and Their Relatives*.
22. Firth *et al.*, *Families and Their Relatives*.
23. P. Willmott & M. Young (1960) *Family and Class in a London Suburb* London: Routledge & Kegan Paul.
24. Willmott & Young, *Family and Class*.
25. M. Komarovsky (1964) *Blue Collar Marriage* New York: Random House.
26. Willmott & Young, *Family and Class*.
27. Adams, *Kinship in an Urban Setting*.
28. Leigh, 'Kinship interaction. . .'
29. G. Baruch & R. Barnett (1983) 'Adult daughter's relationships with their mothers' *Journal of Marriage and the Family*, *45*, 601–12.
30. Adams, *Kinship in an Urban Setting*.
31. H. G. Ross & J. L. Milgram (1982) 'Important variables in adult sibling relationships: a quantitative study' in M. E. Lamb and B. Sutton-Smith (eds) *Sibling Relationships* Hillsdale, NJ: Erlbaum.
32. D. D. Clarke and C. M. B. Allen (unpublished) 'The effects of different types of residential accommodation on individuals' numbers and types of friendships: an exploratory study' Department of Experimental Psychology, Oxford University.
33. Clarke and Allen, 'The effects of different types. . .'
34. Ross & Milgram, 'Important variables. . .'
35. J. Dunn & C. Kendrick (1982) *Siblings: Love, Envy and Understanding* London: Grant McIntyre.
36. Ross & Milgram, 'Important variables . . .'
37. F. F. Schachter (1982) 'Sibling deidentification and split-parent identification: a family tetrad' in Lamb & Sutton-Smith, *Sibling Relationships*.
38. W. Ickes & M. Turner (1983) 'On the social advantages of having an older, opposite-sex sibling: birth order influences in mixed-sex dyads' *Journal of Personality and Social Psychology*, *45*, 210–12.
39. H. Kivnick (1983) 'Dimensions of grandparenthood meaning: deductive conceptualization to empirical derivation' *Journal of Personality and Social Psychology*, *44*, 1056–68.
40. B. L. Neugarten & K. K. Weinstein (1964) 'The changing American grandparent' *Journal of Marriage and the Family*, *26*, 199–204.
41. V. Wood & J. F. Robertson (1976) 'The significant grandparenthood' in J. F. Gubrium (ed.) *Time, Roles and Self in Old Age* New York: Human Science Press.
42. Adams, *Kinship in an Urban Setting*.
43. L. E. Troll, S. J. Miller & R. C. Atchley (1979) *Families in Later Life* Belmont, Cal: Wadsworth.
44. Fischer, 'Mothers and mothers-in-law'.
45. Fischer, 'Mothers and mothers-in-law'.

46. Shanas *et al.*, *Old People*.
47. M. F. Nimkoff & R. Middleton (1960) 'Types of family and types of economy' *American Journal of Sociology*, 66, 215–25.
48. W. J. Goode (1963) *World Revoution and Family Patterns* Glencoe, IL: Free Press.
49. C. L. Johnson (1982) 'Sibling solidarity: its origin and functioning in Italian-American families' *Journal of Marriage and the Family*, 44, 155–67.
50. R. O. Blood (1972) *The Family* London: Collier-Macmillan.
51. T. S. Weisner (1982) 'Sibling interdependence and child caretaking: cross-cultural view' in Lamb & Sutton-Smith *Sibling Relationships*.

Chapter 10

1. T. Keon & B. McDonald (1982) 'Job satisfaction and life satisfaction: an empirical evaluation of their interrelationships' *Human Factors*, 35, 167–80.
2. R. Cohen (1984) 'Laypersons' conceptions of social relationships: A test of contract theory' *Journal of Social and Personal Relationships* (in press).
3. S. Cohen & G. McKay (1984) 'Social support, stress and the buffering hypothesis: an empirical and theoretical analysis' in A. Baum, J. E. Singer & S. E. Taylor (eds) *Handbook of Psychology and Health*, vol. 4, Hillsdale, NJ: Erlbaum.
4. M. J. Kelly (1982) 'Stress among blue-collar workers' in A. Kakabadse (ed.) *People and Organisations* Aldershot: Gower.
5. J. Marshall & C. L. Cooper (1979) *Executives under Stress* London: Macmillan.
6. J. H. Goldthorpe, D. Lockwood, F. Bechhofer & J. Platt (1968) *The Affluent Worker* Cambridge: Cambridge University Press.
7. M. Wish, M. Deutsch & S. J. Kaplan (1976) 'Perceived dimensions of interpersonal relations' *Sociometry*, 40, 234–46.
8. F. C. Mann & H. J. Baumgartel (1953) *Absences and Employee Attitudes in an Electric Power Company* Ann Arbor, MI: Institute for Social Research.
9. R. Stewart (1967) *Managers and Their Jobs* London: Macmillan.
10. Stewart, *Managers and Their Jobs*.
11. H. Mintzburg (1973) *The Nature of Managerial Work* New York: Harper & Row.
12. Stewart, *Managers and Their Jobs*.
13. G. Homans (1950) *The Human Group* London: Routledge & Kegan Paul.
14. F. J. Roethlisberger & W. J. Dickson (1939) *Management and the Worker* Cambridge, Mass: Harvard University Press.
15. Roethlisberger & Dickson, *Management and the Worker*.
16. J. Hage, M. Aiken & C. B. Marrett (1971) 'Organization structure and communication' *American Sociological Review*, 36, 860–71.
17. P. Warr & G. Parry (1982) 'Paid employment and women's psychological well-being' *Psychological Bulletin*, 91, 478–516.

18. C. Cooper & M. Davidson (1982) *High Pressure: Working Lives of Women Managers* London: Fontana.
19. G. Forgionne & V. Peeters (1982) 'Differences in job motivation and satisfaction among female and male managers' *Human Relations, 35,* 101–18.
20. Cooper & Davidson, *High Pressure.*
20a. K. Janman (in press) 'Gender dependency of occupational deviance and role overload as Determinants of fear of Success.' *European Journal of Social Psychology.*
21. G. Popp & W. Muhs (1982) 'Fear of success and women employees' *Human Relations, 35,* 511–19.
22. W. S. Neff (1968) *Work and Human Behavior* New York: Atherton.
23. Mintzburg, *The Nature of Managerial Work.*
24. Mintzburg, *The Nature of Managerial Work.*
25. P. McGill (1983) 'Why Japan sends Samuri managers to a training hell' *The Observer,* 19 June, p. 15.
26. L. Mann (1980) 'Cross-cultural studies of small groups' in H. Triandis (ed.) *Handbook of Cross-cultural Psychology,* vol. 5, Reading, Mass: Addison–Wesley.
27. P. Blumberg (1968) *Industrial Democracy: The Sociology of Participation* London: Constable.
28. M. Argyle (1972) *The Social Psychology of Work* Harmondsworth: Penguin.
29. D. F. Roy (1959) 'Banana time: job satisfaction and informal interaction' *Human Organization, 18,* 158–68.
30. C. Sofer (1970) *Men in Mid-Career* Cambridge: Cambridge University Press.
31. J. H. Goldthorpe, *et al. The Affluent Worker.*
31a. M. Henderson and M. Argyle (in press) 'Social support by four categories of work colleagues: relationship, between activities, stress and satisfaction.' *Journal of Occupational Behaviour.*
32. J. K. Chadwick-Jones (1976) *Social Exchange Theory* New York & London: Academic Press.
33. K. Thurley & H. Wirdenius (1973) *Supervision: a Reappraisal* London: Heinemann.
34. Mintzburg, *The Nature of Managerial Work.*
35. Sofer, *Men in Mid-Career.*
36. E. A. Fleishman & E. F. Harris (1962) 'Patterns of leadership behavior related to employee grievance and turnover' *Personnel Psychology, 15,* 43–56.
37. E. Kaplan & E. Cowen (1981) 'Interpersonal helping behavior of industrial foremen' *Journal of Applied Psychology, 66,* 633–8.
38. R. D. Caplan *et al.* (1975) *Job Demands and Worker Health* US Dept of Health, Education and Welfare.
39. E. A. Fleishman, E. F. Harris & H. E. Burtt (1955) *Leadership and Supervision in Industry* Columbus, Ohio: Ohio State University, Bureau of Education Research.

40. R. M. Cyert & J. G. March (1963) *A Behavioral Theory of the Firm* Englewood Cliffs, NJ: Prentice-Hall.
41. A. Kornhauser (1965) *Mental Health of the Industrial Worker* New York: Wiley.
42. R. L. Kahn, D. M. Wolfe, R. P. Quinn & H. D. Snoek (1964) *Organizational Stress* New York: Wiley.
43. J. Turner & H. Giles (1981) *Intergroup Behaviour* Oxford: Blackwell.
44. F. C. Ile (1964) *How Nations Negotiate* New York: Harper & Row.
45. N. Rackham & J. Carlisle (1978, 1979) 'The effective negotiator' *Journal of European Industrial Training*, 2, no. 6, 6–11 & no. 7, 2–5.
46. B. Rosenshine (1971) *Teaching Behaviours and Student Achievement* Slough: NFER.
47. P. Marsh, E. Rosser & R. Harré (1978) *The Rules of Disorder* London: Routledge & Kegan Paul.
47a. M. Henderson and M. Argyle (1984) 'Endorsed and applied rules of relationships reported by teachers.' *Oxford Review of Education, 10,* 193–202.
48. J. M. F. Jaspars & D. Pendleton (1983) 'The consultation: a social psychological analysis' in D. Pendleton & J. Hasler (eds) *Doctor–Patient Communication* London: Academic Press.

Chapter 11

1. MORI (1982) *Neighbours and Loneliness* London: Market Opinion Research International.
2. T. R. Lee (1968) 'Urban neighbourhood as a socio-spatial schema' *Human Relations, 21,* 241–67.
3. M. Young & P. Willmott (1957) *Family and Kinship in East London* London: Routledge & Kegan Paul.
4. R. G. Barker & P. Schoggen (1973) *Qualities of Community Life* San Francisco: Jossey-Bass.
5. E. O. Laumann (1973) *The Bonds of Pluralism* New York: Wiley.
6. B. Wellman (1979) 'The community question: the intimate networks of East Yorkers' *American Journal of Sociology, 84,* 1201–31.
7. C. S. Fischer (1977) *Networks and Places* New York: Free Press.
8. MORI, *Neighbours and Loneliness.*
9. W. M. Williams (1963) *A West Country Village, Ashworthy* London: Routledge & Kegan Paul.
10. M. Killilea (1975) 'Mutual help systems: interpretations in the literature' in G. Caplan & M. Killilea (eds) *Support Systems and Mutual Help* New York: Grune & Stratton.
11. B. H. Gottlieb, ed. (1981) *Social Networks and Social Support* Beverly Hills: Sage.
12. M. Young & P. Willmott (1973) *The Symmetrical Family* London: Routledge & Kegan Paul.
13. H. E. Bracey (1964) *Neighbours* London: Routledge & Kegan Paul.
14. *Social Trends* (1982) vol. 12, Central Statistical Office; London: H.M.S.O.

15. MORI, *Neighbours and Loneliness*.
16. W. L. Warner (1963) *Yankee City* New Haven & London: Yale University Press.
17. N. Lin, R. S. Simeone, W. M. Ensel & W. Kuo (1979) 'Social support, stressful life events and illness: a model and an empirical test' *Journal of Health and Social Behavior*, *20*, 108–19.
18. S. Chown (1981) 'Friendship in old age' in S. Duck & R. Gilmour (eds) *Personal Relationships 2. Developing Personal Relationships* London: Academic Press.
19. L. Festinger, S. Schachter & K. W. Back (1950) *Social Pressures in informal Groups* New York: Harper.
20. J. M. Mogey (1956) *Family and Neighbourhood* Oxford: Oxford University Press.
21. J. M. Zito (1974) 'Anonymity and neighbouring in an urban, high-rise complex' *Urban Life and Culture*, *3*, 243–63.
22. A. Baum & S. Valins (1979) 'Architectural mediation of residential density and control: crowding and the regulation of social contact' *Advances in Experimental Social Psychology*, *12*, 131–75.
23. O. Newman (1972) *Defensible Space* New York: Macmillan.
24. P. Mullins & J. H. Robb (1977) 'Residents' assessment of a New Zealand public-housing scheme' *Environment and Behavior*, *9*, 573–624.
25. B. Crabbe & K. M. Alexander (1980) 'Social contact and dwelling types' in R. Thorne & S. Arden (eds) *People and the Man Made Environment* Sydney: Sydney University Architecture Dept.
26. H. Newby (1980) 'Urbanization and the rural class structure: reflections on a case study' in F. H. Buttel & H. Newby (eds) *The Rural Sociology of the Advanced Societies* London: Croom Helm.
27. C. S. Fischer (1976) *The Urban Experience* New York: Harcourt Brace Jovanovich.
28. Fischer, *The Urban Experience*.
29. Young & Willmott, *Family and Kinship*.
30. M. Fried & P. Gleicher (1961) 'Some sources of residential satisfaction in an urban slum' *Journal of the American Institute of Planners*, *27*.
31. M. Stacey (1960) *Tradition and Change* Oxford: Oxford University Press.
32. Young & Willmott, *The Symmetrical Family*.
33. Bracey, *Neighbours*.
34. Barker & Schoggen, *Qualities of Community Life*.

Chapter 12

1. M. Argyle (1983) *The Psychology of Interpersonal Behaviour* (4th edn) Harmondsworth: Penguin Books.
2. W. Jones, R. Hansson & C. Cutrona (1984) 'Helping the lonely: issues of intervention with younger and older adults' in S. Duck (ed.) *Personal Relationships 5. Repairing Personal Relationships* London: Academic Press.
3 M. L. Smith & G. V. Glass (1977) 'Meta-analysis of psychotherapy outcome studies' *American Psychologist*, *32*, 752–60.

4. M. Argyle (1981) 'The contribution of social interaction research to social skills training' in J. D. Wine & M. D. Smye (eds) *Social Competence* New York: Guilford Press.

5. S. O'Dell, W. Krug, J. O'Quin & M. Kasnetz (1980) 'Media-assisted parent training – a further analysis' *Behavior Therapist*, *3*, 19–21.

6. W. Jones, S. Hobbs & D. Hockenbury (1982) 'Loneliness and social skill deficits' *Journal of Personality and Social Psychology*, *42*, 682–9. C. Gallup (1980) 'A study to determine the effectiveness of a social skills training program in reducing the perceived loneliness of social isolation' *Dissertation Abstracts International*, *41*, 3424.

7. D. Pendleton & J. Hasler (eds) (1983) *Doctor–Patient Communication* London: Academic Press.

8. M. J. Dunkin & B. J. Biddle (1974) *The Study of Teaching* New York: Holt, Rinehart & Winston.

9. A. Goldstein (1981) *Psychological Skill Training: The Structured Learning Technique* New York: Pergamon.

10. J. Broderick, J. Friedman & E. Carr (1981) 'Negotiating and contracting' in A. Goldstein, E. Carr, W. Davidson & P. Wehr (eds) *In Response to Aggression: Methods of Control and Prosocial Alternatives* New York: Pergamon.

11. Home Office (1979) *Marriage Matters* London: HMSO.

12. J. Brannen & J. Collard (1982) *Marriages in Trouble* London: Tavistock.

13. F. D. Fincham (1983) 'Clinical applications of attribution theory: problems and prospects' in M. Hewstone (ed.) *Attribution Theory: Social and Functional Extensions* Oxford: Blackwell.

14. H. Eysenck (1983) *'I Do': Your Guide to a Happy Marriage* London: Century Publishing and Multimedia Publication.

15. N. S. Jacobson & G. Margolin (1979) *Marital Therapy* New York: Brunner/Mazel. G. Birchler (1979) 'Communication skills in married couples' in A. Bellack & M. Hersen (eds) *Research and Practice in Social Skills Training* New York: Plenum.

16. Broderick *et al.*, 'Negotiating and contracting.'

17. N. S. Jacobson (1977) 'Behavioral treatments for marital discord: a critical appraisal' *Progress in Behavior Modification*, *8*, 169–205.

18. H. Hahlweg, D. Revenstorf & L. Schindler (1982) 'Treatment of marital distress: comparing formats and modalities' *Advances in Behavior Research and Therapy*, *4*, 57–74.

19. A. S. Gurman & D. P. Kniskern (1978) 'Research on marital and family therapy: progress, perspective and prospect' in S. L. Garfield & A. E. Bergin (eds) *Handbook of Psychotherapy and Behaviour Change* New York: Wiley.

20. H. J. Markman & D. Floyd (1980) 'Possibilities for the prevention of marital distress: a behavioral perspective' *American Journal of Family Therapy*, *8*, 29–48.

21. H. A. Otto (ed.) (1976) *Marriage and Family Enrichment, New Perspectives and Programs* Nashville, Tenn: Parthenon Press.

22. D. H. Olson (1975) 'A critical overview' in A. S. Gurman and D. G. Rice (eds) *New Directions in Marital Therapy* New York: Jason Aronson.

23. S. Cobb & S. Jones (1984) 'Social support, support groups and marital relationships' in S. Duck (ed.) *Personal Relationships 5.*
24. R. Butler & M. Lewis (1982) *Aging and Mental Health: Positive Psychosocial and Biomedical Approaches* St Louis, MO: C.V. Mosby.
25. R. D. Glasgow & G. M. Rosen (1978) 'Behavioral bibliotherapy: a review of self-help behavior therapy manuals' *Psychological Bulletin*, *85*, 1–23.
26. H. H. Jennings (1950) *Leadership and Isolation* New York: Longmans Green.
27. Argyle, *The Psychology of Interpersonal Behaviour.*
28. M. Argyle (1975) *Bodily Communication* London: Methuen.
29. P. Noller (1980) 'Misunderstanding in marital communication: a study of couples' nonverbal communication' *Journal of Personality and Social Psychology*, *39*, 1135–48.
30. J. M. Gottman (1979) *Marital Interaction* New York: Academic Press.
31. D. Clarke & M. Argyle (1982) 'Conversation sequences' in C. Fraser & K. Scherer (eds) *Advances in the Social Psychology of Language* Cambridge: Cambridge University Press.
32. M. Argyle (1972) *The Social Psychology of Work* Harmondsworth: Penguin Books.

Further Reading

Adams, B. N. (1968) *Kinship in an Urban Setting* Chicago: Markham

Allan, G. A. (1979) *A Sociology of Friendship and Kinship* London: Allen & Unwin

Argyle, M. (1972) *The Social Psychology of Work* Harmondsworth: Penguin

Argyle, M. (1983) *The Psychology of Interpersonal Behaviour* (4th edn) Harmondsworth: Penguin

Blood, R. O. (1972) *The Family* London: Collier–Macmillan

Blood, R. & Blood, M. (1978) *Marriage* (3rd edn) New York: Free Press

Brace, H. E. (1964) *Neighbours* London: Routledge & Kegan Paul

Burgess, R. L. & Huston, T. L. (eds) (1979) *Social Exchange in Developing Relationships* New York: Academic Press

Campbell, A., Converse, P. E. & Rodgers, W. L. (1976) *The Quality of American Life* New York: Sage

Coleman, J. C. (1974) *Relationships in Adolescence* London: Routledge & Kegan Paul

Cook, M. & McHenry, R. (1978) *Sexual Attraction* Oxford: Pergamon

Dominian, J. (1980) *Marital Pathology* London: Darton, Longman & Todd, & B. M. A.

Duck, S. and Gilmour, R. (eds) (1981–5) *Personal Relationships* (5 vols) London: Academic Press

Firth, R., Hubert, J. & Forge, A. (1969) *Families and their Relatives* London: Routledge & Kegan Paul

Hinde, R. A. (1979) *Towards Understanding Relationships* London: Academic Press

Lamb, M. E. & Sutton–Smith, B. (eds) (1982) *Sibling Relationships* Hillsdale, NJ: Erlbaum

Lynch, J. J. (1977) *The Broken Heart* New York: Basic Books

Pendleton, D. & Hasler, J. (1983) *Doctor–Patient Communication* London: Academic Press

Peplau, A. & Perlman, D. (1982) *Loneliness* New York: Wiley

Pilling, D. & Pringle, M. K. (1978) *Controversial Issues in Child Development* London: Elek

Thornes, B. & Collard, J. (1979) *Who Divorces?* London: Routledge & Kegan Paul

Troll, L. E., Miller, S. J. & Atchley, R. C. (1979) *Families in Later Life* Belmont, Cal: Wadsworth

Subject Index

Author Index